OPEN-ECONOMY POLITICS

OPEN-ECONOMY POLITICS

THE POLITICAL ECONOMY OF THE WORLD COFFEE TRADE

Robert H. Bates

PRINCETON UNIVERSITY PRESS   PRINCETON, NEW JERSEY

Copyright © 1997 by Princeton University Press
Published by Princeton University Press, 41 William Street, Princeton, New Jersey 08540
In the United Kingdom: Princeton University Press, Chichester, West Sussex
All Rights Reserved

Library of Congress Cataloging-in-Publication Data

Bates, Robert H.
Open-economy politics : the political economy of the world coffee
trade / Robert H. Bates.
p. cm.
Includes index.
ISBN 0-691-02655-6 (cloth : alk. paper)
1. Coffee industry.   2. International Coffee Organization (1962–   )
I. Title.
HD9199.A2B27   1997
382′.4′373—dc20   96-20694

This book has been composed in Times Roman

Princeton University Press books are printed on acid-free paper and meet
the guidelines for permanence and durability of the Committee on
Production Guidelines for Book Longevity of the Council on Library
Resources

Printed in the United States of America by Princeton Academic Press

10 9 8 7 6 5 4 3 2 1

To My Students —————————————————————

WHO HAVE TAUGHT ME

Contents

Maps and Figures

Maps

Figures

Tables _____

Preface

COFFEE IS A COMMODITY. Commodities are not merely physical goods, bought and sold in markets; they are also cultural constructs.[1] People in different societies vary in the quantities of coffee they demand, the forms in which they prepare it, and the values they associate with its consumption. Adults in the United States once drank four to five cups daily, but since the 1960s their consumption has fallen by one-half, and youths drink even less. Adults in Finland, by contrast, consume seven to ten cups daily, with little sign of decreased demand by year or age group.[2] In Latin countries, people consume coffee in multiple cups of diminutive size; they savor it as an accompaniment to a cigarette, a glance at a newspaper, or conversation. In northern climates, people consume it by the mug; they take it not solely for pleasure but also as a stimulus to harder work, less sleep, and greater achievement.[3] Only recently have coffeehouses begun to spring up in and around major U.S. cities, attracting new aficionados with exotic blends and special flavors.

People in different cultures differ in their willingness to sacrifice for the pleasures of coffee. When coffee prices rose in the 1950s, for example, consumers in the United States switched from the more expensive arabicas to the cheaper robustas, consumed in soluble form. In the face of price rises in the 1970s, they extracted more cups per pound of coffee, producing a watery brew.[4] In Europe, coffee drinkers appear to be made of sterner stuff and to be willing to sacrifice their consumption of other goods in order to maintain the level and form of their coffee consumption.[5]

As with other cultural practices, the consumption of coffee appears to be historically conditioned. For the eighteenth-century French, coffee connoted refinement of taste and manner; they consumed it in well-appointed parlors, using services made of the finest porcelain. For the English of that era, coffee consumption connoted a rawboned republicanism. Englishmen sipped the beverage in public houses, where they smoked tobacco and heatedly discussed news gleaned from the popular press. For Americans of the nineteenth and twentieth centuries, the consumption of coffee connoted physical energy and industrial expansion; they drank it to refresh themselves from the weariness of labor and to reenergize themselves for renewed effort.[6] And now, in the 1990s, the consumption of coffee is being promoted in the formerly tea drinking countries of Asia. If advertisements are to be believed, in Japan coffee is taken to impel a jolt of energy to white-collar workers in large corporations, propelling them to new heights of productivity and to new production records.

Whether it was because of the rise of republicanism, industrialization, and the large corporation—or, more prosaically, because of the growth of population and per capita income—in the nineteenth century, the growth of coffee demand outpaced the growth of coffee supply. The result was a rise in coffee prices.

In response to rising prices, sources of supply shifted. Originally produced in Ethiopia and the Arabian peninsula, the coffee plant migrated to the East and West Indies, where its production and sale came to underpin the economies of those territories and the revenues of their governments.[7] Almost everywhere it was introduced, the production of coffee launched that territory's export economy, linking its people to the global market and rendering international prices the fundamental determinant of the allocation of land, labor and capital in the domestic economy; of the incomes of its population; and of the revenues of its government.

Coffee is thus not merely a commodity. Its consumption and production illuminate the culture of peoples and the history of nations. More directly relevant to this study, it offers a vantage point from which to study politics. The study of coffee enables us to learn about the politics of trade, the politics of development, and the political origins of institutions.

I began my research into the international coffee market in 1982, when David Leonard of the University of California, Berkeley, offered me the chance to advise on the restructuring of the export of agricultural products from Uganda. Working with Robert Hahn, then a graduate student at the California Institute of Technology, I outlined ways of introducing competition among private buyers into Uganda's coffee market, which had hitherto been dominated by the Coffee Marketing Board, a monopsonistic agency of the Ugandan government. The World Bank made acceptance of our report a condition for further lending. But when they asked me to return to Uganda to implement our recommendations, I demurred; without knowing more about the structure of the international market, I could not in good conscience insist that Uganda stop selling its coffee through a single marketing channel. The World Bank then sent me to New York, London, Hamburg, and Vevey to interview members of the green coffee trade and executives of roasting firms and thus to learn about the structure of the international coffee market. Armed with this knowledge, I returned to Uganda, negotiated the implementation of my report, and left. Despite the blandishments of the Bank and the penetrating insights of its consultant, the Coffee Marketing Board's monopoly remained intact, under the control of the military forces that had placed the government in power. Thus was I introduced to the politics of coffee.

By joining the United States' delegation to the 1984 meetings of the International Coffee Organization (ICO) in London, I gained insight into the international market as well. I wish to acknowledge the assistance I received from representatives of the U.S. Departments of Commerce, Treasury, and State and of the offices of United States Trade Representatives, as well as from representatives of private industry, who served on the United States' delegation.

In later years, I returned to London where I was assisted in my research by Nestor Osorio, Colombia's representative to the ICO; Alexandre Beltrao, the Executive Director of the ICO; and Mr. C.P.R. Dubois, its Information Officer. To Mr. Dubois, I owe special thanks.

The major economic forces driving the coffee market emanate from Latin America. To study this subject, I therefore shifted my research from London and Africa to Colombia and Brazil.

Drawing on years of personal and professional relationships, Charles Bergquist and Sutti Ortiz introduced me to the world of coffee in Colombia. They assisted me with an openhandedness and generosity of spirit that earned my lasting gratitude.

In Colombia, the Directors, Guillermo Perry and Miguel Urrutia; the Assistant Director, Pilar Medina; and the administrative and research staff of Fedesarrollo supported my work and made me welcome. I owe particular thanks to Diego Pizano-Salazar and his colleagues at the Federación Nacional de Cafeteros. It would be invidious to single out particular persons, but no one who witnessed my research could begrudge special mention of the help of Diego Pizano; Clemencia Fajardo Guerra, Jefe, Centro de Documentación; Juan José Echevarria Soto, Director, División de Investigaciones Económicas; or Alberto Ararat Chavez, Subdirector, División de Investigaciones Económicas, all of the Federación.

While working in Manizales, I was based at the Center for Research into Economic Development. The Director, Carmenza Saldias, generously made available to me the facilities of her institute and the results of her research into the history and development of the department of Caldas. I also owe a great debt to the departmental officers of the Federación Nacional de Cafeteros in Caldas.

I wish to thank Roberto Junguito Bonnet, Marco Palacios, Malcolm Deas, María Errázuriz, José Antonio Ocampo, Felipe Jaramillo, Cynthia Rosenberg, Richard Stoller, and Mario Laserna for their help and friendship throughout my many visits to Colombia.

My transition to Brazil was eased by Christopher Welna, Barry Ames, David Collier, and Jeffry Frieden, who generously provided me with advice and suggestions as well as introductions to academics and policymakers. Upon my arrival in Brazil, Amaury de Souza and Bolivar Lamounier introduced me to persons in the coffee sector. I give particular thanks for the assistance I received in Rio de Janeiro from Edmar Bacha, Orlando Corrêa Neto, and Manoel Corrêa do Lago of Marcellino Martins & E. Johnston; the directors and library staff at the Centro do Comércio de Café; and Anna Celia Castro and Guillermo Palacios of the Federal University of Agriculture. Colleagues at the University of São Paulo extended generous assistance and in particular Roberto Macedo, Guilherme Leita da Silva Dias, Basila Aguirre, and Denisard Alves. I also wish to thank Luiz Carlos Bresser Pereira, Claus Floriano Trench de Freitas, and Monica Baer.

Over the course of this study, I have received skilled research assistance from Laura Alvarez, Rosalba Capote, Carlos Contreras, Amy Farmer, Gina Dalma, Catherine Elkins, John Hall, Da-Hsiang Lien, Brian Loynd, Andrew Mason, J. Muthengi Musunza, John Nye, Daniel Restrepo, Dixie Reeves, and Michael Thompson. Da-Hsiang Lien, while a graduate student at Caltech, convinced me, and others, that the patterns I was observing were systematic rather than random and therefore amenable to systematic investigation. Dr. Lien coauthored my first papers on this subject, the results of which are incorporated into this study. I also wish to thank Deborah Jacobs of the Perkins Library and Doris Carr Cross of the Program in Political Economy, both at Duke University. The map of Brazil is reprinted, with permission of the publisher, from Solena V. Bryant, *Brazil* (Santa Barbara, Ca.: Clio Press, 1985).

Part of this work was written while I was John M. Olin Professor at Stanford University's graduate school of business. David Brady, John Roberts, Susanne Lohmnann, and David Kreps provided valuable comments and criticisms. I have presented chapters at the Federal University of Agriculture in Rio de Janeiro; the Federación Nacional de Cafeteros and Fedesarrollo in Bogotá; the Center for Advanced Study in the Behavioral Sciences; and the political economy programs of Duke University; Stanford University; Washington University, St. Louis; and the University of California, Los Angeles. I wish to thank in particular John Ferejohn, Mathew McCubbins, Geoffrey Garrett, Barry Weingast, Diego Pizano, Malcolm Deas, and Douglas Rivers for comments and criticisms.

The manuscript was drafted at the Center for Advanced Study in the Behavioral Sciences, financed in part by NSF Grant SES-9022192. Thanks to Avner Greif, Margaret Levi, James Poterba, Nancy Rose, Jean-Laurent Rosenthal, Barry Weingast, and Michael Whinston for their suggestions and encouragement. Barry, Margaret, Avner, and Jean-Laurent will recognize their impact upon every aspect of this book, especially the conclusion. I redrafted the manuscript following a round of often brutally frank criticism from the "groupies"; Barry Ames, Jorge Domínguez, Robert Keohane, Stephen Krasner, Anne Krueger, Sylvia Maxfield, Andrew Mason, Ronald Rogowski, and David Rowe; and anonymous referees chosen by Princeton University Press.

Jonathan Hartlyn regularly imparted guidance, tips, and counsel. Ronald Archer did the same. And Ronald Rogowski not only set the standard for excellence in this field but also, by sending me Bach's *Coffee Cantata*, reminded me of the pleasures of scholarship.

In closing, I wish to give special thanks to the Department of Government and the Institute for International Development of Harvard University; Duke University; California Institute of Technology; and the National Science Foundation (Grant SES—8821151) for providing the financial support that made this work possible. Thanks too to Humphrey Costello, Beth Simmons, and Melissa Thomas. And, above all, my thanks go to Margaret, who supported me over the many years that went into this project.

Cambridge, Massachusetts
February 1, 1996

OPEN-ECONOMY POLITICS

1

Introduction

WRITING IN 1976, Peter Katzenstein called for an end to the division between the study of international politics and domestic politics.[1] A decade later, Stephan Haggard and Beth Simmons renewed the call. "We suggest," they wrote, "a research program that views international [politics] not only as the outcome of relations among states, but of the interaction between domestic and international games and coalitions that span national boundaries."[2] On the one hand, the interval between these pieces underscores a lack of progress in the program set out by Katzenstein; on the other, it highlights its continued significance. In recent years, Frieden, Rogowski, Putnam, Simmons, and others have contributed to this research agenda, which might be called the search for a framework for research into the politics of open economies.[3] I, too, seek to contribute to this framework and do so by focusing on the domestic politics of the international market for coffee.

Why Coffee?

Currently worth roughly U.S. $10 billion per year, coffee stands next to oil as the most valuable commodity exported from the tropics. For many nations in the tropics, coffee constitutes a major source of foreign exchange (see table 1.1). Everywhere coffee has been grown, the politics of coffee has proved central to the politics of national development.

Because of coffee's significance as an export crop, the politics of coffee focuses not only on domestic issues, such as land rights, marketing controls, and labor contracts, but also on international issues, such as global prices and the terms of trade. Since the first decade of this century, developing nations have sought to intervene in the international market and raise the price of coffee. In the early 1960s, their efforts culminated in the formation of a political agency, the International Coffee Organization (ICO), which regulated international trade in the product. Quick calculations highlight the domestic significance of the ICO. Consider Uganda, for example, one of the major suppliers of robusta coffee: for the coffee year 1981–82, the ICO granted Uganda a quota of roughly 2.8 million bags.[4] Had members of the agency permitted Uganda a 5 percent larger quota, that country could have earned an additional $20 million per year in export markets.[5] Ten more bags of coffee, shipped out by a Ugandan peasant, would have generated an additional in-

TABLE 1.1
Percentage of Total Exports Comprising Coffee Exports in Selected Countries

Year	Brazil	Colombia	El Salvador	Guatemala	Kenya	Côte d'Ivoire	Uganda
1950	63.7	77.8	88.9	66.9	17.4	50.0	28.8
1951	59.8	77.6	88.9	69.4	15.1	55.4	28.7
1952	73.8	80.3	87.9	75.6	24.1	62.6	25.8
1953	70.7	82.6	85.5	68.5	29.3	52.5	34.4
1954	60.7	83.7	87.6	70.8	25.2	64.9	32.9
1955	59.3	83.5	85.6	71.0	31.9	52.9	47.8
1956	69.5	76.9	77.5	75.3	41.5	63.7	37.9
1957	60.8	82.4	80.5	72.2	34.8	57.1	41.4
1958	55.3	84.9	72.5	72.6	31.3	59.6	39.6

Sources: International Monetary Fund, *International Financial Statistics* (Washington, D.C., 1980, 1990, 1992, 1993). FAO, *Trade Yearbook* (Rome: FAO, 1988–91).

come of over $200,[6] an *increase* equivalent to the *average* per capita income in Uganda at that time. Eventually, the ICO broke up. When it did so, prices halved in world markets (figure 1.1) and coffee-dependent economies of the tropics (see map 1.1) suffered accordingly.

These figures illustrate the domestic significance of the international efforts to regulate the market for coffee. Among the central issues to which the ICO gives rise, four stand out:

1. What were the origins of the International Coffee Organization?
2. How did it function?
3. What has been its impact on member nations?
4. And why, ultimately, did it collapse?

In seeking to answer these questions, I turn to two major fields of scholarship: international political economy and developmental politics.

International Political Economy

The field of international political economy is defined by its subject matter: it studies the politics of trade and markets rather than the politics of warfare or security, which constitute the subject matter of security studies. The field is also defined by its premises. Whereas those who study warfare emphasize threat and conflict, those who study markets emphasize exchange and bargaining. Whereas those who study international security emphasize the centrality of states, those who study international trade emphasize the significance of nonstate actors. Most relevant to this book is that those who study international security regard conflict as normal and international agreements as problematic, whereas those who study international political economy re-

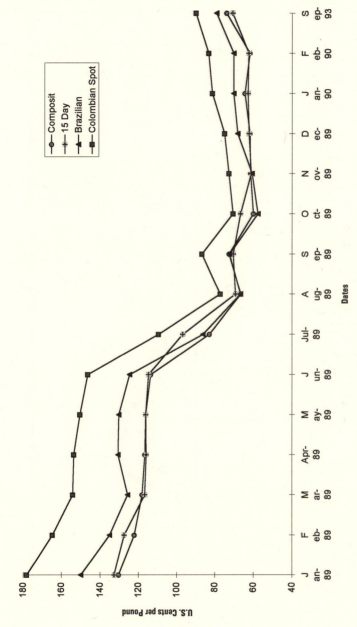

Figure 1.1. The breakup of the ICO—July, 1989. *Source:* Monthly price data from the files of the International Coffee Organization.

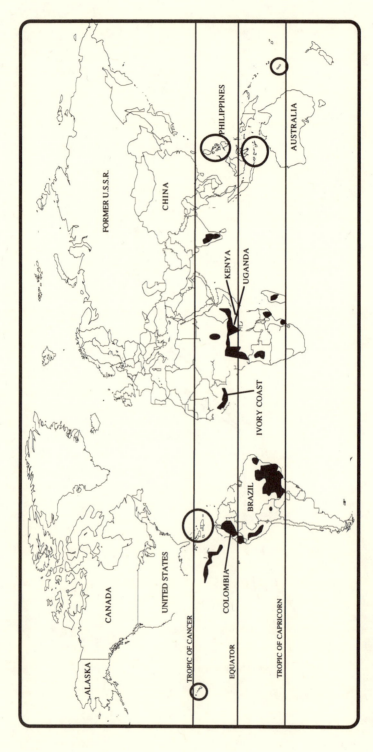

Map 1.1. Coffee Zones of the World

gard such agreements as commonplace. As stated by Oran Young, "Far from being unusual, [cooperative agreements] are common throughout the international system."[7]

A central question addressed by international political economy thus becomes: Where does international cooperation come from? Some who address this question launch their answers from the international level, focusing on the distribution of wealth and power in the global system. The study of hegemons constitutes a case in point. A hegemon is a state that controls such a sufficient portion of the globe's resources that it finds it in its private, that is, national, interest to provide collective goods—benefits that are freely available to other nations in the international system. One such good is military security. Another is an international infrastructure that defends markets, facilitates trade, and thereby secures international prosperity. Hegemonic theory thus accounts for the creation of international institutions by taking account of the global distribution of resources and the incentives those create for large powers.[8]

As initially developed by Kindleberger, hegemonic theory drew its logic from economics and, in particular, from the theory of public goods;[9] as subsequently developed by others, it draws on the closely related theory of collective action.[10] Kenneth Waltz invokes economic analysis when expositing on such system-level modes of reasoning: "In defining a system's structure, . . . the economic analogy [helps]. The structure of the markets is defined by the number of firms competing. . . . If few firms dominate the market, competition is said to be oligopolistic even though many smaller firms may also be in the field."[11] A hegemon stands to world politics as a dominant firm stands to industry: it constitutes a "price setter," the benefits of whose actions are reaped by the "competitive fringe" of lesser powers in the global system. In this instance, the benefits assume the form of international institutions that underpin the international coffee market.

In this study, I argue that such systematic arguments do not work. In the coffee market, Brazil occupied the position of the dominant firm, or hegemon, in the international marketplace; yet, as we shall see, Brazil repeatedly refused to exploit the position of market power conferred on it by its position as the leading exporter of coffee. The United States occupied the position of hegemon in the global state system. Yet, at key moments, it too proved reluctant to act as a dominant power. In the case of the coffee market, the position of states within the global system thus fails to define their behavior within it.[12]

It is Kenneth Waltz who, unwittingly, highlights the central problem: "An international political theory," he writes, "does not imply or require a theory of foreign policy any more than a market theory implies or requires a theory of the firm."[13] But economists have found it desirable and necessary to develop a theory of the firm. By analogy, what is required for the study of international political economy is a domestic theory of politics. Indeed, I will demonstrate that the foreign economic policies of the great powers that created the International Coffee Organization represent the product of domestic political struggles. Brazil's on-again, off-again mobilization of its market power, and the United States' uncertain response to international threats, resulted from the difficulty of forging coherent economic policies in decentralized political systems. The policies of nations toward the international marketplace are not defined, then, by the nations' location in that environment. Rather, they are defined domestically, and in a political process that is structured by institutions.

Hegemonic theory stresses the unequal distribution of capabilities in the global system and the incentives for dominant states to provide collective goods, such as international agreements and regimes. The reasoning originates in economics. So too does the reasoning invoked by a second major approach to the study of international institutions: that of game theory, and, in particular, the theory of noncooperative games in extended form.[14]

The international system, scholars note, is made up of sovereign states. Being sovereign, these states can behave as they wish; for no government exists at the global level that is capable of constraining their choices. In the midst of this anarchy, scholars note, cooperation nonetheless takes place: agreements are reached, regimes are forged, and, as in the case of the International Coffee Organization, institutions are created at the global level. In seeking to explain the emergence of cooperation, scholars cite the incentives created not by the dominance of a particular actor or a government but by the fact of repeated interaction.

These arguments are best conveyed by exploring a canonical game, the so-called chain-store paradox.[15] There exists an established firm, a chain store, in a particular market. In order to retain its monopoly status, the firm seeks to deter entry; it therefore threatens to fight any firm seeking to enter the market. Fighting is costly. The new arrival can choose whether to enter or to stay out. The incumbent firm can choose whether to incur the costs of fighting the new entrant, thereby retaining its monopoly status, or to let it enter and then share the market. The new firm moves first.

On the basis of these premises, scholars then analyze a single play of the game; finitely repeated plays of the game; and then the game when repeated an infinite number of times, or when randomly terminated. For a single play of the game, the outcome is clear: the new firm will enter, despite the incumbent's threats. For fighting is costly; and for a wide range of costs and benefits, the incumbent firm therefore does better sharing the market with the entrant. Its threat to fight is not credible.

This result lays the foundation for the paradox, which becomes apparent when the game is repeated a finite number of times. Intuitively, when the game is repeated, it would seem plausible that the incumbent would fight. A chain store, for example, might be expected to pay the costs of punishment in one market so that it could render its threats credible in others. It could thereby recoup the costs of fighting by reaping monopoly profits in other locations. But the analysis of the game shows that such intuition is violated. In the last market, knowing that the incumbent cannot profit from fighting, the new firm enters. So too in the penultimate market. Through backward induction, the process therefore unravels, such that in the first market, the chain store chooses to share the market rather than to contest entry. Knowing that no future periods of monopoly profits await it in other markets, the incumbent will not incur the costs of fighting in the first. The dominant firm—the chain store—is therefore, paradoxically, powerless. Even in repeated play, its threats are not credible.

There are many lessons to be extracted from this example, and I shall build several major arguments upon them.[16] What is relevant here, however, are the lessons to be learned when the game is repeated not a finite number but rather an infinite number of times (or when it is of uncertain duration). When the game is repeated an infinite number of times, or when its stopping point is uncertain, then there is no knowable last period of play; the game therefore does not unravel. As the incumbent's present costs of fighting can be recovered from the future stream of monopoly profits, albeit ones discounted for lying in the future or for being uncertain, the incumbent firm may well find it in its interests to implement its threat. Knowing that to be the case, the entrant will refrain from contesting the market. Under such circumstances, then, the established firm's threat to punish becomes credible. And the reaping of monopoly profits therefore becomes a sustainable (subgame perfect) equilibrium.

The shift from a finite to an infinite time horizon—that is, the shift to infinitely repeated play—thus yields outcomes that were not sustainable as equilibrium in other settings.[17] It therefore illustrates what is known as the folk theorem.[18] For scholars of international relations, the significance of the folk theorem is obvious and has been rapidly absorbed: cooperation *can* be sustained as an equilibrium, even in a world that lacks a government.[19] International agreements can be sustained as an equilibrium of the infinitely repeated interactions among states at the global level.

Scholars of international political economy thus explain the emergence of international bodies, such as the International Coffee Organization (ICO), by appealing to game theory and to repeated interaction. As with the theory of hegemonic behavior, however, this approach too encounters difficulties. And these difficulties reemphasize the importance of shifting the focus from the international level to domestic politics.

The policy choices of the "players" in the international game are not solely a function of the strategic situation: the distribution of capabilities, in the case of hegemonic theory, or the structure of the game, in the case of noncooperative game theory. They are also a function of the preferences of the players, and thus of the payoffs they assign the outcomes resulting from these choices. These payoffs accrue to domestic political actors. For any choice of foreign policy, there will be winners and losers at the domestic level; what one player values, another may discount. Without information about the domestic politics of the nation, we therefore cannot understand how choices at the international level are arrived at. The analysis of decisions must be based on both preference and constraint. As a theory of international politics, game theory therefore requires an analysis of domestic politics for its completion.[20]

Throughout this study, we will marshal the logic of games in extended form. We will do so in an attempt to comprehend the origins of the ICO. Ultimately we will find game theoretic models of collusion unsatisfactory, however. But we will learn much from their failures. The failure of these approaches will provoke innovation. It will lead us to reconceptualize the problem posed by the ICO as one in *political* economy and international policies as the outcome of domestic political struggles. The domestic political process, and the policies that result from it, I will argue, are governed and structured by institutions. Again and again, throughout this study, I will therefore reaffirm the importance of moving from economics to politics, from the international to the domestic—and toward the analysis of institutions.

Domestic Politics

Thus far I have focused on approaches to the study of international political economy. But a major objective of this book is to isolate and define the elements of what can be called an open-economy approach to the study of politics. With respect to the developing areas, two earlier efforts stand out, the one Marxian in inspiration and the other neoclassical.

The so-called dependency school constitutes a major, earlier effort to create a theory of open-economy politics.[21] In the 1980s, scholars abandoned this approach; they did so too precipitously, I feel. In the developing world, the debt crisis precipitated the conversion to market-based economies; with the rise of Reagan and Thatcher and the collapse of socialism in the advanced industrial economies, the spread of market forces heralded the decline of Marxist thought. But, at the same time, those who supplied international capital gained unprecedented influence over economic policies throughout the developing world. Aligned with the governors of national banks and finance ministries, suppliers of international capital launched an extension of the market system from the core to the periphery of the global economy. Ironically, then, dependency theory fell out of fashion just when it was becoming most relevant. I, too, will critique it; but I will also build off it, rather than ignoring it, as too many others now do.

Developing societies specialize in the production of primary economies, dependency theorists stress, which they exchange in global markets for manufactured goods. With the growth of per capita incomes, the prices of primary products fall in international markets relative to the prices of industrial commodities; and with static production technologies, the result is continued poverty among the developing nations. Dependency theorists therefore argue that the route to development lies in reducing reliance upon the production of primary commodities for export to world markets; it lies in promoting industrial production for the domestic market. But, dependency theorists note, the policies of the state reflect the interests of economic elites. Changes in policy therefore encounter political resistance from those whose economic fortunes are tied to traditional exports. Only by wresting power from the "feudal oligarchy" of export agriculture can domestic industrialists secure the policies that will enable them to transform the economic structures of developing societies, break ties of dependence on foreign markets, and thereby secure economic development.

This book focuses on the coffee industry. It therefore enables us to assess critically the dependency school, which treats Brazil as a critical case.[22] In the "dependency account," the story of Brazilian development becomes a story of political capture. The coffee barons of São Paulo don the garb of feudal oligarchs; the political conflicts between export agriculture and the industrializing elite, including Vargas and Kubitschek, provide a parable from which are drawn lessons about development. Brazil was underdeveloped when dominated by export agriculture; this was the Brazil of the Old Republic. Brazil began to develop when agrarian elites were overthrown by the urban industrial classes; that is the story of Brazil under Vargas and Kubitschek. The lessons are clear: Policy choices reflect the interests of dominant groups, and economic development results when political power is transferred between them.

The dependency school thus provides an interpretation of Brazil's political and economic history. Building from that history, it provides as well an interpretation of the International Coffee Organization. By joining with other coffee producers in founding the ICO, Brazil organized the poor agrarian nations of the south over and against the rich, industrial nations of the north, it claims. Through the ICO, the development-minded elites of Brazil led a producers' alliance that raised the price of primary commodities in international markets, increasing Brazil's export earnings and redistributing income from the advanced industrial nations of the north to the developing nations of the tropics. The international politics of coffee thus represents an extension of Brazil's domestic transformation. The ICO, the dependency theorists argue, constituted a means by which Brazil could reverse its declining terms of trade.

Dependency theorists thus offer an open-economy approach to the analysis of developmental politics. They offer an analysis of Brazil and of the ICO. I endorse their insistence that the analysis of the domestic politics of developing nations be situated within the analysis of international markets. I endorse their argument that foreign economic policy, such as Brazil's support of the ICO, should be viewed as an extension of domestic political struggles. But I concur with the critique offered by those who dissent from the dependency school's interpretation of Brazilian political history.[23] As we shall see, even in the Old

Republic, Brazilian politics was *not* captive. Politics in the Old Republic was dominated by politicians, *not* by interest groups. The policies the politicians favored and the measures they devised to address the needs of the coffee industry reflected the incentives created and the constraints imposed by the political institutions within which they competed for power. Contra the dependency school, public policy is not the result of capture by economic interests, I demonstrate. Public policy is the outcome of the efforts of politicians to gain and retain political office within a structure of domestic political institutions, sometimes to the benefit of particular interests, and other times not.

Trade theory provides a second approach to the study of politics in open economies. Whereas the foundations of dependency theory lie in Lenin's theory of imperialism, those for trade theory lie in neoclassical economics.[24] Recent works by Ronald Rogowski and Jeffry Frieden best illuminate this approach.[25]

Rogowski draws upon the Stolper-Samuelson theorem in trade theory; Frieden on the Ricardo-Viner variant. Employing neoclassical reasoning, both theorems link changes in international prices to changes in the domestic distribution of income, and thus to patterns of conflict among domestic interests. According to both theories, income is determined by the flow of payments to factors used in the production of commodities.[26] Increases in the price of a commodity produce a more than proportional increase in the returns to the factors used in its manufacture; decreases lead to a more than proportional fall. Because nations hold a competitive advantage in the production and export of goods that make intensive use of factors with which they are relatively abundantly endowed, those who derive their incomes from the payments that flow to the relatively abundant factor favor free trade. Those who own relatively scarce factors, by contrast, find their incomes depressed by competition from lower-cost producers abroad and so favor protection. Relative positions of advantage in international markets thus induce domestic political differences.

Thus far, the approaches followed by Frieden and Rogowski follow the same path. Where they diverge is in the assumptions they make about the nature of the factors of production. For Rogowski, factors flow freely among many alternative uses; the release of labor in one industry thus affects the price of labor in others, for example. As a result, changes in international markets animate class interests; they affect the price of factors of production—labor, land, or capital—nationwide. For Frieden, by contrast, factors are specific. Factors that are released from one industry or sector do *not* compete with factors employed by another. When an industry or a sector is adversely affected by foreign competition, the results are recession and unemployment, but for that industry or sector alone. For Frieden, changes in international markets therefore animate specific industries or sectors, rather than classes, in the domestic economy.[27]

Employing the logic of trade theory, Rogowski and Frieden analyze the domestic political significance of international market forces. Rogowski, for example, examines the impact of the lowering of transport costs upon the emergence of political cleavages in Europe and North America in the nineteenth century; he explores as well the domestic effects of the collapse of trade upon class conflict during the Great Depression. Frieden focuses on the impact of the recession and debt crisis of the 1980s on politics in Latin America. He stresses the resultant patterns of sectoral politics where factors are specific, as in the case of Brazil, and class conflict where factors are not, as in the case of Chile.

Ironically, while derived from fundamentally different intellectual traditions, the neoclassical approaches of Rogowski and Frieden and the Marxist approaches of the dependency theorists share much in common. Both seek an open-economy theory of politics and view international markets as fundamental determinants of domestic political conflict. Both treat political actors as agents of economic interests, be they classes, sectors, or industries. Neither accords a significant, much less determinative, role to political institutions. Both offer interest-based, economically deterministic visions of politics. The criticisms I offer for dependency theory therefore extend to the neoclassical approach as well.

Both dependency theory and neoclassical trade theory treat Third World exporters as small nations, that is, as price takers in world markets. For dependency theory, the result is victimization by large multinational firms or by protectionist forces in the markets of the advanced industrial nations; for the neoclassical trade theorists, the result is that world prices can be treated as exogenous, and the domestic distribution of income can be viewed as the product of forces unleashed in international markets. In recent years, however, prominent trade theorists—such as Krugman, Helpman, Grossman, and others—have abandoned the assumption of competitive international markets, noting that particular firms, industries, or nations possess the power to shape prices in international markets.[28] They have produced the so-called "new trade theory," based upon models of imperfect competition. It too offers a theory of open-economy politics.

As we shall see, the international coffee market is highly imperfect. A few nations, led by Brazil and Colombia, dominate the production of coffee; a few firms, led by General Foods and Nestlé, dominate the processing and sale of coffee in consumer markets. Economic agents have responded to market imperfection by attempting to set market prices. This study traces the efforts of producers to exploit their power in international markets and the attempts of processors and consumers to resist producers' efforts; indeed, it shows how the dependency school was born of public reactions to struggles between producer and consumer nations. The imperfect market for coffee inspired the international politics of coffee, as it created incentives to use economic power to redistribute resources at the global level.

Attempts at institution building represent a second result. Some took place internationally: Efforts to build the International Coffee Organization represented attempts to create a context within which smaller producers could credibly pledge to abide by cooperative agreements. Others took place domestically. Particularly when the ICO worked and prices rose, producers of coffee would seek to increase exports, thereby threatening to undermine the accord. Governments therefore needed to constrain and to alter the behavior of farmers, and they devised regulatory institutions to do so.

In keeping with recent work in international trade theory, I therefore adopt an approach that emphasizes the imperfection of international markets; contra both dependency theory and neoclassical trade theory, large coffee producers possess market power. Seeking to reap the benefits to be secured from the manipulation of market prices, the producers created institutions both at home and abroad.[29] In particular, their choice of international strategy led them to transform the domestic political economy and to reshape the structure and behavior of markets. Their ability to do so, and the way in which they do so, is shaped by domestic politics.

To emphasize this last point, note that, as illustrated in map 1.1, coffee production bands the globe. As we shall see, when the International Coffee Organization shocked the world coffee market by requiring each producing nation to limit its exports, similarly situated producers chose ways of restructuring domestic markets that led to different allocations of the costs of adjustment to the ICO's quotas (see table 1.2). Each form of adjustment represents a distinctive political story.

Under one form of adjustment (table 1.2, Policy I), the producers respond to the increase in world prices by producing more coffee. But the government elicits adherence to the international quota by withholding coffee from the market. The government creates institutions that purchase and stockpile surplus coffee. Such a response represents *a triumph for export agriculture; it entails transfers of resources to farmers from the state.*

Alternatively, the government secures adherence to the international quota by imposing an export tax (Policy III). The growers then do not perceive the new world price, created by the ICO's limits on exports; rather, they see that price discounted by the amount of the tax imposed by their government. Given this tax, producer incentives are weakened; and coffee growers therefore reduce production to the assigned quota level. This means of apportioning the costs of adjustment represents *a triumph of the state over export agriculture.*

A third possibility (Policy IV) involves the creation of institutions that enable the manipulation of the exchange rate. Under this form of adjustment, the government creates a domestic price for coffee growers that lies below the world market price by appreciating the domestic currency. Following an appreciation of the national currency, exporters are forced to sell the "dollars" they earn to the national bank for fewer "pesos" than before. They therefore reduce their production of coffee, thereby adhering to the international quota.

TABLE 1.2
Divergent Policy Outcomes

Policy Choice: Limitations of Exports by	Illustrative Cases	Political Implications
Policy I: The government purchases coffee surpluses	Brazil 1906 Brazil under the Permanent Defense	Farmers capture the state
Policy II: The government bans coffee planting	São Paulo 1906	Established producers exclude new entrants Estates triumph over peasants
Policy III: The government taxes coffee exports	The Vargas regime Brazil 1954–64 Brazil under military government Colombia under Rojas Pinilla and the National Front	The state triumphs over export agriculture
Policy IV: The government overvalues the currency	Colombia after World War II Brazil, 1954–64	Import-substituting industry extracts resources from export agriculture
Policy V: The coffee growers tax themselves	Colombia, all periods	Export agriculture left partially autonomous
Policy VI: Unrestricted exports	Colombia, 1930s	Export agriculture left unregulated

Appreciating the national currency acts as a tax on coffee exports; by strengthening the "peso" relative to the "dollar," the government also confers a subsidy on imports, which now appear cheaper, in terms of local currency. In the context of the developing nations, imports are usually demanded by industry; exports are usually furnished by farmers. This mode of allocating the costs of adjustment therefore represents *a triumph of the urban, industrial sector over export agriculture*.

As illustrated in map 1.1, the coffee-producing nations lie scattered throughout the tropics. Each supplies a similar product to a single, or at least a tightly integrated, market; but, as revealed in table 1.2, their governments can, and do, differ in the ways they adjust to the imposition of export limits and therefore in the ways in which they apportion the costs. By focusing on domestic politics, I seek to account for this variation in the way in which governments articulate their domestic economies with the international market. I thereby seek to take advantage of the opportunity provided by the coffee market to integrate the study of comparative politics with the study of international political economy.

Did the ICO Work?

Before launching into an analysis of the ICO—its origins, operations, and impact—we must ask, Did it have any impact? Responding to this question forms a necessary preliminary to any investigation of the agency. For if the ICO had no effect on international markets, then it would not warrant our attention.

The ICO divided the world into two categories: the member and the non-member nations. As seen in table 1.3, over the period 1972–73 to 1981–82, its members—those who had signed the International Coffee Agreement—accounted for virtually all of the world's exports of coffee and, on average, for 90 percent of the world's imports. The nonmember consuming nations included the socialist countries of Asia, Eastern Europe, and the Soviet Union that lacked the convertible currencies so desired by tropical exporters; and the Middle Eastern countries that possessed such currencies but consumed little coffee.

By agreement among its members, the ICO constructed an indicator price and used it to set target prices for coffee. In the later years of its existence, the target interval for the indicator price lay between $1.20 and $1.40 a pound. The agency then set quotas for coffee exports so as to force the indicator price into the target range. When the indicator rose above $1.40 a pound for a predefined period, then quotas were relaxed; when it fell below $1.20 a pound, they were tightened. At times of extreme increases in prices, such as after major frosts in Brazil, quotas were abandoned altogether, until production resumed normal levels and trading took place at prices falling within the target range.

When in effect, the quotas were enforced by the customs authorities of the consuming members. Every quarter of the coffee year—which runs from October 1 to September 30—the secretariat of the ICO would issue stamps to its exporting members; the "value" of the stamps would total the magnitude of that nation's quota. Customs officers in the consuming member nations inspected coffee shipments. They would deny entry to those lacking stamps. And they would collect the stamps from shipments bearing proper documentation, returning them to the secretariat of the ICO. In this way, the secretariat could monitor adherence to the quotas. Shipments to nonmember markets could be made using normal commercial documents, as they did not count against the exporter's quota. Without the stamps of the ICO, however, they could not legally be re-exported to member states.

Did the controls imposed by the ICO work? As suggested in table 1.4, the studies that have directly addressed this question suggest that the ICO's constraints on exports raised coffee prices. The studies are few in number, however.[30] In addition, they appear to rely on methods that may yield erroneous estimates.

TABLE 1.3

Exports and Imports by Member and Nonmember Nations, 1972/73–1981/82 (Millions of Bags)

	1972/73	1973/74	1974/75	1975/76	1976/77	1977/78	1978/79	1979/80	1980/81	1981/82
World Exports	61	58	57	57	53	55	64	61	59	64
Member Exports (by origin)	60	57	57	57	52	51	63	60	59	63
Brazil	18	15	15	13	15	9	13	14	16	17
Colombia	6	7	8	7	5	8	11	12	9	9
Other Americas	19	16	20	19	18	20	22	20	19	20
Robustas	16	18	15	18	14	14	16	15	15	17
Member Exports (by destination)										
To members	54	51	50	50	48	46	57	54	52	52
To nonmembers	7	6	6	7	5	5	6	6	8	9
Exporting Nonmembers[a]	—	—	—	—	—	—	—	—	—	—
World Gross Imports	64	64	62	66	60	56	70	67	67	69
Members	57	57	55	59	53	49	63	60	59	61
U.S.A.	24	23	20	22	18	17	22	20	18	19
E.E.C.	22	22	22	24	22	21	27	25	27	27
Other members	12	12	12	13	13	10	15	14	14	15
Member Imports by Origin	57	57	55	59	53	49	63	60	59	61
From exporting members	54	53	51	55	50	46	59	56	55	56
From importing members	3	3	3	3	3	3	4	4	4	4
From nonmembers	—	—	—	1	—	—	—	—	—	1
Importing Nonmembers	6	7	7	7	7	6	7	7	7	8

Source: International Coffee Organization, *Quarterly Statistical Bulletin, July–September 1982* (London: ICO, 1982), summary table, p.2.
[a]Less than 500,000 bags.

TABLE 1.4
Recent Studies of ICO Impact on World Coffee Prices

Akiyama, Tamassa, and Panayotis Varangis (1990), "The Impact of the International Coffee Agreement on Producing Countries." *World Bank Economic Review* **4, 2 (May 1990): 157–73.**

Model/ Methodology	Simulations based on a multiequation econometric model of the world coffee market. The econometric model used annual data, 1968 to 1986; simulations were run for the 1981–86 period.
Findings	Average prices under the quota system, 1981–85, were higher than if there had been no quotas. If no quotas had been in place during that period, however, 1986 world coffee prices—when Brazil experienced production shortfalls due to drought—would have been 24 percent higher than actual prices, since the quota system induced accumulation of stocks that were released into the world market in 1986. In general, such stock accumulations would reduce coffee prices in years when the quota system was not in operation.
	Overall, the quota system had a stabilizing effect on world coffee prices. Quotas reduced real export earnings for most small exporting countries, but large producers gained. Most small countries gained in terms of reduced variability of export income.

Herrmann, Roland, Kees Burger, and Hidde P. Smit (1990), "Commodity Policy: Price Stabilization vs. Financing," in *Primary Commodity Prices,* **ed. L. Alan Winters and David Sapsford (Cambridge: Cambridge University Press, 1990).**

Model/ Methodology	Simulations based on econometric estimations of the world coffee market. Estimations used 1966–81 annual data. Simulations compared hypothetical nonquota prices in 1982 and 1983 with actual prices under the quota system.
Findings	In 1982 and 1983 world prices in ICO member markets were 47 and 17 percent higher, respectively, than would have been the case without quotas; conversely, prices were lower in nonmember markets. Although higher prices reduced demand in member importing countries, ICO exporters experienced net welfare benefits—as did nonmember importers. ICO member importers and nonmember exporters experienced welfare losses. On net, the world coffee economy experienced welfare losses due to the quota system.

(continued)

TABLE 1.4   (*Continued*)

Palm, Franz C., and Ben Vogelvang (1991), "The Effectiveness of the World Coffee Agreement: A Simulation Study Using a Quarterly Model of the World Coffee Market," in *International Commodity Market Models*, ed. Orhan Gurenen, Walter C. Labys, and Jean-Baptiste Lesourd (London: Chapman and Hall, 1991).

Model/ Methodology	A model of coffee-producing and coffee-importing countries that included trade on spot and futures markets as well as inventory accumulations was estimated using quarterly data from 1971 to 1982. Experiments were run to simulate the effects of different production and policy scenarios.
Findings	Under an ICO quota system, price levels and export earnings were higher than without quotas; exported quantities, disappearance, and inventories were lower. In the long run, coffee prices in member markets would be 42 percent higher with a quota system than without one.

To appreciate the origins of such errors, consider periods in which the coffee price rose above $1.40 a pound; under the rules of the ICO, in such periods, prices were formed by the interplay of supply and demand. Now consider a period in which the price fell into the defense range; under the rules of the ICO, prices would be formed by the interplay of demand and quantity constraints. There is thus a change in regime, that is, in the way in which prices are determined. There is also an element of simultaneity. Without properly specifying the process of price formation, estimates of the relationship between quotas and prices might misleadingly suggest that the quotas that constrained export quantities produced a decline in price. In addition, there remains the problem of censoring: When the ICO regulated the coffee market, we rarely observed the impact of market forces at low price levels. It is thus extremely difficult to determine statistically whether the ICO produced prices that differed from those that would have prevailed in an unregulated market. By the same token, it is difficult to generate unbiased estimates of the impact of the agreement.

Given that the econometric studies of other researchers fail to address these problems, their findings cannot be relied upon. I have attempted to build a properly specified econometric model of price formation. Annual data offered too few observations, however; and while I was able to secure monthly data for some variables, I was not able to do so for others. I have therefore had to settle for a less direct approach. For the ICO to work, it needed to fulfill two necessary conditions: it had to restrict arbitrage between the member and nonmember markets and competition among the producers of coffee. The evidence suggests that it succeeded in both tasks.

Arbitrage

Figure 1.2 presents evidence concerning the effectiveness of the ICO. The horizontal axis displays the dates in which quotas were in effect: August 1965–October 1972 and October 1980–August 1985. The vertical axis records the ratio between coffee prices in the markets of member and nonmember nations, expressed as a percentage.[31] When the ratio exceeds 100 percent, then prices in member markets exceed those in the markets for nonmembers, arbitrage has been prevented, and barriers to trade have been put in place effectively. The evidence in figure 1.2 suggests that when the ICO imposed quotas, it was able to enforce them, yielding a higher price in the coffee markets of member nations.

While visually satisfying, were these effects statistically significant? To answer this question, I calculated the means and variances of coffee prices in member and nonmember markets in periods in which the ICO did and did not impose quota restrictions.[32] I constructed a variable, call it D, which measures the difference in the mean value of prices in the member and nonmember markets in each period. D can be transformed into a test statistic that possesses a t-distribution. The null hypothesis is that the mean of D is zero, or that there is no statistically significant difference between the mean of the prices in the two markets. We reject the null if we observe values for the test statistic that fall into a critical range—a range where its value would be highly unlikely (one chance in one hundred), were it determined by chance.

In this instance, I chose a critical range appropriate to a one-tailed test of the null hypothesis; I wished to reject the null when the value of the test statistic is highly and significantly positive—that is, when the mean price of coffee in the member market exceeds that in the nonmember market by a level significantly greater than would be likely by chance. Given the number of observations available, the critical region in which one can reject the null hypothesis begins at 2.33. The results of the test, presented in table 1.5, enable us to reject the hypothesis of no difference in the mean price of coffee in the two markets at the .01 level of confidence in periods in which the ICO quotas were in place. The imposition of quotas appears to generate a significantly higher price in member markets.[33]

Rivalry

Thus far I have focused on the impact of the ICO on average price. At least as important is its impact on relative prices. For competition between coffee producers takes the form of competitive price cutting by producing nations. If average prices are to stay high—if the marketing agreement is to work—then such competition would have to cease.

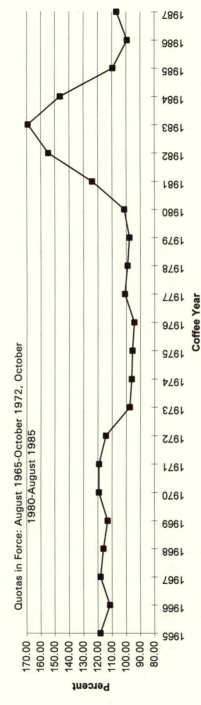

Figure 1.2. Price of Coffee Exported to Members as Percentage of Price of Coffee Exported to Nonmembers. *Source*: Monthly price data from the files of the International Coffee Organization.

TABLE 1.5
Testing for the Impact of the Quota

	Number of Observations	Mean for D	t-Statistic
Periods in Which Quotas Were in Place			
August 1965–October 1972	600	2.342	5.295
October 1980–August 1985	299	18.742	6.571
Periods in Which Quotas Were Not in Place			
November 1972–September 1979	420	−1.516	−1.264
September 1985–August 1988	240	−9.150	−1.923

Source: Monthly price data from the files of the International Coffee Organization.

Loosely speaking, coffee markets recognize four major types of coffee. At the top of the market stand the coffees of one dominant producer, Colombia.[34] Accounting for 15–20 percent of the world's coffee exports, Colombian coffees tend to fetch the highest average price in international markets. Brazil, with 20–30 percent of the world's exports, produces coffee valued in the middle range of the market.[35] Positioned between the coffees of Brazil and Colombia are the "other milds"; produced largely in Central America, they tend to be preferred to the coffee of Brazil but to be regarded as of lower quality than that of Colombia. Robusta coffees, produced largely in Africa, occupy the bottom rung of the coffee market.

From the point of view of Colombia, the other milds constitute the competitive fringe; from that of Brazil, the other milds and robusta coffees. For, within limits, the different types of coffee can be substituted for one another. Should Colombia raise the price of its coffee and the producers of other milds not follow, then consumers would switch to other milds; the ratio of the prices would be less than the ratio of the marginal utilities. Should African producers reduce robusta prices, Brazil would have to follow suit; for, given a suitable price differential, consumers could switch to the lower quality coffee without suffering a decrease in their utility. And should Brazil seek to raise the price of its coffee while the producers of other milds maintained their prices, then consumers could increase their utility by switching to the higher quality washed arabicas of the other milds group.

A second test of the effectiveness of the ICO, then, is its impact on relative prices. For the agency to work, it had to enable Brazil and Colombia, the dominant producers, to raise their prices without being undercut by the competitive fringe. Figure 1.3 illustrates the pattern of relative prices for a period when quotas were in effect. Overall, price differentials remained stable. The pattern contrasts with that exhibited in figure 1.4, which portrays relative

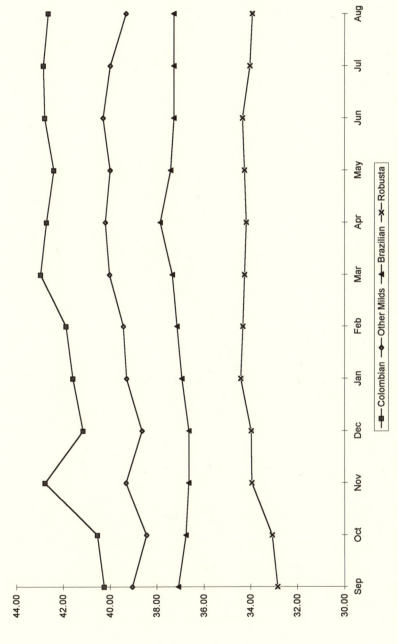

Figure 1.3. Coffee Prices, 1967–68. *Source:* Monthly price data from the files of the International Coffee Organization.

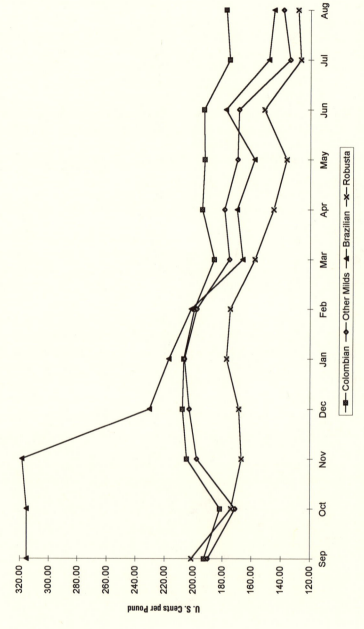

Figure 1.4. Coffee Prices, 1977–78. *Source*: Monthly price data from the files of the International Coffee Organization.

prices in a period when quotas were suspended following a catastrophic frost in Brazil. Given Brazil's size in the market, the frost produced a massive rise in prices (compare the prices on the vertical axes of figures 1.3 and 1.4). It also produced a massive distortion in relative prices. Upon recovering, Brazil sought to reposition its coffee at a price level intermediate to that of the other milds and robusta coffees. But, as can be seen in figure 1.4, African producers resisted, cutting their prices to keep Brazil from closing the gap. So too did the producers of other milds, who lowered their prices below those charged by Brazil. The competitive response posed a challenge to Colombia as well, for the growing price differentials between other mild and Colombian coffee encouraged consumers to abandon the higher quality Colombian product. Colombia therefore joined in the price cutting. In the face of the kind of competitive behavior portrayed in figure 1.4, the dominant producers sought to reimpose the quantity constraints that would generate the evenly spaced price differentials exhibited in figure 1.3.

The Collapse of 1989

Restraint of competition represents an essential prelude to price-setting behavior. The evidence contained in figures 1.3 and 1.4 therefore suggests that the ICO was an effective institution.

I offer one last piece of evidence: the behavior of coffee prices at the time of the breakup of the ICO. As will be recounted in the narrative that follows, in June and July 1989 the ICO collapsed. As seen in figure 1.1, when the ICO broke up, coffee prices plummeted. The spot price for Colombian milds, for example, fell from $1.80 a pound in June to less than $1.00 by July—and stayed below $1.00 a pound for several years thereafter.

In data not presented here, I have also analyzed the behavior of prices for future coffee contracts.[36] Through June 1989, the spread between future prices and spot prices remained negative, suggesting that agents perceived a scarcity of supplies and sought to sell rather than to store coffee. In June and July, however, the relationship between future and spot prices reversed. Immediately upon the breakup of the agreement, spreads became positive, implying that agents in the market perceived an abundance of supplies.[37]

The data thus suggest that not only had the ICO been effective, but that it had also been perceived as effective by those making decisions in the marketplace. When the ICO was no longer in place, relative prices reflected the end of its restrictions upon the availability of coffee.

Where did the ICO come from? How did it operate? How did it impact upon member nations? Why did it collapse? To these questions we now turn.

2

Brazil as Market Maker

IN THE nineteenth century, leaf rust invaded the coffee plantations of Ceylon, one of the largest producers in the East Indies; by 1890, the disease had affected two-thirds of the island's plantations. As recounted by Jacob: "By the middle of the eighteen-eighties, Hemileia vastatrix (the leaf rust) had conquered. [And] in the devastated coffee-plantations, a new crop was grown—tea."[1] "The last coffee-crop harvested in Ceylon was in the year 1900, and amounted to no more than 7,000 sacks. For years, the island had been one of [the leading producers of coffee], but it no longer took part in the competition."[2]

In the 1880s, the leaf rust spread to the plantations of the Dutch East Indies. It struck with particular force in Java, an island that produced a superior grade of coffee and that so dominated the coffee market that it lent its name to the beverage.[3] As coffees from the East Indies became scarce, their prices rose; as the supply of Brazilian coffees increased, the price declined. The price differential between coffees from the two origins widened, and people therefore switched to Brazil's cheaper coffees. By the mid-1800s, 60 percent of the coffee purchased in world markets came from Brazil, a figure that rose to 70 percent by the early 1900s (figure 2.1). With the collapse of exports from the east, Brazil became a giant in the world coffee market. It became the dominant producer of the world's coffee.

But Brazil did not immediately respond to its position of market power. And when it did so, it launched, and then abandoned, policies of market intervention. It is precisely this inconsistency in response that renders its behavior significant.

Systemic theories locate the behavior of nation states in the global distribution of resources. From such a perspective, Brazil constitutes an extreme case: few states have ever so thoroughly dominated a particular market. Under the assumptions of systemic theory, Brazil would therefore be expected to act as a market maker, transforming its position of market power into a position of economic advantage.[4] And yet, for long periods, Brazil's power remained only potential; lacking organization, its coffee sector could not exert influence over market prices. Brazil, then, did not respond as systemic theories would predict. Brazil's behavior challenges game theoretic approaches as well. Game theoretic models of international politics take states as unitary actors, with well-defined preference orderings and coherent choices of strategy. But, as we shall see, Brazil's coffee industry sometimes combined and cohered,

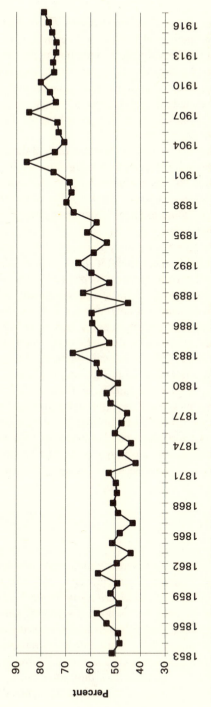

Figure 2.1. Brazil's Share of World Exports by Year. *Source:* Robert Carlyle Beyer, "The Colombian Coffee Industry: Origins and Major Trends, 1740–1949." Ph.D. diss., University of Minnesota, 1947, Appendix, table 5.

while at other times its industry remained disorganized, with its members competing against each other as well as with foreign producers in international markets. Internal conflicts signaled conflicting preferences over coffee policy. And, when lacking coherence and organization, Brazil was incapable of implementing the sophisticated strategies that game theorists would expect. Brazil's behavior also violated the expectations of the new trade theory; with a preponderant share of the market, Brazil was slow to adopt domestic policies that would maximize its export earnings.

The evidence from this chapter makes clear that each of these approaches to the study of international political economy requires the analysis of domestic politics for its completion. It was not until the domestic industry was organized that Brazil behaved internationally in ways that conform to theoretical expectations formed in response to either systemic or strategic approaches to the study of international politics.

The variability in Brazil's trade policy not only evokes modifications in theories of international political economy; it elicits reappraisals of theories of domestic politics as well.[5] Until recently, dependency theory provided the dominant explanation of Brazil's domestic development. More recently, scholars have shifted to neoclassical approaches.[6] Both variants seek to explain political choices in open-economy settings; both appeal to interest-based explanations. In the context of Brazil, they treat economic policies as resulting from the capture of the state by large-scale interests. And yet, as we shall see, contrary to the expectations of both theories, the coffee planters often failed to capture the state. And the climax of Brazil's market intervention resulted from the actions of politicians, rather than from lobbying by coffee growers. The complex and decentralized institutions of the state made it difficult to capture; they also shaped the content of interventionist programs. From an interest-based explanation, we thus move to one based upon political institutions and the incentives they create for—and the constraints they impose upon—politicians.

The Old Republic

The Old Republic of Brazil was a federal republic: the constituent states possessed the attributes of sovereignty—the power to tax, to borrow, to make international commitments, and to place armies in the field.[7] The states were grouped into a national confederation whose government was characterized by a division of powers. The president's constituency was the nation; that of a legislator, the state. The states sent equal numbers of representatives to the Senate; the number of representatives each sent to the lower house depended upon its population. Policies became laws only after bills proposing them secured a majority in both chambers of the legislature and received the assent

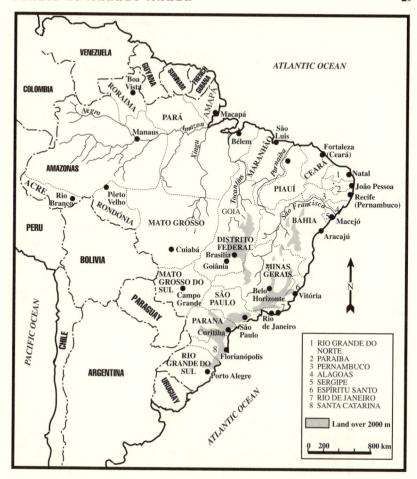

Map 2.1. Brazil. *Source:* Solena V. Bryant, *Brazil* (Santa Barbara, Calif.: Clio Press, 1985), p. 245.

of the national president. By refusing its approval, each branch of government could, in effect, veto the legislation. The president appointed a cabinet that superintended the executive departments of the national government, the most significant of which were the Ministry of Finance and the armed forces.

The military deserves special mention. Brazil and Argentina constitute the giants of Latin America; they competed for territory as well as status, battling for control over lands lying along Brazil's southern border. The Brazilian army was therefore a large one, and a major portion of its forces was located in the south, particularly in the state of Rio Grande do Sul (see map 2.1). The army was professionalized to a greater degree than other national bureau-

cracies. Driven by its military mission, it demanded that the state establish
policies designed to transform the economic and technological capabilities of
the nation, the better to equip it for war. When supported by the armed forces,
the national president became a formidable figure with the ability to overawe
even the largest of the member states. When opposed by his army, he was
politically and physically in peril.

The armed forces antedated the Old Republic; indeed, by overthrowing the
government of the Empire, they helped to create it. The power of the central
military helped to induce a political preference for federation. When alienated
from the policies of the national government, individual states nonetheless
sought to accommodate themselves to its dictates; they sought to modify its
policies rather than to secede from its jurisdiction.

This structure of political institutions posed fundamental challenges to any
interests, such as the coffee interests, that sought to capture power at the
national level. An interest would have to capture a majority in both houses of
the legislature, and secure the backing of the executive branch as well—
including, and especially, the military forces. To do so, the interest would also
have to gain the support of the powerful states that dominated the federal
system.

The Federal Regime

At the end of the nineteenth century, coffee production was concentrated in
São Paulo; the state accounted for nearly 60 percent of Brazil's total exports.
Furthermore, it was concentrated among a small portion of the planters within
that state: data from the 1920s suggest that the largest 12 percent of the plantations in São Paulo controlled nearly two-thirds of the productive potential of
the industry (table 2.1). These data should be viewed against the narrative
evidence marshaled by Holloway and Font, which underscores the rapid
growth of smallholder production, particularly in the 1920s in São Paulo.[8]
Given the rapid multiplication of smallholdings in the 1920s and their increased significance in the industry, the industrial structure must have been
even more concentrated in earlier periods.

Within the federal structure, each state sought to use its power at the national level to secure key policy objectives; in the case of São Paulo, that of
course meant to secure policies that favored the producers of coffee. Each
state also sought to use its power to defend against attempts by others to use
the national government to seize its resources. For a wealthy state, such as
São Paulo, security from predation constituted a core political interest. To
secure such objectives, states therefore sought to render presidents dependent.
They could do so by delivering or withholding large blocks of votes in presidential elections or in a large and unified congressional delegation, able to use

TABLE 2.1
Distribution of Plantations in São Paulo According to Size, 1927

Estates With	Number of Estates	Cumulative Percentages of Farms	Number of Trees (millions)	Cumulative Percentage of Trees
1 million trees and over	21	0.05	34.0	3.01
900,000 up to 1 million	12	0.08	11.4	4.02
800,000 up to 900,000	7	0.10	5.9	4.54
700,000 up to 800,000	16	0.14	12.0	5.60
600,000 up to 700,000	27	0.21	17.5	7.15
500,000 up to 600,000	37	0.30	20.3	8.94
400,000 up to 500,000	73	0.48	32.8	11.84
300,000 up to 400,000	160	0.88	56.0	16.80
200,000 up to 300,000	451	2.02	112.7	26.77
100,000 up to 200,000	1,615	6.06	242.2	48.19
50,000 up to 100,000	2,390	12.05	179.2	64.04
20,000 up to 50,000	5,659	26.24	198.0	81.56
10,000 up to 20,000	7,489	45.01	112.3	91.49
5,000 up to 10,000	8,189	65.53	61.4	96.92
Under 5,000 trees	13,751	100.00	34.4	99.96
Total	39,897		1130.1	

Source: J.W.F. Rowe, *Studies in the Artificial Control of Raw Material Supplies, No. 3: Brazilian Coffee* (London: HMSO, 1932), p. 89.

its voting power to pass desirable policies—and to block harmful ones. In order thus to tame the executive and legislative branches of the federal government, politicians at the state level used their control over state-level political parties. They employed their control over patronage to mobilize unified political delegations, and thereby to influence the legislative process and the selection of presidents at the national level.[9]

Given the incentives operating within the federal system, political elites therefore placed a premium on securing unified political delegations in the legislature and unified political parties "back home," at the state level. The value of political unity increased with the size of the state. The apportionment of votes among key states is shown in table 2.2.

Clearly, not even the largest state—Minas Gerais—could by itself dominate the Chamber of Deputies. It would have to recruit allies. Its ability to extract concessions when bargaining with other delegations would depend upon the number of votes it could deliver—or withhold. The larger the number of votes, the greater the ability to convert legislative coalitions into legislative majorities; and the larger the number of votes, the greater the ability to threaten to defect from majorities, rendering them losers in the competition for control over legislative outcomes. The larger the number of votes in a state

TABLE 2.2
Size of State Delegations in Chamber of Deputies

Delegation Size	Minas Gerais	São Paulo	Bahia	Rio Grande do Sul	Pernambuco	Pernambuco and Satellites	Total[a]
Number of Deputies	37	22	22	16	17	42	214
Percentage of Deputies	17	10	10	7	8	20	72

Sources: Compiled from Robert Levine, "Pernambuco e a Federação Brasiliera, 1889–1937," and John Wirth, "Minas e a Nação," in *O Brasil Republicano,* ed. Boris Fausto (Rio de Janeiro: Editora Bertrand Brasil, 1989), pp. 89 and 124.
[a]There were 58 Deputies from other states in Brazil.

delegation, then too the greater the value to that delegation of remaining unified.[10]

Unity was valuable for another reason: When parties competed for seats in the Chamber, they would send forward rival delegations. Members of the Credentials Committee in the federal legislature could then choose which delegation to admit. From the point of view of a state, this led to a decrease in its power; having others choose the state's delegation weakened the state's ability to bargain. For the elite, political disunity at the state level thus represented a prelude to disaster, for rivals within the state could ally with forces external to it and use the Credentials Committee to install themselves in power.[11]

Minas Gerais furnished the largest national delegation. By all accounts, the members of this delegation operated in unison, mobilizing in serried ranks behind legislative proposals advanced by the state's governor and checking the advance of political forces hostile to their interests. In seeking to control legislative outcomes, the delegation from Minas Gerais worked closely with the delegations from São Paulo—the next largest—and Rio Grande do Sul. Rio Grande do Sul was significantly smaller than either Minas Gerais or São Paulo; but, by judicious control over the Credentials Committee, on the one hand, and appropriations for the military (so heavily concentrated in the state), on the other, Rio Grande do Sul accumulated a fringe of dependent, satellite delegations, thereby expanding its political weight. By targeting selected smaller delegations, the leaders of Minas, São Paulo, and Rio Grande do Sul gained a bloc of votes sufficient to control policy-making by the national legislature.

In the late nineteenth century, Brazilian leaders were aware of the coffee industry's newly won position in world markets and appreciated its significance. Cincinato Bragga, a representative of São Paulo in the national legislature and an influential spokesman for coffee interests, frequently cited Brazil's "monopoly" in the world market and advocated that the nation exploit the resultant potential for increased revenues by driving up prices in the international market.[12] Members of the Senate Finance Committee advanced similar arguments in 1905, urging the government to abandon "classical economic theory" and market-based reasoning: "Due to Brazil's almost monopolistic position in coffee production," the Committee reported, Brazil "is in an exceptional position" and should not simply take market prices as given but rather set them by withholding coffee from export.[13] Dr. Augusto Ramos, a professor and consultant on coffee, offered a similar assessment. After studying the productive potentials of regions elsewhere in South and Central America, Ramos reported: "Brazil continues and will continue to have no competitors in the world."[14] Brazil was free, he contended, to capitalize upon its position by driving up the international price of coffee.

In the nineteenth century, then, Brazilian coffee achieved a distinctive position in the international coffee market. Its position engendered a sense of a national interest and created the opportunity to pursue an international economic policy in pursuit of that interest. But political action was required to realize Brazil's economic potential. Brazil achieved the capacity to act strategically and to extract the value of its market domination only after the Paulistas, as São Paulo's elite were called, solved the problems posed by Brazil's decentralized political system. The Paulistas did so by bundling coffee policy with exchange rate policy, thereby attracting the support of politicians from other states and, in particular, providing the leaders of Minas Gerais, the largest state, with a means of providing a unified—and therefore powerful—national political delegation.

Side Payments and Coalition Formation

Brazil's coffee growers possessed market power; the quantity of their exports influenced market prices. By withholding coffee supplies, they could raise the price of coffee in international markets; given that Brazil faced an inelastic demand for coffee, they could thereby increase its foreign earnings. An increase in "dollar" revenues—I shall refer to all foreign currency earnings as dollars—would yield an equivalent increase in local currency revenues only if the exchange rate—the number of mil-réis issued per dollar—did not decline. But precisely at this point, the coffee growers confronted a dilemma: the very factor that gave them control over the price in dollars—the huge size of the Brazilian crop—weakened their ability to increase their earnings in local currency. For as the dollars earned from coffee exports flooded into Brazil, they became relatively abundant by comparison with mil-réis; mil-réis became relatively scarce; and the local currency therefore appreciated in value. With each dollar earning fewer mil-réis, the coffee growers found the benefits resulting from their use of market power eroded by changes in the exchange rate.[15]

When coffee growers demanded policy measures to enable them to affect prices in international markets, they therefore demanded as well policy interventions that would enable them to maintain the value of the mil-réis. The two policies complemented each other economically. More importantly for this discussion, they complemented each other politically as well. For while the impact of changes in the earnings of coffee producers would be regionally concentrated, the impact of changes in the exchange rate would spread throughout the nation. The mil-réis was, after all, the national currency.[16] By raising the exchange rate, the political representatives of São Paulo's coffee producers could generate benefits for their constituents while generating benefits for interests in other regions. In seeking to secure national support for coffee legislation, São Paulo's political representatives therefore emphasized and exploited the macroeconomic effects of exchange rate policy. They bundled government intervention in coffee markets with the reform of the exchange rate.

The Paulistas pointed out that the producers of other exports would benefit from the depreciation of the local currency demanded by the exporters of coffee. Sugar producers in the northeast, the exporters of cotton from the northern and central states, the rubber industry of the Amazon, and cocoa growers and mineral exporters: these too would gain. While the producers of these commodities might not be able to influence the "dollar" price of their exports in global markets, as could the producers of coffee, all would benefit from a depreciation of the mil-réis, for the foreign currency they did earn would then convert for greater amounts of local currency.

While it would be misleading to argue, as many have, that sugar, rubber, cocoa, coffee, and other export crops were produced in enclaves, nonetheless their production was regionally concentrated. Far more widely distributed was the production of food crops. Rice was grown along the coast and on river margins; beans, maize, and manioc along the coast and inland; and cattle were raised in the Pampas and the interior of states farther north. Each of these "crops," while destined for the domestic market, nonetheless was internationally traded. The growth of urban centers spurred increases in the demand for food; urbanization took place most rapidly along the coast and rivers; and the domestic producers of agricultural commodities therefore encountered competition from imports, which could be delivered at low cost to the port cities. One response was to demand tariff protection; indeed, political careers were built by advocating protection to agriculture.[17] A second was to demand public works to lower transport costs and, in particular, railways to link the agrarian interior to the coastal cities, with rate structures that favored farm products.[18] A third was to back the Paulistas' demand for a depreciation of the mil-réis. With a devalued currency, domestic consumers would face a higher price for imported food products. Demand would shift to local products. And the growers of food for local consumption could increase the value of their sales in the domestic market.[19]

By packaging the proposals for intervening in coffee markets with proposals to depreciate the mil-réis, the coffee producers were thus able to forge an alliance with other exporters and with the producers of import-competing commodities, particularly the producers of food.

Rio Grande do Sul stood among the most important of the food-producing states, exporting to other states not only rice but also beef, particularly dried beef, a staple of the urban diet.[20] Pinheiro Machado, head of Rio Grande do Sul's delegation, diligently backed São Paulo's proposals to raise coffee prices. São Paulo, in turn, backed policies promoting the interests of Rio Grande do Sul's producers of food crops.[21]

Minas Gerais, an important producer of coffee, also produced cotton, dairy products, and tobacco in the central sections and lumber, dairy products, and beef in the west. The São Paulo representatives therefore forged close ties with David Campista, leader of the large bloc of delegates from Minas Gerais. He championed São Paulo's coffee policies; São Paulo backed his demands for tariff protection and railways, both targeted at the food-producing regions of Minas Gerais. It was São Paulo's demand for currency reform, however, that consolidated the alliance. Pinheiro Machado and David Campista vigorously backed São Paulo's demand for the depreciation of the currency, which would benefit not only the export-oriented coffee sector but also the producers of import-competing agricultural products destined for national markets.

The linking of valorization policies with the manipulation of the value of Brazil's national currency thus enabled the representatives of the coffee industry to politically transcend the confines of their region. By tying the withholding of exports to the depreciation of the mil-réis, the champions of São Paulo were able to transform a proposal that they found politically desirable into a policy that was politically feasible, given the federal structure of Brazil's political institutions.

Recall an earlier point: that the game of politics defined by the federal system placed a premium upon state unity. Fragmented states lost bargaining power in the coalitional politics of the center and became vulnerable to external intervention. Recall, too, that the value of state unity increased, all else being equal, with the size of the state's delegation. These factors help to account for the depth of the appeal of the use of exchange-rate policy in Minas Gerais, but the limits of its appeal in Rio Grande do Sul. They therefore also help to explain the limits of its use in constructing a national alliance in support of interventionist policies.

Minas Gerais impaneled the largest bloc of delegates in the national legislature; its political leaders therefore derived great benefits from political unity.

But Minas Gerais was highly vulnerable to fragmentation. As argued by Wirth, "Minas is not a natural economic unit."[22] It had been created as "an administrative convenience of the mother country";[23] that is, by Portugal during the colonial period. As underscored by Wirth, the political leaders of Minas Gerais therefore sought every means possible to promote state unity. One was by controlling the distribution of federal patronage, granting projects—roads, railways, and other public works—as rewards to those who were politically loyal and withholding them from those who were not.[24] As stated by Wirth: "Each year what has been called the 'political budget' was received by the Finance Committee, where deputies from Minas were well entrenched. To put it gently, they assured that the interests of Minas would not be overlooked."[25] The state leadership used its influence in the national legislature to gain control over this "political budget" and thus over the allocation of jobs, projects, and other distributive benefits. Another way was by backing measures to depreciate the currency, thereby creating advantages for both the regions in Minas Gerais specializing in the production of coffee exports and the regions specializing in the production of goods destined for the local market that could also be imported from abroad.

Rio Grande do Sul, like other states with large delegations, also derived great benefits from political unity. But exchange-rate policy that elicited unified backing throughout Minas Gerais failed to do so in Rio Grande do Sul. Rio Grande do Sul contained regions specializing in the production of food for the growing urban market, especially rice, produced on the coast, and beef, produced inland. But it also contained a large number of military bases; much of Brazil's army was stationed close to the country's southern border. As with the food producers in Minas Gerais, the producers of food crops in Rio Grande do Sul stood to benefit from the depreciation of the currency; as producers of import substitutes, they would then face less competition from abroad. But the members of the military consumed but did not produce food products. Increased prices for foreign crops, brought about through the depreciation of the mil-réis, made possible increased prices for domestic food; but in doing so, they reduced the real value of the military's salaries. The depreciation of the mil-réis undercut the standard of living of the members of this powerful bureaucracy.

The tensions within Brazil's political economy represented conflicts between the "traded" and "nontraded" portions of an open economy, in the terms of the so-called Australian trade model.[26] The depreciation of the currency shifted relative prices in favor of the producers of exports and importable products; by the same token, it shifted relative prices against those in the "untraded sectors," such as providers of governmental services. The model thus provides insight into the preferences of key actors in Brazil's political economy and into the fragility of the political foundations for its coffee policy. Because the policies championed by the Paulistas would exacerbate conflicts within the leadership of Rio Grande do Sul, they could weaken the state at the national level. Rio Grande do Sul's alliance with São Paulo therefore remained problematic, depending in large part on the strength and degree of politicization of the armed forces and the way in which they reacted to the inflationary consequences of coffee policy.[27] As we shall see, this factor proved to be of very great significance in explaining the political sustainability—and nonsustainability—of Brazil's economic policy.

The Valorization of 1906

The difficulty of forging domestic political coalitions that spanned both states and branches of the government helps to explain the lag with which Brazil exploited its market power.[28] In the late nineteenth century, São Paulo's political leaders repeatedly introduced bills in the national legislature proposing government intervention: "Beginning in 1889," Holloway reports, "and in every legislative session from that time to 1906, at least one bill was proposed in one or both houses of Congress."[29] In 1906, reports from early in the crop year suggested a harvest of magnitude never before seen (see figure 1.3). The Paulistas redoubled their efforts.[30] Jorge Tibiriçá, governor of the state of São Paulo, not only dominated the politics of his state; he also exercised control over its parliamentary delegation. In unison with his legislative team, he lobbied vigorously for national backing for a national marketing strategy.

Despite their efforts, the Paulistas lost out, for a majority of votes in the legislature did not suffice, given the division of powers; the president also had to concur. And the incumbent president, Rodrigues Alves—himself from São Paulo!—fearing the costs to the government, refused to add the assent of the executive branch to the approval of the legislature. Tibiriçá and his confederates therefore began to maneuver, pressing forward in two arenas: the back rooms of Congress and the party caucuses selecting the president's successor.

In the Congress, the Paulistas played their next card: they proposed the creation of a Caixa de Conversão, a monetary body that would purchase foreign exchange for notes that could be used as domestic currency. By reducing the quantity of foreign currency in circulation and augmenting the supply of domestic currency, the Caixa would elicit the depreciation of the mil-réis. The Paulistas were able to recruit David Campista, head of the massive delegation from Minas Gerais, as floor leader for their scheme. And in September of 1906, they were able to gain as well the public endorsement of Pinheiro Machado, head of the delegation from Rio Grande do Sul.[31]

Tibiriçá and his followers also maneuvered in the arena of presidential politics. Rodrigues Alves was scheduled to leave office in 1906; he chose Bernardino de Campos as his successor. In an interview widely quoted in the Brazilian press, however, Campos revealed his opposition to "the projects of the valorization of coffee [in association] with the 'disvalorization' of the currency,"[32] and the Paulistas therefore mobilized to derail Rodrigues Alves's plans. They switched their backing to a more compliant presidential aspirant, Afonso Pena, who was willing to commit federal resources to their program and to support the depreciation of the currency.[33] Pinheiro Machado and David Campista joined in the effort to unseat Bernardino Campos and to install Afonso Pena. With the backing of the leaders of the three great congressional delegations—those from São Paulo, Minas Gerais, and Rio Grande do Sul—the maneuver succeeded. In 1906, Pena assumed the presidency, bringing Campista into his cabinet as Minister of Finance. The president signed the coffee legislation and Campista, as Minister of Finance, set in motion the operations of the Caixa de Conversão. The exchange rate stabilized at roughly 15 (British) pence per mil-réis in 1907.[34] And in 1907, the federal government arranged for its bankers to loan, in its name, 3 million pounds sterling to the state of São Paulo for "obligations assumed with the valorization of coffee."[35]

The 1906 valorization converted Brazil's coffee industry from a price taker to a price setter in world markets, enabling it to function as a unitary actor, pursuing sophisticated economic strategies. The valorization enabled Brazil to act hegemonically in world markets, converting its potential into actual market power. The adoption of the policy demonstrates the power of the coffee interests. But it also demonstrates that neither Brazil's economic power, nor its ability to behave as a unitary actor, nor the power of major economic interests over trade policy—none of these—could be assumed. Rather, they had to be constructed. Their construction required the skillful solving of the political challenges posed by the institutions of the Old Republic: the problems posed by federalism, that necessitated cross-state alliances, and by the division of powers, that necessitated coordination across the branches of government. The challenges posed by these institutions shaped as well the content of economic policies, for they required the construction of coalitions, thus accounting for the bundling of export with exchange-rate policy in the construction of "coffee power."

The So-called Permanent Defense of Coffee

When alluding to the capture of the Brazilian political system by export agriculture, most scholars refer to a second major period of market intervention: the period of the Permanent Defense of coffee, initiated in October 1921 by Epitácio Pessoa, who proclaimed: "Coffee accounts for the largest share of the value of our exports. . . . The defense of coffee constitutes, therefore, a national problem, whose solution requires that Brazil impose sound economic and financial policies."[36] And yet, proposed by the national government in 1921, the policy was abandoned shortly thereafter. Taken up again in 1922, it was again abandoned in 1923. The national government recommitted itself to the defense of coffee in 1925 and maintained that commitment until the program's spectacular collapse in 1929. An examination of the politics of the so-called Permanent Defense reveals the fragility of the power of the planter elite and clarifies the factors that account for changes in their ability to control national policy.

A massive frost in 1918 had destroyed nearly 40 percent of Brazil's coffee harvest and, as a consequence, nearly 30 percent of the world's crop. The shortfall brought the global market close to equilibrium, with roughly 20 million bags being produced and consumed annually.[37] The absence of surplus coffee encouraged Brazil's coffee growers once again to aspire to set market prices; and the sharp recession of 1920 and the resultant collapse in commodity prices spurred renewed demands for government intervention.[38] The representatives of coffee interests in Congress pushed for the issue of treasury notes with which to purchase and stockpile coffee; the president, Epitácio Pessoa, resisted. The leader of the government in the legislature backed the planters' demands. After heated clashes between the two branches of the government, the president surrendered to the demands of the coffee growers and announced his backing for measures to raise the price of Brazilian coffee in the international market.[39]

The successful valorization of Brazilian coffee in 1906 had required the overcoming of institutional divisions in the national political structure: divisions between states, promoted by the federal system, and between branches of the government, promoted by the separation of powers. By the 1920s, these divisions loomed too large to be readily spanned by politicians. The policy announced by Epitácio Pessoa—the Permanent Defense of coffee—therefore turned out not to be so permanent after all.

As with any major policy initiative in the Old Republic, the new programs required cooperation among the political leaders of three states: São Paulo, which initiated policies in favor of intervention in coffee markets; Rio Grande do Sul; and Minas Gerais. By the 1920s, those advocating an interventionist coffee policy had encountered increased difficulties in building this coalition.

New Interests

The rise of industry in Brazil took place most rapidly and dramatically in the coffee zone. As stated by Villela and Suzigan: "As late as 1905, when the first systematic industrial survey was made, the Distrito Federal was still the main industrial center in the country. By 1919, however, [it was São Paulo]."[40] Once launched, industrial growth accelerated rapidly; as shown in table 2.3, by the end of World War I, São Paulo had become not just the center for coffee production, but also the center for industrial production in Brazil.[41]

TABLE 2.3
Brazil: Value of Industrial Production and Industrial Employment by State,
1907 and 1919 (Percentage of National Total)

	1907		1919	
State	Value of Production	Employment	Value of Production	Employment
Distrito Federal	30.3	23.4	22.4	20.3
Rio de Janeiro	7.5	8.9	6.1	6.1
São Paulo	15.9	16.0	33.1	30.6
Rio Grande do Sul	13.5	10.1	11.8	9.0
Others	32.8	41.6	26.6	34.0
Brazil	100.0	100.0	100.0	100.0

Source: Annibal V. Villela and Wilson Suzigan, *Government Policy and the Economic Growth of Brazil, 1889–1945* (Rio de Janeiro: IPEA/INPES, 1977), p. 129.

Insofar as the mil-réis appreciated at times of increased coffee earnings, the industrialists' costs of imported capital equipment declined. Rates of capital formation in industry increased, as dollars could be purchased more cheaply by entrepreneurs. And when the political representatives of coffee bundled measures to depreciate the local currency with measures to raise coffee prices in international markets, then industries producing for the domestic market, like their agricultural counterparts, were protected from foreign competition by the increased prices of imported goods. Either way, then, industrialists could seize advantages from the impact of coffee exports on the value of the national currency.[42] The complementarity of sectoral interests is emphasized as well by those who document the extent of the investment of coffee "dollars" into projects that supported the growth of industry, be they railways, banks, or firms themselves. Warren Dean, Caio Prado Júnior, and others emphasize the degree to which coffee planters invested in the creation of urban industry, either by taking equity positions in industrial firms or by placing their savings in the capital market, where banks and other institutions could on-lend them to investors in industry.[43]

Despite the complementary interests of urban industry and export agriculture, it is clear that the rise of industry also provoked political conflict. The urban sector demanded high levels of public expenditures and therefore favored increased taxes on exports; in addition, it demanded a composition of services that differed greatly from that preferred by farmers. The rise of industry also created a growing number of consumers whose preferences clashed with those of industrialists and agricultural exporters. Producers might benefit from a depreciated currency—one raising the price of foreign products—but consumers did not. While exporters and the producers of import-competing goods therefore might not welcome the depreciation of the currency, the growing number of wage and salary earners in São Paulo increased the political costs of employing exchange-rate policy.

Increased Costs of Coalition Formation

The Paulistas not only incurred increased costs at home—that is, within São Paulo; they also encountered increased costs of forging the coalitions necessary to secure national power. The protests of consumers in São Paulo against the increased prices of imported goods echoed those from the military in Rio Grande do Sul, exacerbating political tensions between the states.

In 1910, Pinheiro Machado, Rio Grande do Sul's leading politician, had maneuvered Marshal Hermes de Fonseca, also from Rio Grande do Sul, into the presidency, against the opposition of the Paulistas. The latter retreated to their powerful state, literally fortifying its defenses so as prevent its take over by the alien forces that had seized national power.[44] In 1919, the politicians from Rio Grande do Sul struck again, successfully running Epitácio Pessoa for president. And in 1922, they unsuccessfully backed ex-president Nilo Peçanha against Artur Bernardes, the candidate favored by São Paulo and Minas Gerais. Clearly, Rio Grande do Sul had become an increasingly restive political ally. One reason was the growing dissatisfaction of the military, sparked in part by the inflationary impact of national economic policies. In 1922, the garrison in Copacabana revolted against the national government. When military units joined urban demonstrations in São Paulo in 1924, "The manifesto of the army rebels . . . complained about inflation."[45] The military focused on other issues as well, of course, particularly the growing disillusionment with electoral fraud and corruption. But, as Boris Fausto writes, "The *tenentista* rebellions of the 1920s were to point to inflation and budgetary imbalances as evils as serious as fraud."[46]

The growing militancy of the military reduced the value of exchange-rate policy as a means of roping Rio Grande do Sul into a cross-state coalition.[47] The Paulistas therefore found it increasingly difficult to form a coalition capable of mobilizing legislative majorities in favor of the coffee industry. Having bullied Epitácio Pessoa into announcing the Permanent Defense of coffee, they failed to secure the backing of a sufficient number of state delegations to pass the legislation.

Lower Prospects for Internal Unity

In the institutions of the Old Republic, political unity at the state level constituted a prerequisite for power at the national. It increased the bargaining power of state elites, enabling them to form or decisively to defect from legislative coalitions and rendering them less vulnerable to countermoves by political rivals. The elites of São Paulo had been weakened by the increasing difficulty of using exchange-rate policy to forge national political coalitions. They were further weakened in the Brazilian game of politics by their increasing disunity within their own state.

Given the growth of an increasingly vigilant consumer population in the rapidly expanding urban sector, São Paulo's political elites could champion currency depreciation—the instrument once used to entice other states into a national "coffee coalition"—only at the risk of exacerbating divisions within their state. Adding to the potential for internal conflict was the changing structure of the coffee sector.

In the 1920s, coffee production swept into the western regions of São Paulo. Given that coffee trees extract nutrients from the soil, and that the soils of the new region were more fertile than those of the old, the farms in the western coffee zones were more productive than those in the east.[48] Immigrants or workers from the coffee estates made up the bulk of the migrants to the coffee frontier, but the new farms were smaller than the established plantations. The result was the creation of the size distribution of production recorded in table 2.1, with a small number of extremely large farms, concentrated in the old coffee zones, and a large number of much smaller ones, lying in the frontier. Assigning all farms in a given category the value of the midpoint, we obtain the distribution portrayed in figure 2.2. The mean size of the farms—between 250,000 and 350,000 trees—lies well above the mode—5,000 trees or less—with the median falling close to the lower level (in the range of 5,000 to 15,000 trees).

In 1926, an opposition party, the Democratic Party, arose in São Paulo. Those who view Brazilian history in economic terms attempt to portray the Democratic Party as a vehicle of the interests of a rising bourgeoisie or a growing industrial sector. But more recent studies suggest that rather than being a social movement or a champion of class interests, the Democratic Party instead appears to have been a political party, pure and simple, intent upon choosing candidates and devising programs in a effort to win elections.[49] While moderate in its intentions and behavior, the Democratic Party was nonetheless revolutionary in its consequences.

The open emergence of partisan cleavages within São Paulo posed an urgent political threat to São Paulo's political elites. To defend themselves, the elites had to consolidate their political base, if only by matching or outbidding the new political entrants in their appeal to key constituencies. Under the spur of party competition, politicians were driven to a competitive search for votes. The number of smallholders in the interior far exceeded the number of large plantations, and the smallholders tended to concentrate in the new coffee zones. Politicians therefore increasingly promoted the colonization, subdivision, and settlement of the frontier and the public provision of services in the

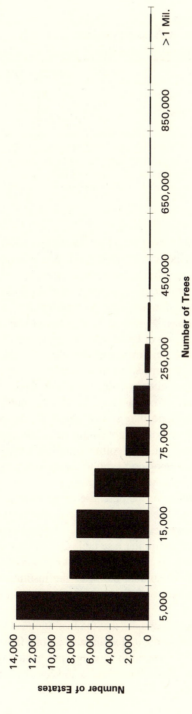

Figure 2.2. Size Distribution of Coffee Farms, 1927. *Source: J.W.F. Rowe, Studies in the Artificial Control of Raw Material Supplies, No. 3: Brazilian Coffee* (London: HMSO, 1932), p. 89.

TABLE 2.4
Costs of Production by Region
(Mil-réis per 60-kg Bag)

Region	Costs per Bag
New	132
Intermediate	143
Old	171

Source: Ronato Augusto Frederico, "Brazil: Stabilization of the Exchange Rate and Coffee, 1927–
1929." M.Sc. thesis, Department of Economic History, London School of Economics and Political Science, 1985, p. 40.

new coffee zones.[50] In his pursuit of the governorship of São Paulo, Washington Luís, for example, vigorously campaigned on a platform of smallholder
development, promising to provide "surveying teams free to plantations wish-
ing to subdivide, credit facilities for the purchase of farm inputs, free distribution of land in the public domain, and the construction of access roads in
newly opened frontier areas."[51] And in 1926, backed with funding obtained
from foreign loans, the governor took over the Instituto do Café, which managed the purchase, storage, and export of São Paulo's coffee.

Announcing that the guarantees given foreign bankers "demanded unfet-
tered control" over the Instituto do Café, the government of São Paulo took
control of all voting positions on the council of the Instituto.[52] The state governor transformed the Instituto into an instrument for his own political sur-
vival, rendering it an adjunct of the governing party. He appointed his secretary of finance as its president. The political pressures brought to bear upon
the Institute, and therefore upon coffee policy, were structured by the logic of
electoral competition and the search for votes.

The program put in place for the purchase of the crop of 1927 reflects the
impact of these pressures. The institute calculated the costs of production in
the old, intermediate, and new coffee zones, the last lying in the newly
planted regions of the coffee frontier (see table 2.4). The institute then set the
farm-gate price at between 30 and 35 mil-réis per 10 kilograms. Given that a
bag of coffee weighs 60 kilograms, the price the institute sought to defend
precisely matched its estimate of the costs of production of the old—and most
costly—coffee producers.[53]

At least as important as the choices that the Instituto made were those that it
did not; in particular, it chose not to discriminate among farmers, paying them
all the same price. Having covered the costs of production of the established
coffee elite, the institute could have paid a lower price to the lower-cost,
small-scale producers. But it did not choose to do so.

When the object of group pressures is prices, as it was in coffee policy, then the incentive to lobby is a function of economic size; all else being equal, the larger the producer, the larger the benefits of an increase in price. In such circumstances, then, we can think of the "mean" of the size distribution of farmers as governing the choice of coffee policy. In São Paulo in the 1920s, this meant that the outcome favored the larger farmer.

With the switch to a competitive party system, however, politicians had to respond to the competition for votes. The vote of a small farmer would count as much as that of a large one. In such circumstances, then, we can think of the median of the size distribution of farms as governing coffee policy. As suggested in figure 2.2, this meant a shift in policy in favor of the more numerous, smaller coffee farmers. It is therefore not surprising that when the Instituto became an economic wing of the governing party, it adopted a pricing policy that channeled the majority of its benefits to the mass of the smallholders. The smallholders may not have been large in economic scale or influential as lobbyists; but, being numerous, they carried weight in the electorate and, under the spur of electoral competition, the government tailored its policies accordingly.

São Paulo's political elite thus advocated economic polices to counter the political threat posed by the rise of partisan conflict within the state. But these policies proved in the longer run both economically and politically costly. For, given the institute's policies, producers in the new coffee zones planted more coffee. The defense of coffee prices therefore required the purchase of larger stocks. As we shall see, the economic repercussions generated a split between São Paulo's national political leaders and the leaders of other delegations.

The Crumbling Coalition

In 1926, Washington Luís, former governor of the state of São Paulo, followed Artur Bernardes to the presidency of the republic. A Paulista, Washington Luís was backed as well by the powerful elites of Minas Gerais; and he was the first president since 1919 not to face a challenge emanating from Rio Grade do Sul. With support from the three key states, Washington Luís could aspire to mobilize a congressional coalition of sufficient size to enact new legislation; and simply by occupying the presidency, he was in a position to span the division of powers on behalf of policies favored by São Paulo, thereby securing the adoption of these policies by the national government.

Washington Luís recommitted Brazil to the Permanent Defense of coffee. The national government therefore sought to back São Paulo's intervention in the market for coffee. Washington Luís created a Caixa de Estabilização to intervene in the market for foreign exchange. The government of São Paulo, through the Instituto do Café, purchased and stockpiled increasing volumes of coffee. When the Instituto purchased coffee, the "dollar" price of coffee rose and so too did Brazil's foreign exchange earnings. As had the Caixa de Conversão before it, the Caixa de Estabilização purchased foreign exchange with mil-réis (convertible to gold certificates), shifting the relative supply of foreign and local currencies and countering the appreciation of the mil-réis.[54]

By capturing the national presidency, the Paulistas thus gained the political power to orchestrate interventions in both the coffee and currency markets, using the national government's control over the market for foreign exchange to underpin the state of São Paulo's control over the physical supply of coffee. The twin interventions proved politically unsustainable, however, for both imposed costs on other members of the national political coalition.

In order to drive up prices in the world coffee market, São Paulo had to prevent the export of coffee. It did so by controlling shipments to the port of Santos. It required farmers to deliver coffee to the Instituto's warehouses inland, where it was stored for later emission into the world market. In partnership with the Instituto, the government created the State Bank of São Paulo to finance the purchase of the crop. The institute paid the farmers in promissory notes, backed by the proceeds to be realized from the subsequent sale of the coffee. And the bank formed a market in the notes issued by the institute; despite the notes' long and uncertain maturity—the coffee might not be shipped for up to twenty months or more—the bank was allowed to discount the notes, enabling the farmers to receive cash payment.

The government of Minas appears not to have created financial institutions similar to those created in São Paulo. The banks of Minas could only discount notes of short and certain duration. To secure cash payment, the farmers of Minas therefore pressured the Instituto to secure positions at the head of the queue for export.[55] The Instituto was controlled by the state of São Paulo, however, and did not respond with alacrity to their demands. As production increased in response to the new pricing policies, stocks mounted, and so too did delays in transshipment. Conflict between Minas Gerais and São Paulo rose in direct proportion.

Washington Luís also had to retain the political elites of Rio Grande do Sul within the "coffee coalition." But the latter's ability to cooperate was limited by the demonstrated sensitivity of the armed forces to inflation. Washington Luís was now politically constrained by having to restrain the rate of inflation. To depreciate the currency while avoiding inflation, Washington Luís therefore strove to reduce government spending. "In early 1928," Frederico notes, Washington Luís "went so far as personally reducing budget estimates from his Ministers' departments if they indicated expected deficits."[56] In the period 1923 to 1929, expenditures on public capital "fell abruptly in both relative and absolute terms," according to Villela and Suzigan.[57] "The restrictive monetary and fiscal policy of these years," they stress, "were clearly carried out at the cost of public works."[58]

By reducing inflation, Washington Luís's cutbacks generated political bene-fits: they helped him to retain the backing of the military and Rio Grande do Sul. But the cutbacks also inflicted political costs; for they threatened the ranks of the political elites of Minas Gerais, the guardians of the Old Repub-lic. As a consequence of the fiscal stringencies imposed by Washington Luís, the "political budget" was radically reduced in magnitude. Political leaders in both the coffee and noncoffee regions of Minas therefore suffered the costs of the stabilization policies. The benefits appeared to concentrate in São Paulo.

In an earlier era, by bundling the depreciation of the currency with inter-vention in export markets, politicians could provide the political foundation for a "coffee coalition." But the military members of the political block from Rio Grande do Sul placed one constraint on the use of this instrument: that the increased supply of local currency not generate too high a rate of inflation. And the machine politicians of Minas Gerais imposed another: that the supply of money not be curtailed by reducing the budget for public projects. The political institutions of the Old Republic required the simultaneous imposition of these constraints; only in this way could São Paulo secure national backing for coffee policy. But in the circumstances that prevailed in the 1920s, the two constraints ruled out any politically feasible common ground. The political foundations for a national coffee policy had crumbled.

Frustrated by limitations placed on him by the rules of the game, Washing-ton Luís sought to alter them. Not only did he try, through reapportionment, to gain control over the legislature; he also tried to secure São Paulo's succession to the presidency. In opposition to Washington Luís's attempts, Rio Grande do Sul put forward its own candidate for the presidency: Getúlio Vargas. Vargas enjoyed the support of the military; he had also forged close ties with the opposition party that had formed in São Paulo and with dissident factions in Minas Gerais. When the electoral counts failed to confirm the popular percep-tion of Vargas's victory, the army rebelled, placing Vargas in the presidency. Their action marked the end of the Permanent Defense of coffee, and of the Old Republic.

Conclusion

This chapter critiques major approaches in political economy, while under-scoring the utility of an alternative: one based upon the power of political institutions to shape and constrain the choices of political leaders.

Systemic theories appeal to the global distribution of capabilities to explain the choices of states. But Brazil, although a giant in international markets, was hobbled by its inability to choose or to implement policies consistent with its potential economic power. Game theoretic approaches stress the capacity of states to implement sophisticated strategies in international settings; they assume a coherent definition of national interests. So too does strategic trade theory, which, when applied to this case, would treat Brazil as a single producer with a single marketing strategy. But the political institutions of Brazil, as we have seen, rendered it difficult to adopt and maintain sophisticated market strategies or to formulate a coherent definition of national economic policy. Rather than behaving as a single, unitary actor, with well-defined notions of its national interest, Brazil instead often operated as a disaggregated entity, in which the producers of its primary export product, coffee, competed not only with producers elsewhere in the globe but also with themselves. As a consequence, Brazil often failed to pursue a sophisticated trade policy; rather, its individual producers maximized their incomes by selling competitively in global markets.

Domestic politics often overrode incentives arising from systemic forces in shaping Brazil's trade policies; proponents of national coffee policy often failed in their attempts to solve the challenges posed by the decentralized structure of power. And political barriers often frustrated attempts to render Brazil a unified actor, capable of exploiting its economic power; the structure of Brazil's institutions raised the costs of creating national political coalitions. The decentralized nature of those institutions—their federal structure and the division of powers—placed extraordinary demands on the size and nature of the domestic coalitions necessary to capture control of the government and thus to shape national policy.

The case of Brazil thus calls for the incorporation of domestic politics into the study of international political economy. The materials of this chapter suggest, moreover, the limitations of prominent forms of domestic political analysis. The history of the Old Republic is often written as the history of the power of export agriculture. Such an interpretation is in accord with both dependency and neoclassical approaches to open-economy politics, which stress the political role of economic interests and their power in shaping policy; it is also in accord with the new trade theory, which implies that a government is the agent of an industry or firm. Clearly, the Paulista coffee elite did exercise great power. But coffee policy was not imposed by an all-powerful elite. It was the result of complex political maneuvers, and the Brazilian state often escaped capture by the coffee interests. Once again, it is the structure of political institutions that helps to explain the unexpected weakness of economic interests. Brazil's political institutions imposed requirements that often made it impossible for São Paulo's politicians to harness the state to the interests of the large coffee growers. The nature of Brazil's political institutions helps to explain not only why politicians were less than perfect agents of economic principals in Brazil, but also the manner in which they packaged and structured public policies. It helps to explain why sectoral—coffee— policy was bundled with macro—exchange rate—policy. The structure of

Brazil's political institutions thus helped to define which economic policies were politically sustainable—and which were not.

Transition

In many respects, Vargas's coffee policies paralleled those of his predecessors. Initially politically vulnerable, Vargas needed, after all, the support of São Paulo's coffee growers. Nonetheless, Vargas soon initiated major policy changes. A major reason was changes in the costs, and the benefits, of Brazil's policy.

Vargas had been placed in power with the backing of Brazil's military. The depreciation of the mil-réis that accompanied market interventions shifted relative prices in a way that lowered the real value of the military's incomes. Insofar as the emission of notes also led to increases in money supply, domestic consumers were subject to additional sources of inflation; but insofar as the government cut spending to avoid inflation, it incurred political unpopularity.

The costs of Brazil's policy thus remained high. So too, however, did the benefits. When Brazil intervened, it successful defended against falls in the coffee price, at times of larger than normal harvests, or secured increases in coffee prices when supplies were low. Given Brazil's size in the market, and the inelasticity of coffee demand, the result was increased dollar earnings, and a redistribution of income from consumers in the north and planters in Brazil.

Changes in the world coffee market led, however, to an erosion in the benefits of Brazil's marketing strategy. For under the shelter of Brazil's costly intervention, Colombia vigorously entered the market and expanded its exports of coffee. Colombia free rode, reaping the benefits of the higher coffee prices created by Brazil. Brazil was thus left with an eroding share of the market, and a smaller share of the benefits of its interventionist policies. In response to the continuing costs and reduced benefits of Brazil's economic policy, Vargas transformed the structure of relations between planters and the state in the domestic political economy and the structure of relations with other members of the global coffee market. While previous governments had been willing to use taxpayer funds to remove coffee from the market and thereby drive up its price, Vargas required that the growers shoulder a greater portion of these costs; his government raised the export tax on coffee and compelled the farmers to surrender a part of their crop for storage or distribution. The government also shifted a greater portion of the costs to new entrants who might seek to exploit—and thereby undermine—its program: it imposed a "prohibitive" tax on new plantings.[59] In addition, Vargas's diplomats convened a series of conferences at which they sought to persuade producers abroad to restrict exports, rather than marketing their total production of coffee at prices created by Brazil.

Vargas's diplomats determined to secure an international marketing agreement. Failing the achievement of an agreement, his government announced, Brazil would retaliate: by abandoning its export limitations on exports and dumping its coffee on the market, it would launch a price war, thereby sanctioning the opportunistic behavior of other producers. On November 1937, Vargas acted on these threats. All coffee produced could now be exported, he announced; the government would no longer compel producers to surrender coffee for stockpiling or destruction. In addition, the government reduced the export tax; it thereby strengthened the incentives to move coffee stocks into the international market. Following the change in policy, Brazil increased its monthly shipments by 50 percent.[60] The price of Brazilian coffee (Santos 4) fell from 11.04 cents per pound to little more than 7 cents per pound,[61] a historical low on world coffee markets.

Brazil thus implemented its threat to revert to a competitive strategy, thereby seeking to elicit help from its competitors in bearing the costs of raising the international price of coffee. In so doing, Brazil began to use its economic power to restructure the international market, transforming it from a (imperfectly) competitive economic arena into a rule-governed organization. The chapters that follow will analyze this transformation.

3

Colombia's Entry

BEFORE LAUNCHING Brazil's valorization programs, Jorge Tibiriçá—the governor, booster, developer, and vigorous defender of the wealth and power of São Paulo—had dispatched Dr. Augusto Ramos to examine and report upon coffee production in the other nations of Central and Latin America. Professor Ramos had long served as a consultant to São Paulo's coffee industry. Everywhere he traveled, he found political disruption and economic disarray. In most nations he encountered rampant inflation and labor shortages. In others, warring armies created "apprehension and terror of the morrow," laying waste to plantations, railways, ports, and warehouses.[1] For these reasons, Dr. Ramos stated, "The coffee production of our competitors is . . . doomed to remain stationary."[2] As he concluded: "No appreciable increase of production need be expected from them. We must follow with the greatest interest the affairs of those nations and visit them at every opportunity. Nothing more. Concerning the increase in the production of coffee, Brazil continues and will continue to have no competitors in the world."[3] The implication was clear: should Brazil seek to raise the price of coffee in international markets, its efforts would not be undercut by the opportunistic behavior of competitors.

Among the countries visited by Dr. Ramos was Colombia. It too had been wracked by conflict, with over 100,000 persons dying in the so-called War of 1,000 Days.[4] But soon—much sooner than Tibiriçá or his advisers had anticipated—Colombia turned into a powerful competitor. As shown in Figure 3.1, Colombia increased its exports from less than 300,000 bags in the early 1890s to over 3 million bags in the early 1930s. And, as shown in figure 3.2, Colombia increased its share of the world market from less than 2 percent in the early 1890s to roughly 10 percent in the early 1930s. Colombia rapidly became Brazil's biggest trade rival.

In effect, Colombia had no marketing policy; its coffee growers competed in the global market, exporting all that they grew and undercutting the prices set by Brazil and other exporters. While market oriented, however, Colombia's policy was not apolitical. As this chapter will argue, Colombia's competitive strategy abroad represented the outcome of a political struggle at home, in which the coffee growers gained extraordinary influence over national economic policy. A major reason they could do so, I argue, is because the structure of political institutions, and in particular the structure of party competition, rendered them pivotal, giving them power over the political fortunes of those with ambition for office and enabling them to make or break

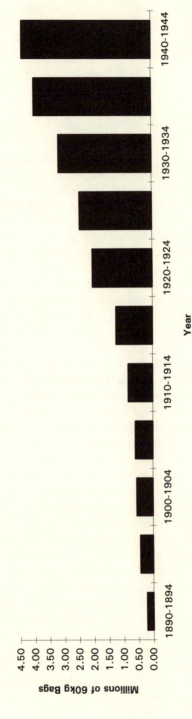

Figure 3.1. Colombia's Entry. *Source:* Edmar Bacha and Robert Greenhill, *150 Years of Coffee* (Rio de Janeiro: Marcellino Martins and E. Johnston, 1992), Appendix, table 1.1.

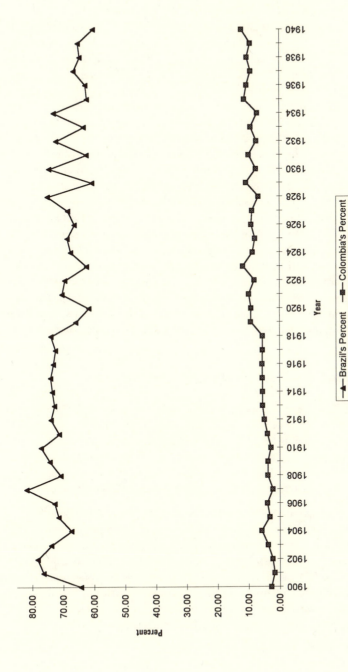

Figure 3.2. Changes in Share of World Exports. *Source:* Edmar Bacha and Robert Greenhill, *150 Years of Coffee* (Rio de Janeiro: Marcellino Martins and E. Johnston, 1992), Appendix table 1.1.

governments. They thereby gained the power to defeat government officials who sought to orchestrate or to constrain their behavior.

A major lesson of the Brazil case was that the dependency school's interpretation of Brazil's political history was wrong: Brazil's politicians frequently eluded capture by economic interests. Given the tendency to equate large with powerful in interest-based explanations, the weakness of Brazil's plantation agriculture posed a puzzle for political analysis, which I resolved by exploring the structure of Brazil's political institutions. This chapter further challenges interest-based explanations by exploring another case: that of Colombia, in which coffee producers were numerous and small. Being numerous and small, Colombia's coffee producers, like peasants elsewhere, encountered formidable costs of collective action. In most similar instances, such difficulties have rendered smallholders politically powerless.[5] And yet, as we shall see, Colombia's peasants elicited favorable policies from politicians, who at key moments themselves bore the costs of collective action, provisioning the coffee sector with economic institutions and delegating public powers to coffee interests. The explanation, I argue once again, lies in the way in which political institutions structure politics.

This chapter begins by exploring the Brazilian origins of Colombia's coffee industry. It emphasizes its smallholder structure and the nature and power of its major economic institution: the Federación Nacional de Cafeteros. And it addresses the basic question: From where did the power of the coffee growers arise?

The Mobilization of Colombia's Coffee Industry

When Jorge Tibiriça, governor of São Paulo, formed a domestic coalition in support of the "valorization" of coffee, his successful efforts to raise global prices imparted impetus to a trend that had already begun: the movement of capital and people down the central cordillera and into the western regions of Colombia (see map 3.1). Discussing the wave of optimism that swept Colombia after Brazil first intervened in the coffee market, Beyer notes:

> The coffee outlook after 1906 rapidly changed from one of depression to one of feverish enthusiasm. . . . Beginning with this period, it became the manifest destiny of Colombia in the eyes of many to sweep into the unsettled lands suitable to coffee, plant the trees, increase Colombia's production from 600,000 bags to 1,000,000, to 5,000,000, to 10,000,000 bags, to dominate the world market in mild coffees—even to replace Brazil. By 1909 even General Uribe had set the slogan "Colombians *sembrar* (plant) coffee!" It embodied the spirit of the cry "Go west, young man!" and might well have translated "Plant coffee or bust!"[6]

With the increase in coffee prices, people responded as if they had heard Beyer's injunction, "Go west, young man," and had gone west to plant coffee.[7] Histories of settlement in the new regions document the migrants' re-

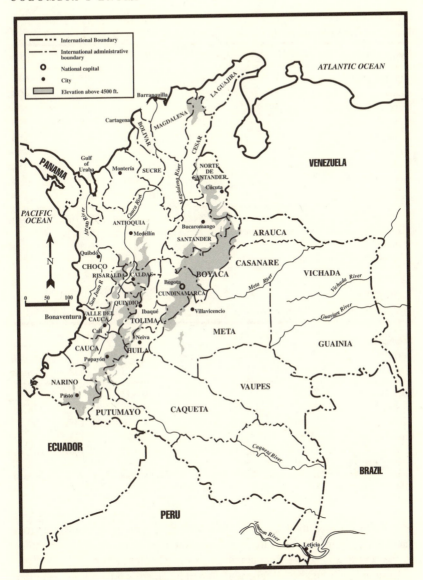

Map 3.1. Colombia. *Source:* Leon Zamosc, *The Agrarian Question and the Peasant Movement in Colombia* (New York: Cambridge University Press, 1986), p. xx.

liance on coffee.[8] Coffee did poorly in the extreme heat of the valley bottoms; it thrived in the cool, moist climate that prevailed in the mountains. Coffee could be grown on steep slopes; other "crops," such as cattle, could not adapt to such conditions. Coffee could therefore be grown on land for which there were few alternative uses—on land that was cheap. In addition, coffee was

TABLE 3.1
Production by Department, 1874–1932 (Thousands of 60-kg Bags of Green Coffee)

Department	1874	1890	1900	1913	1932
Antioquia	1	6	90	185	618
Caldas	a	a	a	199	1,004
Cundinamarca	3	40	230	200	406
North Santander	95	120	150	200	270
Santander	10	60	120	105	150
Tolima	b	b	b	60	448
Valle	1	4	20	50	354
Other	—	—	—	70	204
Total	110	230	610	1,069	3,454

Source: José Antonio Ocampo, "Los Orígenes de la Industria Cafetera, 1830–1929," in Nueva Historia de Colombia, vol. 5, ed. Alvaro Tirado Mejía (Bogotá: Planeta, 1969), p. 214.
a Included in Antioquia.
b Included in Cundinamarca.

TABLE 3.2
Production by Size of Coffee Farm in Eastern and Western Zones, 1923–32 (tons)

Size of Coffee Farm (Hectares)	Western Zone			Eastern Zone		
	1923	1932	Percent Change	1923	1932	Percent Change
Less than 3	20,540	37,434	82.2	6,333	16,030	153.1
3–12	26,572	44,074	65.9	8,685	24,151	178.1
12–15	14,649	30,640	109.2	7,586	15,138	99.6
Greater than 35	9,815	14,384	46.6	15,789	22,473	42.3
Total	71,576	126,532	76.8	38,393	77,792	102.6

Source: Absalón Machado, El Café: De la aparcería al capitalismo (Bogotá: Tercer Mundo Editores, 1988), p. 123.

one of the few commodities that could withstand the cost of transport from such relatively inaccessible areas. Coffee therefore became the crop of choice in the central and western mountain ranges of Colombia.[9]

Responding to the boom generated in part by Brazil's intervention in coffee markets, coffee production increased; the geographical center of the industry shifted from the eastern to the central and western portions of Colombia, and production shifted into the hands of smallholders (tables 3.1 and 3.2). The consequence, as shown in table 3.2, was not just a shift in the geographical location of coffee plantations in Colombia but also, with that shift, an accompanying transformation in industrial structure.

Special notice must be taken of Caldas, the department of Colombia lying immediately south of Antioquia along the central cordillera. Immigrants spread

TABLE 3.3
External Loans (Thousands of Dollars)

Year	National Government	Departmental Governments	Municipalities	Banks	Totals
1923	21,085	—	3,000	—	24,085
1924	18,530	—	8,970	—	27,500
1925	17,273	2,963	9,725	—	29,961
1926	14,501	27,132	12,939	8,922	63,494
1927	37,252	40,938	17,303	31,449	126,942
1928	71,125	63,497	24,008	44,484	203,114

Source: Jesús Antonio Bejarano, "El Despegue Cafetero (1900–1926)," in José Antonio Ocampo, *Historia Económica de Colombia* (Bogotá: Siglo Ventiuno Editores, 1988), p. 193.

into Caldas from Antioquia. In 1835 Caldas contained scarcely 12,000 residents; by 1851 its population had risen to 35,000; it then doubled to nearly 72,000 by 1870. By 1912, the population of Caldas had risen to over 340,000 people.[10]

Caldas lacked the expanse of plains that surrounded the coffee-growing regions in central Colombia, so useful for large-scale ranching. Nor did Caldas possess the rich bottomlands of Valle, suitable for the production of rice or sugar. It lacked the high, cold savannas of the east, on which could be grown wheat or barley.[11] Few gold deposits, so important to the economy of Antioquia, were to be found in this department. Caldas held a relative advantage in but one activity: the production of coffee. And the thousands of peasant families that migrated there specialized in the production of that crop. By the 1930s, as shown in table 3.1, Caldas was producing roughly 30 percent of Colombia's coffee. As we shall see, the spokesman for coffee from Caldas provided the "ginger group" in the coffee industry. In conflicts with the government and other sectors, Caldas's leaders furnished the industry's political core.

The Permanent Defense of Coffee

The development of Colombia's coffee industry received renewed impetus from Brazil's subsequent "Permanent Defense" of coffee. The boom of the 1920s, spurred on in part by Brazil's trade policy, reinforced the position of the smallholders. It also led to the creation of a new actor in Colombia's coffee industry—the Federación Nacional de Cafeteros (FNC).

Some historians refer to the 1920s as the period of Colombia's renaissance; others as the "dance of the millions."[12] As seen in table 3.3, the foreign private lending rose more than eightfold, from $24 million to over $203 million per year. Governments, too, transferred capital into Colombia. Over the period 1923 to 1926, the United States paid $25 million to the government of Colombia as reparations for backing the secession of Panama in order to secure a canal to the Pacific: $10 million in 1923 and $5 million annually for the next three years. In the words of Vernon Fluharty:

> It was, undeniably, a period of . . . material progress. The nation's foreign trade increased from 63 million pesos to 260 million between 1913 and 1928; by 1927 real estate was worth 2,000 million pesos; telephone line mileage went from 5,095 to 34,680 between 1913 and 1927; instruments in use from 11,860 to 20,066, and messages from 2 to 6 million. The volume of mail quadrupled, railroad track mileage doubled, and the volume of freight rose 800 percent.[13]

The annual rate of growth in the net national product per capita reached 5.2 percent in the late 1920s, the highest rate hitherto attained in Colombia and one of the highest in Latin America.[14] The inflow of capital further strengthened smallholder production in the coffee industry, and in two ways: by reducing the costs of exporting from the western and central portions of the nation, wherein smallholder production was concentrated, and by raising the costs of labor on the estates in the east, thereby reducing their profitability and promoting their subdivision.

In the west, the government used the infusion of capital to construct railways; the largest linked the new coffee zones of the west to the port of Buenaventura, strategically positioned to take advantage of the opening of the Panama Canal.[15] The smallholders in the new coffee regions could then supply foreign markets at lower cost and greater profit.[16]

The inflow of capital and resultant growth of the economy led to a sharp increase in the demand for labor. In industry, workers in the oil fields, the railways, and the ports and harbors formed unions and struck in an effort to exploit their bargaining position.[17] In agriculture, workers targeted the coffee estates. With the growth of the economy and increased demand for labor, workers in agriculture no longer needed to work for the owners of an estate. They could produce food and other products for sale to wage laborers; or they could work for other tenants, who themselves were producing food or providing services to those in paid employment.[18] In response to their enhanced bargaining position, employees on the coffee estates demanded better terms of service. Many demanded the right to cultivate their own plots of coffee.[19] One result was rural radicalism, as peasants sought to redefine the terms under which they gained access to land. Other results included an increased rate of fragmentation in the estate sector and the further spread of smallholder production.[20]

The Creation of the Federación Nacional de Cafeteros

The increase in coffee production thus led to economic growth in Colombia while creating a peasant-based, smallholder coffee economy. It also led to the creation of the Federación Nacional de Cafeteros (FNC).

The impetus for the creation of the FNC came from the western and central

TABLE 3.4

Data on the Structure and Political Significance of the Federación Nacional de Cafeteros

Department	Production 1932[1]		Number of Properties[2]	Percentage of Properties	Estimated Number of Adults		Representation in Coffee Congress[3]		Votes Actually Cast in 1930[4]
	Thousands of Bags	Percentage			Number[a]	Percentage of Voters	Number	Percentage	
Antioquia	618	17.90	28,589	19.14	28,589	31.18	5	16.67	91,687
Caldas	1,004	29.08	40,174	26.89	40,174	53.26	6	20.00	75,425
Valle de Cauca	354	10.25	20,289	13.58	20,289	64.64	3	10.00	31,387
Tolima	448	12.97	12,771	8.55	12,771	25.37	3	10.00	50,335
Cundinamarca	406	11.76	13,812	9.25	13,812	9.90	3	10.00	139,450
Santander Norte	270	7.82	7,972	5.34	7,972	17.68	3	10.00	45,095
Santander Sur	150	4.34	3,045	2.04	3,045	3.77	2	6.67	80,740
Magdalena	98	2.84	682	0.46	682	2.47	1	3.33	27,618
Cauca	56	1.62	12,447	8.33	12,447	22.46	2	6.67	55,416
Huila	51	1.48	4,471	2.99	4,471	23.39	2	6.67	19,111
Nation	3,453		149,384		149,384	18.12	30		824,530

Sources: [1]From data from the Censo Cafetero of 1932 reported by Jose Antonio Ocampo, "La Consoldiación de la industria cafetera, 1930–1958," in *Nueva Historia de Colombia,* ed. Alvaro Tirado Mejiá (Bogotá: Planeta 1989), p. 236. [2]FNC, "Censo Cafetero de 1932," reported in Mariano Arango, *Café y Industria, 1850–1930* (Bogotá: Carlos Valencia, 1977), p. 165. [3]Data from Federación Nacional de Cafeteros, IX Congreso, *Actas, Acuerdos, y Resoluciones,* Bogotá 1938, Acta No. 1. [4]Data calculated from archives of the Registraduria Nacional del Estado Civil.

Note: Columns will not total, as data from some departments are not included.

[a]Assuming one adult per property.

portions of the coffee zones: the areas dominated by smallholder production. As the FNC later became the embodiment of the power of Colombia's producers, the site of its creation is at first surprising; peasants, being "small," experience weaker incentives (even if greater needs) to organize.[21]

The key to unraveling this anomaly lies in recognizing that politicians, not peasants, organized the Federación. Taxes and fees paid by the producers helped to fund departmental and municipal governments in the coffee zones. The growth of the railways, the funding of public utilities, and the financing of roads: all significantly depended on revenues derived from the coffee industry. The governments in the coffee regions thus had strong financial reasons to promote the fortunes of the coffee industry. The department of Antioquia, in league with the municipalities and agricultural societies of adjacent regions, such as Caldas, convened a national Coffee Congress. The Congress petitioned for easier credit; better infrastructure, such as roads, railways, bridges, and harbors; greater facilities, such as docks and warehouses; and the reduction of transport costs, by reducing charges levied by the railways and barge owners. The Congress also called for the creation of an association that would represent the industry's interests, to be named the Federación Nacional de Cafeteros.

The FNC was structured as a mass organization. Membership was restricted to coffee producers, and the requirements for membership were such that even the smallest producer could join. The rank and file selected representatives to the municipal units of the FNC by ballot, and the municipal officials selected the departmental committees who then chose the delegates to the Coffee Congress: the sovereign core of the Federación that was convened periodically, or at moments of crisis, and whose assent was required for the decisions of its leadership to become FNC policy. The Coffee Congress chose the members of the executive committee, the Comité Nacional, that recruited and organized a professional staff and managed the finances and affairs of the organization.

While democratic in its structure, the FNC also abided by commercial principles. The membership chose the local leaders by ballot; but the number of representatives that a locale sent forward to the Coffee Congress—and the number of representatives that a department could therefore expect to place on the Comité Nacional—depended on that locale's contribution to the national harvest (see table 3.4). Members therefore gained representation not purely by dint of their numbers but also by dint of their volume of production. Both factors, it will be noted, favored the smallholders.

The Vigorous New Entrant

The Federación Nacional de Cafeteros rapidly emerged as a leading proponent of the virtues of unrestrained competition in world markets. Its early reports resemble the promotional materials of an aggressive and expansionary firm.

That of 1930 stresses the Federación's commitment to an international advertising campaign, keyed on the slogan "Buy Colombian when buying coffee,"[22] and the signing of contracts with advertising agents and prominent restaurants in Madrid, Barcelona, Prague, Stockholm, Brussels, Rome, Naples, and Berlin. As a result of this campaign, the phrase "Colombian coffee" would soon appear on posters in restaurant windows and on placards outside coffee shops in the major cities of the industrial world. The FNC also began a systematic effort to evaluate its position in world markets. It established offices in New York and London to analyze coffee demand, breaking down the market by sales in specialty shops, chain stores, and restaurants and by use in the home and workplace. It focused in particular on the demand for Colombian coffee and on its use in major blends. As the champion of Colombia's entry into the world market, the FNC undertook a far less public measure: it inserted an industrial spy in Brazil—an agent whom the government listed as its consul in São Paulo but whose primary job was to file reports on Brazil's coffee industry to the Federación in Bogotá.[23]

The Public Origins of Private Power

The FNC was also active at home. Within the coffee regions, it sought to provide essential infrastructure: warehouses, credit facilities, and information about prices in foreign markets. It also sought to improve the preparation and presentation of Colombia's coffee, so as to enhance its reputation for quality. In both activities, the FNC confronted organizational challenges. For individual producers possessed incentives to act in ways that undercut the collective interests of the industry.

Created by local and regional politicians, the FNC was then endowed with the public power to curtail opportunistic behavior. It was given the power to compel its members to act in ways that enhanced the productivity of the industry as a whole. It was made an economic institution.

In seeking to finance its projects and activities in the coffee region, the FNC faced a dilemma. Its membership was restricted to producers, the vast majority of whom were small and poor. Its members therefore could not afford to make large contributions; and as they could rationally believe that their contributions would have little effect on the capabilities of the organization, they had little incentive to do so. The founders of the organization therefore sought to make contributions compulsory; rather than charging a fee, they sought to levy a tax. The power to tax falls within the province of governments, not civic associations, however. And for the FNC to secure that power, the government had to confer it.

In Law 26 of 1927, the government of Colombia imposed an export tax on coffee, the proceeds of which were granted to the FNC. In effect, the coffee growers thereby acquired the power of the state, as the customs authorities and excise department now served as agents of the organization. The government's delegation of these powers was made contingent, however, upon the Federación's fulfillment of an explicit contract. Upon approval by the growers' representatives (usually the Comité Nacional, with the approval of the more broadly based Coffee Congress) and by the representatives of the government (usually the Minister of Finance; but also, upon occasion, the Minister of Agriculture or the national president), the contract set out the terms under which the government would agree to a 10-cent levy on each 60-kg bag of coffee exported onto world markets.[24] The terms of the contract stipulated the uses to which the Federación would apply its resources: the promotion of Colombia's coffee in world markets, for example, or the provision of specified services to growers. The contract ran for a fixed period and had to be renewed periodically. Only insofar as the Federación continued to fulfill the agreement could it continue to secure operating revenues. In effect, Law 26 gave access to a private organization to the power of the state. It thereby enabled it to counter incentives for smallholders to free ride, empowering them to engage in collective action. The government conferred further powers upon the FNC when it enabled it to curtail externalities in the marketing of the coffee crop.

Coffee production in Colombia sprawls from the northeastern portion of the country, bordering on the Caribbean, to departments in the southwest lying on the Pacific. Growing conditions vary greatly by geographic area. Owing to differences in soil type, length of growing season, and the temperature under which coffee ripens, Colombia's coffee varies in taste according to the location in which it is grown.

From the buyers' point of view, such variability represents an advantage. For tastes in coffee differ, and some purchasers would place a premium on the coffee produced, say, in Risaralda, while others might instead want that grown in Santander. In addition, purchasers often seek a diverse selection of coffees; by combining them in different proportions, they can then generate distinctive blends. As the physical bean exhibits few clues as to its chemical composition, its quality cannot be directly observed, however. And it is therefore prohibitively costly for buyers to sort shipments of coffee into lots possessing similar attributes. It is far cheaper instead to infer the quality of coffee from its place of origin, that is, where it is grown. A given amount of coffee, sorted by origin, is therefore worth more than the same amount in which the types have been mixed together in unknown proportions. It was therefore to the industry's collective advantage to segregate its coffee by origin before marketing it abroad. By adopting a system of classifications and "brands," it could secure increased revenues.

Initially, growers themselves attempted to separate the distinctive origins. Coffee exports from the northeast were marked "Bucaramanga," for example;

those from Antioquia, "Medellín"; and those from Caldas, "Manizales." But it soon became obvious that voluntary controls would not work. It was in the interest of merchants to ship coffee from an inferior origin under the name of a prized origin, or for producers in a coffee zone that produced lower grade coffee to transport their coffee to a more favored zone for processing and export.

The resultant adulteration of brands threatened to undermine the FNC's efforts to maximize Colombia's earnings in international markets. It weakened Colombia's ability to build reliable reputations for its exports. The point was sharply registered in a report filed by the New York office of the Federación, where the FNC's agent worked feverishly to promote coffee sales in the North American market: "So great is the importance of this matter," he wrote "that when talking with me about it, the commercial representative of a well known foreign country told me that in his way of thinking the matter is of as great an importance to the life and future of the Colombian industry as had been the introduction of the first coffee plant."[25]

To enhance the reputation for quality, the officers of the Federación therefore sought regulatory powers. They sought the power to create brand names, to assign them to coffee produced in particular regions, and to penalize those who sought to ship inferior coffee under the label of a superior brand. Their initiative precipitated a series of disputes within the ranks of the Federación, as the areas that exported superior coffee sought the power to protect their reputations by excluding coffee of lower quality, while those who produced in less privileged regions sought to maintain their right to ship under the "brands" of origin of their more advantaged neighbors.[26]

The protests were for naught. The officers of the FNC acquired the necessary power from the state. They inserted into the Federación's contract with the government a clause establishing a registry of marks of origin. Forwarding to the government the list of marks, they secured a presidential decree making it illegal to ship coffee from one region under the mark established for another and authorizing the creation of a network of inspectors to enforce the decree. The members of the national committee then served as a virtual court of law, judging appeals against the assignment of particular municipalities to particular marks and ruling on such tricky issues as whether coffee grown in one region but processed in another should bear the mark assigned the location of the farm or the processing plant.

Through the empowerment of the FNC, the industry achieved the capacity to penalize those within its group who placed their immediate short-run interests above those of the industry as a whole, be it by avoiding their share of the costs of export promotion or by marketing their inferior coffee under the label of a superior brand. The industry acquired an agent that could resolve the contradictions between individual and social rationality that arose in markets made imperfect by the presence of public goods and costly information. By gaining access to public power, the FNC became an economic institution.[27]

Private Power versus Public Power

Energized by Brazil's interventions in world markets, Colombia's coffee industry was based not only upon smallholders, but also upon a major private organization: the Federación Nacional de Cafeteros. The FNC was created by politicians, who conferred public power upon private interests in the coffee sector. In the years following its creation, however, the institution battled with the government that created it. The coffee industry and the government fought over three major issues: currency valuation; taxes, of course; and trade policy. Of greatest interest to this study is trade policy. In this section we shall see that in each policy domain, the industry triumphed, or, at least, did far better than one would expect, given its smallholder foundations. In the next, we shall try to account for its power.

Overvaluation of the Currency

During the Great Depression, prices for coffee fell to the same degree as did those for other raw materials (refer to figure 3.3). Coffee exporters therefore demanded a depreciation of the national currency, such that the fall in local currency prices would be less than the fall in "dollar" prices. This demand was opposed, however, by the government. Colombia was indebted to banks abroad; this debt had to be paid in foreign currencies, and a depreciation of the national currency would increase the fiscal costs of repaying foreign creditors.[28]

When the industrial nations abandoned the gold standard, the government of Colombia abandoned the free convertibility of the peso; imposing exchange controls, it fixed the exchange rate at a level that represented an overvaluation of the national currency, thereby enabling it to purchase foreign exchange on favorable terms. By law, all foreign exchange had to be sold to the government; but all exporters, including the coffee growers, now received fewer pesos than they could have received in the open market. In response to the measures taken by the government, the Federación Nacional de Cafeteros mounted a vigorous campaign to secure a depreciation of the national currency. In the words of one of its officials, the "artificial fixation of the exchange rate implies for the producers of coffee an expropriation of their labor."[29] And in the words of another, Señor Salazar, one of the departmental representatives: "The FNC, as the entity representing the nation's coffee industry in this matter, must search for ways to defend the freedom that is our

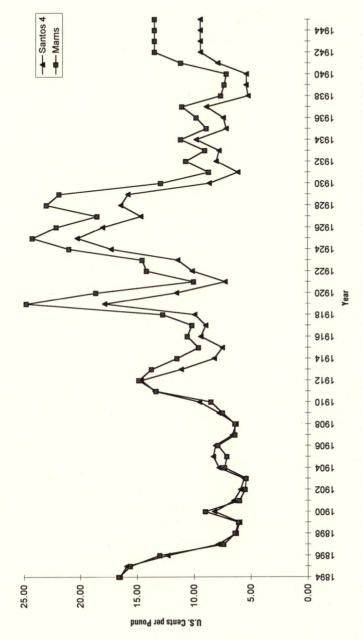

Figure 3.3. Prices by Year, 1894–1945. *Source*: Edmar Bacha and Robert Greenhill, *150 Years of Coffee* (Rio de Janeiro: Marcellino Martins and E. Johnston, 1992), Appendix, table 1.8.

TABLE 3.5
Manizales Coffee: Variation in the Internal and External Price and the Nominal
Exchange Rate (1938 = 100)

Year	Index of Price in United States Dollars	Index of Exchange Rate	Index of the Internal Price in Colombian Pesos
1928	248.2	57.9	103.3
1929	207.3	57.9	83.9
1930	156.4	57.9	67.8
1931	141.8	57.9	77.4
1932	103.6	58.7	64.6
1933	95.5	69.6	67.8
1934	124.5	90.9	116.1
1935	93.6	99.7	93.6

Source: Mariano Arango, *El Café en Colombia, 1930–1938* (Bogotá: Carlos Valencia Editores, 1982), table 1.2, p. 119.

right: to sell foreign exchange, at the price that they could attain in a free market, not at one lowered by means of force. The cafeteros should not agree to *any* proposal that implies the acceptance of the expropriation of the product of our labor."[30] In an effort to communicate these sentiments, the FNC formed delegations to lobby every critical branch of government: the Ministry of Finance, the Chamber of Deputies, and the Office of the President. They also met with the press and the leaders of the political parties in an effort to publicize their demands.

In March 1932, the government devalued its currency, but only by 10 percent; in March 1933, it devalued again. Under continued pressure from the FNC, it devalued once more the following September and again at the end of the year. By the end of 1934, the official rate had converged to the market rate, leading once again to free convertibility of the Colombian peso. From the point of view of the coffee producers, the result was a stabilization of their export earnings.

Manizales is the capital of Caldas, the heart of the smallholder region, and the source of the bulk of Colombia's coffee exports. As seen in table 3.5, whereas the United States' price for coffee exported from Manizales fell by over 60 percent from 1928 to 1935, adjustment of the exchange rate obviated a proportionate fall in the internal (i.e., peso) price of Caldas's coffee. The vigorous lobbying of the coffee exporters thus defended the economic fortunes of the coffee sector, at the expense of those, like the government, who now had to purchase dollars at a higher price in pesos.

It will be recalled that in seeking the depreciation of the mil-réis, the coffee exporters in Brazil sought an alliance with domestic producers of food; they needed such an alliance to secure government backing for the measure. It will be recalled as well that exporters in Colombia faced rapidly rising costs of production, as the boom of the 1920s led to an increased demand for labor and therefore to a rise in the wage rate. To counter the demand for higher wages, Colombia's coffee growers, unlike those in Brazil, appear to have forsaken an alliance with food producers. While seeking a depreciation of the currency, they also called for a reduction in tariffs and in transport charges for food imports.[31] So confident of their power were Colombia's coffee exporters, it would appear, that, in contrast with their counterparts in Brazil, they felt less of a need to form political alliances with other agrarian interests.

Export Taxes

The rise of labor in the 1920s and the subsequent shock of the Depression influenced the balance of political forces in Colombia. It strengthened the political opposition, the Liberal Party, and weakened the incumbent political party, the Conservatives. When, in 1930, the Conservatives split into two factions, each backing its own candidate, they lost the presidential election, bringing to power the first Liberal government in the twentieth century. Liberal hegemony was assured when, in 1934, the party's candidate, Alfonso López Pumarejo, succeeded Enrique Olaya Herrera (the winner in 1930). Under López Pumarejo, the Liberals adopted a political rhetoric in support of an activist government, promoting economic equality and the rights of workers and emphasizing the social obligations of those with wealth. The Liberal government supported health and education and more direct regulation of the workplace and the conduct of firms. But the activist role it prescribed required money. It required foreign exchange. It therefore required higher levels of taxes, some to be raised from the export sector.

Adding to the demand for taxes were the costs of a brief, but costly, war. In 1932, Peru, activating a long-simmering border dispute, invaded a remote Colombian port on the Amazon.[32] Colombia's military was ill prepared, and Colombia's infrastructure—roads, ports, and railways—had to be upgraded rapidly to facilitate movement to the southern front.

President López Pumarejo, motivated by an urgent need for public finance, therefore launched a campaign for tax reform. Colombia, he argued, relied excessively on indirect taxes, the burden of which fell disproportionately on the poor. There was no tax on property, none on capital, and none on incomes. The rich paid but a minuscule portion of their incomes to the state, he argued; the burden of state finances therefore fell largely on the masses. Using figures compiled by his finance minister, López Pumarejo publicly disclosed how small a portion of the state revenues came from the wealthy. And referring to the war with Peru, he called into question the patriotism of the upper classes. The poor had done their part to defend the nation; they had sent their sons to die. Where were the sacrifices of the wealthy? Did not they too have an obligation to society?[33]

The campaign for tax reform resonated politically with other issues of the time. Those who backed the reformist campaign of López Pumarejo saw the rights of those who owned land and capital as circumscribed by other rights: the right of workers to organize and to bargain over wages and rules governing the workplace; the rights of peasants to own land; and the rights of all citizens to services from their government. Those who opposed his campaign saw the rights of property as standing above the claims of others, including those of the workers and the poor.

When in 1935 the Supreme Court ruled unconstitutional all taxes on income and capital, the conflict further intensified. To reform taxes, López Pumarejo would have to amend the constitution. The Liberal Party, seeking the majorities necessary for the passage of constitutional amendments, campaigned vigorously in the 1935 congressional elections; the Conservative Party, sensing defeat, refused to put forward candidates, thereby sheltering the party from the onus of the reforms. The nation thus entered a period of single-party rule. With control over both the legislature and the executive, the Liberal Party was able to change the constitution, redefining the rights of property so as to stress the social obligations of the owners of property and thus, by implication, their obligation to share in the costs of government.[34]

The government's legislation was opposed by the coffee growers. Meeting in the Federación's offices in Cundinamarca, a coterie of large planters organized a powerful political group and broadcast their opposition to the Liberals' reforms.[35] But the government was opposed by the smallholders as well, for the government sought not only to tax property, income, and capital but also the foreign-exchange earnings of *all* coffee growers.

The government introduced a new tax, called the *impuesto de giros*. When coffee exporters cleared their earnings through the banking system, they found that, while receiving the market exchange rate for most of their export earnings, the first 15 (later 20) percent of their export earnings was converted into pesos at the *old*, less favorable rate of exchange. Through the *impuesto de giros*, the government thereby confiscated a portion of the dollars earned by coffee growers.

The new tax inspired an avalanche of protest from the departmental committees of the coffee federation. The Comité Nacional dispatched high-level delegations to the Ministry of Finance and the national president, while publicizing to the rank and file its actions on their behalf.[36] The Managing Director then began writing the government on a regular basis, pushing for a reduction in the tax; at one point he secured an informal agreement by the Minister of Finance to a phased reduction, only to find the Minister reversing himself shortly thereafter.[37]

In June 1935, the FNC determined to bring the issue to a head. It convened an extraordinary Coffee Conference in Bogotá. The Federación scheduled its virtual invasion of the national capital to coincide not only with National Coffee Day—a national holiday set aside to honor the coffee industry—but also with the climactic legislative debates over the reform of the constitution.[38] The Coffee Conference resolved to remain in session as long as the legislature, the better to influence its proceedings.[39] In the face of such pressures, the Minister of Finance assured the Comité Nacional that the *impuesto do giros* would not become a permanent part of the nation's tax system: it would be but a temporary fiscal measure, designed to offset the costs of the war. The Coffee Conference passed a resolution noting this pledge. When the government presented its budget to the national legislature, however, its fiscal projections included revenues from the tax on coffee. Indeed, the revenues were projected to increase by 50 percent in the year ahead![40]

News of the budget infuriated the delegates to the Coffee Conference. Delegations of coffee growers virtually invaded the offices of ministers and legislators alike. The government, in turn, dispatched nervous teams of emissaries to explore grounds for reconciliation. At the climax of the controversy, the government backed down. It agreed to lower to 12 percent the portion of foreign-exchange receipts subject to the higher exchange rate—and to hand over 80 percent of the proceeds of the tax to the Federación. Two years later, the tax was renewed, but with a smaller percentage of the export earnings being subject to the discriminatory exchange rate and at a more favorable rate than before. And the totality of the proceeds from this tax were now given to the Federación.[41]

Once again, the FNC had demonstrated its ability to defend the interests of the coffee growers and the magnitude of its political power.

Trade Policy

The government and the Federación Nacional de Cafeteros fought over a third issue: Colombia's strategy in the international coffee market.

Under the Permanent Defense of coffee, Brazil incurred large costs from its efforts to manipulate international prices. Led by the FNC, Colombia's farmers cheerfully and rapaciously capitalized on the higher prices by increasing their output of coffee. As proposed in an international conference, which it convened in June 1931, Brazil therefore sought to share in the costs of defending international prices by getting its competitors to reduce their production and exports of coffee. The government of Colombia endorsed Brazil's proposal; the FNC did not. This debate led to a third major clash between the government and the coffee industry.

The policy of unbridled market competition held few attractions for President López Pumarejo. Because it promoted specialization, it appeared risky and shortsighted; locked into the production of coffee, he argued, Colombia's resources would be drawn away from the new industries that promised economic progress. Specialization would also leave Colombia vulnerable to external, and therefore uncontrollable, economic forces: changes in tariff policies, strikes by workers in the ports or railways—or alterations in the marketing strategies of its competitors.[42] The national interest was therefore better served by diversification, the president claimed. Increasing production in order to take advantage of the artificial conditions created by Brazil only deflected Colombia from that objective.

López Pumarejo not only viewed the national economic interests as distinct from the interests of the coffee industry; he also placed a high value on maintaining close political relations with Brazil. Before assuming the presidency, he had served as a diplomat. On behalf of his predecessor, Olaya Herrera, he had negotiated the treaty ending the war with Peru; and assistance from Brazil had helped him to achieve a highly favorable political settlement. Coming from a background in international diplomacy, López Pumarejo tended to view trade policy in political terms and, in particular, to regard it as a means of securing the continued friendship of Brazil.

López Pumarejo was elected to the presidency in 1933; he took office in 1934. While president-elect, he had headed Colombia's delegation to the World Economic Conference, where the developing nations pushed for international agreements designed to offset the economic power of the advanced industrial nations.[43] While serving as a counselor in Colombia's legation in New York, López Pumarejo had specialized in the promotion of coffee; as a consequence, he was deeply aware of the high degree of concentration in the United States' roasting industry and the economic power that concentration conferred upon those who sought lower coffee prices. López Pumarejo therefore deeply sympathized with the efforts by the developing nations to use the World Economic Conference to secure international agreements to stabilize the prices of raw materials. Cuba pushed for a sugar agreement; Brazil for an agreement on coffee. Strongly predisposed to subscribe to Brazil's initiative,[44] López Pumarejo bombarded the FNC with dispatches urging support for Brazil's position. The Federación remained intransigent, resolving: "We believe it indispensable that Colombia's delegates in London manifest that our country would be gravely wounded by any limitation or regulation of production, for from any point of view it is Colombia that today possesses the most favorable prospects for increases in production and export."[45]

When in 1935 Brazil again approached its competitors to orchestrate the international sale of coffee,[46] López Pumarejo resolved to gain control over export policy. To transform the coffee sector into a servant of the national interest, he argued, the state had to take control of the Federación. As stated in the opening challenge issued by the Minister of Agriculture:

> I believe that in the face of the difficulties presently faced by the industry, a force stronger than that of the Federación is necessary. What is necessary is the full power of the government. . . . One can see the economic war in which the country is presently engaged. In the face of it, we, as in the United States, must mount interventionist policies. Economic problems must become a matter of state.[47]

The members of the Federación were outraged by the government's position. They dispatched telegrams, petitions, and delegations from every nook and cranny of the coffee-producing regions in opposition to the government's proposal. But the government was determined. As the Minister of Agriculture declared, "Today the functions of governments are not the same as in other times. The great economic problems of the world have assumed such proportions that the governments have had to take direction of their economies. . . . [I]ndividuals were fine up to the present epoch, but today it has become necessary to give their prerogatives to a more powerful force, to government."[48]

The Comité Nacional convened to debate the government's demand that the Federación become a virtual department of the government, and that it alter its economic policies. Finally, in August 1935, the government lost patience and played its highest card: it ceased releasing to the Federación the export tax receipts that it collected on its behalf. The Federación, it argued, no longer remained in compliance with the terms of its contract. As outlined in a speech by Alejandro López, a member of the national committee and a prominent spokesman of the Liberal Party, "The opinion of the Chamber of Deputies and the majority of the Senate supports the government and is against the Federación and when we sound out the private opinions of the representatives, we find that support of the Federación would be thin."[49] Under these circumstances, he argued, the Federación could not afford to be intransigent; the "real alignment of political forces was against" the coffee industry, he declared.[50] He therefore proposed that the FNC capitulate to the government's demand. Starved of funds, the Federación could not continue to function. And the FNC therefore agreed with Alejandro López.

The conflict between the government and the coffee industry focused on the Federación's marketing strategy. Seeking to change the Federación's policy, the government changed its structure. Previously, the coffee growers had chosen all the members of the Comité Nacional. Now five members of the Comité Nacional were to be chosen by the Coffee Congress and five by the government; in the case of tie votes, the president of the Republic was to caste the deciding ballot. In addition, the Managing Director was now to be chosen by the president of the Republic from among three candidates nominated by the Coffee Congress.[51] The nominee chosen was Alejandro López—the government's principal defender within the ranks of the coffee industry.

Attempts to change the FNC's international marketing strategy followed, but not until after a long struggle within the ranks of the Comité Nacional—a struggle that pitted the representatives of the coffee industry against those of the national government.

Figure 3.4 captures the base for this debate. It represents the strategic interdependence between the rival coffee-producing nations and the implications of Colombia's choice of market strategy. Colombia could either compete or collude; depending on the choices made by Brazil, there were four possible outcomes. What should Colombia's trade strategy be? The representatives

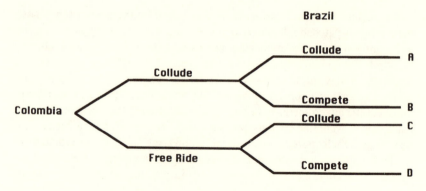

Ranking of Outcomes by:

Representatives of the coffee industry: C > D > A > B

Representatives of the Government: A > C > D > B

Figure 3.4. The Strategic Decision Problem

of the government and the coffee growers differed in their answer to that question.

The government wanted Colombia's coffee industry to cooperate with Brazil, to stop free riding and to collude by withholding coffee from the market, and thereby to drive up the international price of coffee. It wanted the producing nations to offset the consumers' market power; it wanted to preserve close political relations with Brazil. In terms of figure 3.4, *A* therefore stood as the government's preferred outcome; it preferred *A* to *C,* the status quo. The government feared open competition with Brazil. It had long ago learned that when the price of coffee fell, demands to depreciate the peso soon followed; domestic coffee prices were thereby stabilized at the cost of the treasury, which bore the burden of repaying Colombia's debt. The government therefore preferred *C* to *D*. Even worse, from the government's point of view, would be the "sucker's payoff": the payoff resulting when Colombia withheld coffee while Brazil increased its exports. In terms of the diagram, then, the government ranked the outcomes in the following order: A > C > D > B.

To be noted is that the government's ranking implied a contingent strategy: collusion with Brazil was best, if Brazil continued to withhold its coffee production from export markets. That the sucker's payoff lay last in its ordering highlighted the perils of this strategy; for were Colombia to cooperate and

Brazil then to revert to a competitive strategy, Brazil could then grievously harm its erstwhile competitor. Naturally, the government therefore focused on attempting to discern Brazil's capabilities and intentions.

The coffee growers preferred the status quo, C: the policy of free riding. They reaped the profits and Brazil bore the costs of this policy; and, not being politicians or diplomats, they attached little value to the political costs inflicted by their opportunistic behavior. Preferring C to A, the representatives of the coffee industry also preferred D to B. Outcome B led to the sucker's payoff: the losses that would result were Colombia to cooperate but then be betrayed by Brazil. D implied the diminished returns to be gained from open competition. But open competition held few terrors for the coffee growers. In the words of the Managing Director of the FNC:

> Owing to the small size of the coffee farms in Colombia, the diverse crops grown on each farm, Colombia is in a favorable position, should there be a price war. In the small farms, we grow plantains, which, while shading the coffee trees, are also consumed as food; maize, sugar cane, beans, the products of vegetable gardens and fruit trees, etc., greatly aid in feeding the owners of the small farms and those who work on them.[52]

Should the dollar price of coffee plummet, he argued, Colombia's productive potential would remain intact: producers could withstand the competitive onslaught, remain on their farms, and consume the food products while tending to their coffee. Not mentioned by the Managing Director was another reason for welcoming competition: the prospect of cushioning the fall in dollar prices by depreciating the local currency—something that enabled the coffee growers to face the prospects of a price war with Brazil with far greater equanimity than could the government.

Given their evaluation of the payoffs resulting from their choice of strategies in their encounters with Brazil, the representatives of the coffee growers therefore ranked the outcomes $C > A$ and $D > B$. They thus possessed a dominant strategy. For them, Colombia did best competing, regardless of the policy pursued by Brazil. As stated by the Federación's Managing Director, "The clear conclusion . . . is that Colombia, by the special circumstances of her territory, her population, the quality of her coffee and its preparation, as well as by the development of her transport and commerce, is the country that had developed with the greatest intensity and success her coffee production in recent years and therefore has the clearest future in the industry."[53]

The government and the coffee growers therefore conflicted in their evaluation of the possible outcomes of their rivalry with Brazil. Differences in these rankings generated contrasting strategy choices, with the coffee growers regarding a competitive strategy as unconditionally best while the government contingently preferred a strategy of collusion. Being contingent, the government's choice depended upon its forecasts of Brazil's behavior. Its policy made sense only if Brazil's promise to cooperate if Colombia were to collude could be trusted.

In their debates with the government's representatives on the Comité Nacional, the representatives of the coffee growers marshaled the evidence collected by their industrial spy—the representative of the FNC who had been placed in the consulate of São Paulo. Before a skeptical audience of government officials, they quoted from his reports, citing evidence of the mounting debts of Brazil's coffee growers and government; of mounting opposition to the costs of Brazil's interventionist policies; and of growing pressures— financial, administrative, and political—to reduce the stocks accumulated in defense of international prices:

> The conflicts within Brazil and the lack of cohesion between the different states [he reported], conflicts within the coffee sector and between it and the states themselves, have created a ambiance of uncertainty which threaten to destroy all the measures taken up to now in defense of coffee.[54]

To the "industrial spy," his duty was clear:

> We believe it our duty to inform the coffee growers of Colombia that while the political situation of Brazil remains fluid and the mountains of coffee fail to disappear . . . we remain exposed to the gravest dangers.[55]

The coffee growers thus argued that the government was enlisting the aid of an unreliable partner. In meetings that ran hour after hour, generating transcripts that filled volumes, the coffee growers debated, cajoled, and verbally assaulted the government's representatives, seeking to convince them of Brazil's inability to fulfill its commitment to cooperate with Colombia by orchestrating a common policy in defense of higher coffee prices. The result of offering to collude, they declared, would be to be taken as a sucker.

The government's representatives on the Comité Nacional remained unruffled and unmoved in the face of the arguments so vigorously marshaled by the representatives of the coffee growers. They appear to have seen little point in mounting elaborate counterarguments, partly, perhaps, because such arguments would do little to deflect the coffee growers. Nor do they themselves appear to have been persuaded, even by the detailed evidence marshaled by their opponents. The representatives of the government appear to have instead discounted their opponents' declarations as arguments mounted to bolster decisions already arrived at. Given the resolve of the coffee growers to compete no matter what their competitors might do, calculations of Brazil's intentions and capabilities could be of little consequence. So why, the government seemed to feel, should the government give much credence to the coffee growers' assessment of the reliability of Brazil?[56] Even in the face of the reports of the industrial spy, then, the government remained steadfast in its commitment to colluding with Brazil.

Implementing a New Trade Policy

Having appointed Liberal Party leader Alejandro López as head of the FNC in 1936, López Pumarejo initiated negotiations with Brazil. He convened a conference of coffee producers in Bogotá, installed the Brazilian delegate as its chair, and there agreed in principle to coordinate with Brazil the placement of Colombia's coffee in world markets. Two months later, in December 1936, the coffee-producing nations met once again, this time in New York, where Brazil and Colombia agreed to the terms of their joint strategy.[57]

The basis of the accord was the maintenance of a price spread of 1.5 cents between the principle coffees of Brazil and Colombia: Santos No. 4 and Manizales. Brazil would continue to limit exports and so support the price of its coffees at 10.5 cents per pound; and Colombia would reciprocate by restricting exports so as to raise the price of Manizales to 12 cents per pound. Consumers preferred the coffee of Colombia to that of Brazil; were the price differential too narrow, then consumers would switch to Colombian coffees, enabling Colombia once again to free ride on Brazil's efforts.[58] Maintenance of the price spread thus represented a precondition for the cooperative efforts to raise the price of coffee.

Entering into effect in December, the accord almost immediately ran into difficulties. Some originated from Colombia's lack of finances; others from the behavior of those seeking to exploit its program; still others from the inability of Brazil or Colombia to monitor the agreement effectively and thereby to determine when the other party was living up to the accord—or failing to perform. In the judgment of many, however, the agreement ultimately foundered on one basic fact: the power of the coffee growers, as evidenced by their ability to limit the capacity of the government to commit to its implementation.

Financial Constraints

Even before signing the agreement in New York, Alejandro López, the government's choice as Managing Director of the FNC, expressed concern over the fiscal costs of a marketing agreement. Speaking in a meeting of the national committee in November 1936, he "indicated that . . . in the months of December, January, and February, during which the main part of the Central American harvest is shipped, the speculators in New York, who will be damaged when the Federación begins forcing up the price of Colombia's coffee, will try to break our policy."[59] "The Federación better be prepared to purchase coffee on a grand scale," he argued, "even up to 300,000 bags," so as to raise the price of coffee in accord with the price defended by Brazil.[60]

The government had consigned to the Federación the proceeds of the *impuesto de giros*. The Federación still had access as well to the finances generated by the export tax that had underwritten its formation. Neither source of finance, however, could cover the costs of stockpiling 300,000 bags.[61] The Federación therefore approached the Bank of the Republic for a loan of 500,000 pesos.[62]

The Federación received its loan. From November to mid-January, it purchased nearly 100,000 bags of coffee; from the tenth to the twenty-third of January, nearly 15,500 more. Given existing resources, its leaders calculated that they could sustain this rate of purchase for twenty days more.[63]

The Federación then met a series of challenges, each of which imposed further strains on its revenues. With the higher price of coffee, other countries increased shipments—most notably the producers in Central America and "the colonies," as they were called: nations in south Asia and Africa.[64] Speculators also exploited Colombia's marketing policy. Not believing that the Federación could sustain its purchasing program, merchant houses and exporters stopped buying coffee; indeed, they started selling it to the Federación, expecting to be able to buy it back at a lower price.[65] Their efforts redoubled, once reports of the Federación's problems appeared in the press; producers and traders rushed to benefit from the Federación's policies while it still had the funds to implement them. As a consequence, the financial requirements for the Federación's policies rose dramatically.[66] The Managing Director of the Federación responded by returning to the Central Bank with a plea for further loans: "The psychological effect that would be produced in the market if it became known that the resources of the Federación had been amplified by the Bank of the Republic would guarantee 60 percent of the success of the policy that we are mounting," he contended.[67]

The bank was reluctant to advance such loans without an increase in the export tax for coffee—a tax that would both reduce the level of exports, thereby abetting Colombia's collusive strategy, and provide collateral for the advance.[68] Under pressure from the coffee growers, the government failed to raise the export tax further.

Costs of Monitoring

Adding to the problems of the Federación was that it was difficult to evaluate adherence to the agreement. Both Brazil and Colombia closely monitored each other's sales; immediately after the agreement was signed, for example, Brazil reproached Colombia for major sales in the New York market—an act that called into question Colombia's commitment.[69] The terms of the agreement specified prices, not quantities, however; unfortunately for its stability, the agreement failed clearly to specify whether it was relative or absolute prices that counted. Colombia interpreted the agreement as requiring that it maintain the price of Manizales at 12 cents a pound, that is, 1.5 cents above the price of Santos 4 at the time of the signing of the agreement. Brazil interpreted the agreement as requiring that Colombia maintain the price of Manizales at 1.5 cents a pound above the price of Santos 4 at all times. And insofar as specific prices were maintained in the agreement, Colombia interpreted them as minimum prices; it felt no obligation to raise its price in concert with Brazil when prices lay above 12.5 cents per pound for Manizales or 10 cents a pound for Santos 4. When in January of 1937 the price of Brazilian coffee began to rise, while that of Manizales remained at 12 cents a pound, Brazil therefore accused Colombia of failing to implement the accord—an accusation that Colombia branded as unjust.[70]

By the end of March, Colombia's efforts to coordinate with Brazil lay in disarray. The Federación had exhausted its financial resources in attempting to defend the price of Colombia's coffee. And Brazil had become disillusioned with the ability—and determination—of Colombia to collude in the exercise of market power. In the face of mounting evidence of the failure of Colombia's new marketing strategy, Alejandro López resigned as Managing Director.[71]

Tying the Delegates' Hands

In June 1937, President López Pumarejo approached Brazil once again. Requesting that the coffee producers convene an international conference in Havana, he sought to coordinate their marketing strategies.[72]

The fall of Alejandro López was of symbolic significance, for he had been one of the leading publicists of the Liberal Party and one of the most visible spokesmen for the president's program. His fall was of practical significance as well. For the ranks of the government in the Comité Nacional were weakened, and the representatives of the coffee growers were able to dominate the next round of negotiations.

To shift the FNC to a policy of cooperation with Brazil, the government had restructured the Comité Nacional; it appointed one-half of its members. The Coffee Congress, however, remained under the control of the producers themselves. In an effort to gain control over export policy, strategists in the coffee industry therefore shifted the locus of policy-making from the Comité Nacional to the Coffee Congress. And in an effort to constrain the policy outcome, the Congress tied the hands of the FNC's delegates to the meeting with Brazil.

The Congress, deferring to the government, empowered its delegates to negotiate export quotas. But it instructed the delegates to ensure that the agreement included not only Brazil but also those members of the competitive fringe who, by free riding, had raised the costs of implementing the earlier accord. The Coffee Congress would not agree to restrain coffee exports until countries producing 90 percent of the world's coffee exports agreed to similar

limitations. The Congress further instructed its delegates to report in a detailed manner and on a daily basis; it would remain in session for the duration
of the negotiations to monitor and superintend their conduct.[73] By tying the
hands of Colombia's delegation, the coffee growers sought to recapture control over the making of national policy.[74]

Trade War

The Colombian delegation found Brazil's delegate to the Havana conference
in a belligerent mood. Brazil, he declared, remained committed to a policy of
cooperation, based on the setting of quotas and the maintenance of relative
prices. But an agreement had to be made soon; Brazil was suffering greatly as
a consequence of its single-handed efforts to maintain coffee prices. And it
must be made on terms favorable to Brazil. Brazil, he indicated, could not
accept an agreement in which the price spread between milds and Santos 4
was less than 1.5 cents a pound. Failing a favorable agreement, quickly arrived at, Brazil would withdraw from the conference. And, when it did, it
would initiate a price war.

The negotiations broke off. Efforts at an agreement had failed. And Colom-
   Without the cooperation of other delegations, Colombia's representatives to
the Havana conference were powerless to agree to Brazil's demands; they
were bound by the terms of their mandate to secure ratification by countries
who accounted for at least 90 percent of the world's output. Even with pledges
of support from other countries, however, the delegation was unable to convince its principal—the Coffee Congress, in session in Bogotá—of the ability
of the smaller nations to perform. The nations of Central America, Africa,
and south Asia lacked the institutional and financial capacity to regulate exports, accumulate stocks, and thereby adhere to the quotas. In addition, while
Brazil wanted a price spread of at least 1.5 cents a pound, the Coffee Congress
wanted one no greater than 0.5 cent. And Colombia's coffee producers refused to accept any limitation in their right to grow coffee.

The conference in Havana broke up without an agreement. Colombia and
Brazil met again, this time in hurried negotiations in New York. Still, they
could not achieve an agreement on terms that Colombia's coffee producers
could accept. As the delegates wired back to their headquarters:

> It appears that it is absolutely impossible for us to reach an accord within the instruc-
> tions within which we are proceeding. . . .
>   It appears that our mission is reduced to terminating these negotiations in as
> favorable an ambiance and amiable a manner as possible, trying to elude the respon-
> sibility [for their failure] falling on Colombia.[75]

The negotiations broke off. Efforts at an agreement had failed. And Colombia resumed its competitive marketing strategy—the strategy favored by the
coffee growers and championed by the FNC.

Explaining the Power of the Coffee Growers

Once again, the coffee growers had won. They had earlier defeated the government in the fight over the exchange rate. They had then forced the government to reduce the level of export taxes; or, failing that, to return the proceeds to their own Federación. And, in the area of export policy, they had resisted, and then undermined, government attempts to end the policy of free riding on Brazil's costly efforts to raise the international price of coffee.

In the 1920s, the government had delegated public powers to the private agency formed to defend the interests of Colombia's coffee producers. In the 1930s, the Federación turned its power against the government. In doing so, it demonstrated the magnitude of its power by successfully countering government efforts to impose policies that it opposed. The question thus arises: From whence did that power arise?

Interest-Group Politics

Publicists for Colombia's coffee industry, as well as official spokesmen, project a portrait of the industry that contrasts sharply with that in Brazil. They emphasize its small farmer, indeed peasant, base; its typical member more closely resembles, say, Juan Valdez than a Brazilian planter. Scholars such as Palacios, Le Grand, Machado, and Arango offer a radical critique of this populist image of the Colombian coffee industry.[76] For these scholars, the power of Colombia's coffee growers rested on the same foundations as the power of export agriculture in Brazil: the willingness and ability of privileged elites to mobilize the backing of the industry in defense of their interests.

Although the data from Brazil (table 2.1) and Colombia (table 3.2) fail to provide identical measures, they nonetheless suggest that, objectively, production was more highly concentrated in Brazil.[77] Viewed comparatively, the structure of production in Colombia more closely resembled the peasant-based industries of Africa than the plantation-dominated industry of São Paulo. Given this industrial structure, it is therefore difficult to invoke the logic of collective action and to explain the political defense of the industry's interests as a by-product of an agrarian elite's defense of its private interests. Interest-group explanations would appear not to account for the power of the coffee sector.

Skepticism of the "elite interpretation" of the power of the coffee industry, based upon comparative analysis, is reinforced by evidence collected from within Colombia itself. The rules of the Federación highlight its independence from plantation agriculture. Within the FNC, each producer receives one vote; and the branches gain representation within the organization according to the value of their production. The first provision equates a peasant with an estate owner. Because smallholders are more productive than plantations, the departments containing smallholders account for the larger share of the coffee produced; by the second provision, they therefore gain a larger share of the seats controlling the affairs of the FNC. As revealed in table 3.4, Antioquia and Caldas, both important centers of smallholder production, sent the largest number of representatives to the Coffee Congress in the 1930s. Controlling the largest number of seats in the Congress, they controlled the largest number of positions in the Comité Nacional. Political power in the FNC thus rested in the smallholder regions of the western and central portions of the industry.[78]

The FNC acts as an association charged with the defense of the common interests of the industry. Even in the period when the FNC appeared most closely tied to the owners of the coffee estates—when the large growers used its offices to organize opposition to López Pumarejo's constitutional reforms—its leadership behaved in ways suggesting their relative autonomy from the private interests of the coffee elite. Rather than blocking the process of land reform, as some owners of estates would have preferred, the Comité Nacional instead lobbied for the creation of a mortgage bank to assist in the "parcelization" of the large estates. With finance advanced by the bank, smallholders could buy the plots on which they formerly had worked as tenant farmers. Rather than the FNC resisting land reform, it eased the "democratization" of coffee production.

If coffee interests were as powerful in Colombia as they were in São Paulo, then, it was not for the same reasons. In particular, it was not because the plantation elites dominated the organization representing coffee interests in Colombia. Rather than invoking the theory of interest groups, then, I turn instead to other explanations. In particular, I focus on the role of party competition.

The National Structure of Power

The constitution of the Old Republic in Brazil, it will be recalled, was highly federalist. The benefit to the coffee growers was that they could operate behind the defenses provided by the near-sovereign state of São Paulo; the cost was the necessity of forging cross-regional alliances when seeking to influence national policy. In contrast, the constitution of Colombia was highly centrist; political institutions were national, not federal, in structure.[79] Those seeking to exercise power at the national level therefore faced lower costs; they did not need to broker complex, cross-regional alliances.

In Brazil, coffee production was regionally concentrated; for coffee interests to prevail, they had to secure backing from organized interests in other regions. In Colombia, by contrast, coffee production spread throughout the highlands. Even in such heavily populated and politically significant lowlands where coffee was not grown—such as the departments on the Atlantic and Pacific coasts—the industry carried political clout. Its performance affected the prosperity of the ports, banks, and commercial houses, all of which, while located on the coast, were deeply dependent upon the prosperity of the inland coffee regions. The result of the geographic spread of coffee production and nationalization of politics was the greater ease with which the FNC could exercise power at the national level, in comparison with the leaders of the coffee industry in Brazil.

National governments were elected to power in Colombia, and the Federación aggressively sought to exploit the electoral system. As the Managing Director stated in the early 1930s:

> It is necessary that . . . in every election for the legislative bodies, in every legislative action, the interests of the industry must be taken into account. It is not a matter of founding a "coffee party," but rather of giving policy a favorable orientation toward coffee. . . . You [the members], with your well-deserved influence in diverse sections of the country, are in a position to impart an irresistible impulse to such an orientation in the parties that contest for political hegemony in this nation.[80]

Reviewing the FNC's efforts two years later, he reported: "As you, we have obtained favorable results in . . . that the party lists include candidates who are spokesmen for our industry, which gives them the opportunity of giving a timely nudge to the progress of our initiatives in the assembly that should directly benefit our industry."[81] Geographically widespread within a national political system designed to promote rather than to impede cross-regional organization, the coffee growers readily secured political representation at the national level. As stated by a member of the legislature, "Everyone in this Chamber has links with coffee . . . ; many of us possess plantations, others are thinking of acquiring them; some deal in coffee, many have relations in the industry, and the rest, with few exceptions, have connections of one kind or another with it."[82]

Given the composition of the coffee industry, it is tempting to attribute its electoral power to its numerical predominance within the electorate. The small farmers may have numerically dominated the coffee industry; however, they clearly did not dominate the electorate. According to the coffee census of 1932, there were over 140,000 coffee farms in Colombia; but, according to the records for the presidential election of 1930, there were over 800,000 voters (see table 3.4). There is no straightforward way to convert the number of farms into the number of voters. A given family could—and many surely did—own more than one farm; conversely, a single farm could contain more than one voter. The data contained in table 3.4 imply electoral dominance for the coffee industry, however, only under a highly implausible series of assumptions about ownership, occupancy, and electoral cohesion, as well as equally unlikely assumptions about relative rates of voter turnout between

poor rural peasants and the urban middle class—the most active and organized branch of Colombia's electorate in the 1930s.[83] While coffee growers
constituted a substantial portion of the national electorate, they did not approximate a majority of it. Their electoral power was amplified, however, by
their location in the structure of political competition in Colombia, as defined
by the electoral system.

Party Competition

By location, I refer to *strategic* political location, as defined by the rules
for competing for power, not geographical placement. Colombia possessed
competing political parties; rival parties contested along a surprisingly well-
defined political dimension; and the spokesmen for the coffee industry occupied a strategically powerful position along that dimension. The coffee growers
occupied a location that enabled them to convert their considerable numbers
into political clout.

Two parties dominate politics in Colombia: the Liberals and the Conservatives. They compete for power by contesting elections at all levels of government. The parties compete for the patronage monopolized by the state—jobs,
licenses, and public contracts, for example—and, in the 1930s, at least,
championed contrasting visions of the appropriate structure and role of government. The Conservatives favored a strong central government and the Liberals a more federal structure of power. The Conservatives favored protection
for domestic industry and the Liberals openness to international markets.[84]
The Conservatives defended Catholicism as the established religion, protected
church property, and, when in power, signed a concordat granting the church
extensive powers over public education. The Liberals, by contrast, opposed
the paramountcy of the Catholic church; favored secular education; and, when
they held power, seized church lands and sold them to private interests.[85]

In the late nineteenth century, the Liberals had rebelled against a Conservative government in power, plunging the country into civil war. After the Conservative victory, the Liberals withdrew to the relative safety of local politics
and refrained from running candidates for the national presidency. The prosperity of the 1920s, and the resultant labor protest, provided Liberal organizers with political opportunities, however. Workers were numerous;
increasingly, they were well organized; and worker organizations were geographically widespread, being located in the ports, harbors, and municipalities that dotted the coast and river valleys inland, and in the countryside,
where they promoted the fortunes of the campesinos in their struggles against
the estates. The appeal of labor issues spread beyond the working class, moreover, as foreign companies stood among the most visible of labor's targets: the
oil companies, for example, were owned in part by Standard Oil and the

Figure 3.5. The Structure of Political Competition

banana plantations by United Fruit, both United States corporations. Liberal politicians, seeking power at the national level, therefore found that they could link the class interests of the workers with the nationalist sentiments of all Colombians. When the Conservative Party split in the late 1920s, the Liberal Party reentered the lists and, exploiting these issues, recaptured the presidency of Colombia.

In maneuvering for power at the national level, the coffee growers therefore operated within a competitive, two-party system. The parties differed over the role of the church, the rights of labor and property, and openness to foreign markets. Stands on the one issue strongly correlated with positions on the other. As a consequence, as suggested in figure 3.5, partisan cleavages tended to fall along a single, well-defined dimension, one captured in the names of the parties.[86]

While occasionally driven to the point of violent conflict, neither of the parties could afford to remain sectarian. Faced with the need to win elections, partisans grudgingly put aside extremist positions and yielded to the necessity of seeking votes from those less passionately committed to the cause. Each party contained a militant core, violently opposed to the suzerainty of the other; but, driven by the necessity of seeking electoral majorities, each also accommodated more moderate factions.

The irreconcilables of the two parties tended to locate in the central and eastern portions of the country. It was there that their armies had clashed in the nineteenth century; political hatreds from earlier periods still reverberated in the local politics of these areas. Moreover, as the departments of eastern and central Colombia remained relatively poor, government strongly impacted on economic life; to dominate the government in those areas was to control economic opportunity. Political competition for jobs and control over public services gave renewed impetus to age-old conflicts, rendering the region the battleground for partisan struggles between the Liberal and Conservative parties.

Such conflicts were moderated, however, in Antioquia. Antioquia voted Conservative. It certainly was Catholic; its towns and cities vigorously supported their local dioceses and celebrated religious holidays with elaborate displays of piety.[87] But Antioquia also possessed a burgeoning private sector. Within it lay the low cost and therefore rapidly growing portion of the coffee industry; the banks and merchant houses that serviced that industry; the artisanal shops that forged inputs used in the industry—hoes, cutlasses, and steel implements; and the manufacturers that produced the consumer items purchased by coffee farmers.

Given the relative prosperity of Antioquia, the region therefore produced a distinctive form of politics. Rather than being dominated by warlords, left over from the civil strife of the nineteenth century, Antioquenian politics was instead dominated by lawyers and businessmen, with close ties to the banks, trading companies, and manufacturing establishments. They regarded economic issues to be as important as partisan loyalties or as the relationship between church and state, and placed a greater premium on political stability than upon ideological rectitude. Politicians in Antioquia sought a policy environment favorable to business, and to coffee. Indeed, politicians in Antioquia appear to have been less concerned with which party held power than with the policies they adopted. As their clients and constituents did not depend upon the public sector for employment, they could afford to live under a government run by another party, so long as it adopted policies producing prosperity for the private economy. As stated by Abel:

> Between 1910 and 1930, Antioquia defined its own identity in the political life of Colombia. It conserved a de facto regional autonomy, succeeding because of its isolation, the influence of Antiquenians in the central government, and the relative sophistication of the department's governmental machinery, as well as because of the development which permitted the region to maintain itself without relying on the resources of the central government.[88]

From Partisan Conflict to Coffee Power

The conflict between the Liberal and Conservative parties dominates, as it should, much of the literature on the political history of Colombia. These accounts also note, but less frequently emphasize, the capacity of the moderate wings of the two parties to transcend partisan differences and to form governments. Thus they note that in order to terminate the civil wars of the late nineteenth and early twentieth centuries, Conservative and Liberal moderates joined forces to commit Colombia to a future as a commercial republic.[89] They record that the moderates coalesced again in 1910, joining in a Republican government of national unity and overthrowing the incipient dictatorship of General Rafael Reyes.[90] At the beginning of the 1920s, Liberal political leaders had joined with Conservatives to overthrow the government of the Conservative president, Dr. Marco Fidel Suárez. They also note that his successor, the Conservative general Jorgé Holquín, drew López Pumarejo, Eduardo Santos, and Olaya Herrera into his cabinet—all leading Liberals and each a future Liberal president. According to Thomas Tirado, Pedro Nel Ospina, the next Conservative president, "saw himself as being obligated to appease the Liberals by passing progressive economic legislation."[91] His successor, the Liberal Enrique Olaya Herrera, was even more strongly committed to interparty cooperation; when offered his party's presidential nomination, he at first refused, taking it only when elements from both parties besought him to run.

If partisanship forms the central theme of Colombian politics, then coalition forms its principal counterpoint. Its significance appears to have been most fully recognized by the two leading practitioners of partisan politics in the 1930s, López Pumarejo and Laureano Gómez, themselves drawn from the militant wings of the Liberal and Conservative parties, respectively. Upon becoming president in 1934, Alfonso López Pumarejo mounted the "Revolución en Marcha," championing constitutional reforms to limit the privileges of the church, regulate private property, promote the rights of labor, and impose direct taxes. Laureano Gómez led the conservative counterattack, joining with the church, landowners, and proto-Fascists in attacking the Liberal government. In the midst of the bitter invective exchanged by the two partisan leaders, historians have noted—and romanticized—an intriguing anomaly: the surprising degree of personal friendship between López and Gómez. This friendship is far less surprising when taken as a sign that the two leaders appreciated the structure of the political game in which they were involved: one in which the most serious danger to each lay not in the opposition but within his own party. While attacking each other, the two helped each other; their partisan attacks upon each other strengthened their own positions within their parties by energizing the militants while weakening the moderate factions that, by coalescing, could overthrow them.

For López Pumarejo, the moderate threat originated in the "right wing" of the Liberal Party with Olaya Herrera, who could return to the presidency, or with Eduardo Santos, who aspired to it. For Laureano Gómez, the threat lay in the Antioquenian wing of the Conservative Party, with Róman Gómez— who repeatedly revealed an ability to work with the Liberal government, delivering key Conservative votes in the Senate for the governments of Olaya Herrera and López Pumarejo—*and* with Mariano Ospina Pérez: scion of the Ospinas of Antioquia (see figure 3.5).

Antioquia lay in the core of the coffee region. It had been the departmental government of Antioquia that had promoted the creation of the Federación Nacional de Cafeteros. Antioquenian businesses had organized the settlement of Caldas and financed the expansion of coffee growing in that region. And in

1930, Mariano Ospina Pérez, a member of one of Antioquia's most prominent political families—a family that had provided Colombia with two presidents —became the Federación's Managing Director. The coffee sector therefore stood at the pivot of partisan politics in Colombia. By being willing to pivot between the two parties, or to broker a coalition between their moderate factions, the coffee sector could make—or unmake—national governments.

Conclusion

Throughout the period before World War II, Colombia's coffee industry successfully resisted the overvaluation of the currency, eluded distortionary taxes, and achieved a competitive trade policy in international markets. Moreover, the coffee sector created an economic institution that overcame free riding, provisioned the sector with public goods, and maximized the value of exports by creating conditions under which specific origins could build reputations for quality. The result was the rapid growth of coffee exports. Colombia vigorously entered the world coffee market. It became Brazil's biggest trade rival.

Economic efficiency in Colombia was achieved as a political outcome. It resulted from the power of the coffee industry. And this power resulted from the incentives for politicians to provision it with an institution that could solve collective action problems. Politicians delegated power over coffee policy to the leaders of that institution.

A major lesson of the chapter on Brazil was that the interest-based explanations of dependency theory were wrong; the state eluded capture by economic interests. The explanation of Brazil's trade policy lay, rather, in an understanding of Brazil's political institutions, which, by creating political incentives and imposing constraints, made the state difficult to seize. Neoclassical trade theory offers an alternative to dependency theory. And it offers a possible explanation for Colombia's trade policies. Colombia clearly held a competitive advantage in coffee production. And its major producing regions, such as Caldas, possessed fixed and specific factors whose quasi rents motivated heated political lobbying in favor of "free trade," as the Ricardo-Viner version of neoclassical trade theory would suggest. The lesson of this chapter, however, is that neoclassical theory is also wrong, or at least misleadingly incomplete. An explanation of Colombia's trade policies must also take into account its domestic politics and the political significance of its domestic institutions.

The incentives created by Colombia's position in world markets did not directly translate into favorable trade policies. Rather, those interested in free-market policies had first to politically organize. And once organized, the industry had to elude capture by politicians and bureaucrats, who, driven by notions of modernity and interests that diverged from those of the coffee industry, sought to deflect the industry from its competitive orientation toward world markets.

Electoral institutions help to explain the coffee growers' power. Comparisons with peasant agriculture elsewhere help to make the point.[92] But so too does internal evidence. For the greatest threat to the Federación took place in 1935, when the Conservatives had withdrawn from the electoral arena. It was then that the Minister of Agriculture sought to render the FNC a department of the government. When the Conservative Party reentered the electoral arena, and when Ospina Pérez entered the Conservative directorate, however, then the government backed down.[93] Rather than taking over the Federación, as the government of Brazil had taken over the Instituto, the government of Colombia thus instead left it a private entity, endowed with public powers. And rather than forcing a change in external trade policy, the government instead deferred to the wishes of the FNC, which tied the hands of Colombia's trade delegation.

Neoclassical trade theory deploys market-based reasoning. It assumes that exporters are "small" and international markets therefore competitive. Domestically, it largely ignores the impact of nonmarket institutions. As this chapter has shown, however, political institutions matter. In Colombia, incentives created by the electoral system led to the empowerment of coffee producers; the political position of the coffee sector rendered it in the political interests of politicians to serve the economic interests of peasants.[94]

The new trade theory contrasts with neoclassical trade theory in that it recognizes the noncompetitive nature of international markets. Dropping the "small nation" assumption of neoclassical trade theory, it focuses on the choice of trade strategy. The choice of strategy depends upon the definition of the nation's interests, however. And, as we have shown, in Colombia, there was no single notion of those interests; their definition was contested. On the one hand lay the national interest, as defined by the government; on the other, the national interest, as defined by the coffee growers. The definition that prevailed was the outcome of domestic politics.

Transition

And yet, domestic political choices did, as these open-economy theories would suggest, respond to changes in the international environment. In the case of Brazil, as we have shown, Vargas altered coffee policy in response to the competitive pressures of Colombia and the resultant erosion in the benefits of Brazil's interventionist policies. And in the case of Colombia, shocks originating in the global market led to greater government control over the coffee industry, and to a change in marketing policy.

The first shock originated from Brazil's implementation of its threat to re-vert to a competitive marketing strategy. Vargas's government, weary of bear-ing the costs of defending the international price of coffee, sought the cooper-ation of other producers. When Colombia failed to agree to collude, Vargas released on to the market stocks accumulated during the Permanent Defense. A month later, the Comité Nacional surveyed the damage inflicted by its trade rival and proclaimed: "In the face of the gravity of the situation, the Comité Nacional of the Coffee Growers believes it advisable . . . to accept a policy of international cooperation between countries producing."[95]

The second shock was global war. The European market consumed over one-third of Latin America's exports; nearly 9 million of the 25 million bags exported from Latin America were shipped to Europe.[96] Had these shipments been diverted to the United States' market, the result would have been the collapse of coffee prices. Competitors though they may have been, Colombia and Brazil therefore shared the common objective of preventing an abrupt increase in the supply of coffee in the United States.

In earlier attempts, Brazil's diplomats had failed to secure collusion by others with its marketing strategy. They had succeeded, however, in achieving a more limited objective: the funding of a Pan-American Office of Coffee in the United States. Soon the Pan-American Office of Coffee was producing impressive reams of statistical data: tables, charts, and graphs documenting the amount of coffee sold in the United States by each coffee-producing na-tion, the price at which it was sold, and the point of entry, with the numbers running back to the previous decade.[97] With the outbreak of the war, the "coffee diplomats" used these data to devise export quotas. Their efforts re-sulted in the Inter-American Coffee Agreement, which limited the export of coffee to the United States' market and divided the market among the major producers. The director of the Departamento do Café in Brazil, at least, was convinced that Brazil's earlier punishment of Colombia's free riding had eased the way for this agreement. "The policy of competition which Brazil had been obliged to follow," he argued, "among other merits had that of demonstrating to our competitors what we had not achieved by verbal means": the strength of Brazil's commitment to achieve international cooperation in the marketing of coffee.[98]

To orchestrate its coffee marketing in concert with Brazil, Colombia had to negotiate binding international agreements. In search of such agreements, the president deputized the Managing Director of the Federación, conferring upon him official diplomatic status and empowering him to commit the nation to the necessary international accords.[99] The Managing Director thus became a Co-lombian diplomat, negotiating with the Minister of Foreign Affairs of Brazil—and the Secretary of State of the United States of America.

The change from a competitive to a collusive marketing strategy also re-quired the financial empowerment of the Federación: the transfer to it of the capital necessary to purchase coffee and withhold it from the market. With the entry of Colombia into the International Agreement, the government created El Fundo del Café: the fund was managed by the Comité Nacional of the FNC. The government issued 10 million pesos in bonds, crediting the proceeds to the account of El Fundo; it also imposed a tax on the dollar earnings of coffee exports, the proceeds of which were also credited to this account.[100] Backed with a massive new infusion of capital, the Comité Nacional launched a campaign to acquire and stockpile Colombia's coffee.

The FNC thus became a branch of the Colombian government, empowered to represent the state abroad and to manage public revenues at home. It became the single largest purchaser of Colombian coffee. And it began to implement a collusive, rather than competitive, policy with Brazil, Colombia's major trade rival.

In the world of open-economy politics, choices made for domestic political reasons unleash economic forces abroad. Economic forces, originating from the global economy, in turn affect the costs and benefits of domestic political strategies. And when they vastly alter the costs and benefits of such choices, external forces can provoke a change in the structure of domestic institutions.

4

The Demand for an Institution:
The Producers Maneuver

IN THE FIRST decades of the century, Brazil had acted the part of a price maker, raising the price of coffee on international markets, and Colombia had acted the part of a new entrant, undercutting the efforts of Brazil. During the Second World War, they colluded in their marketing strategies. Under the terms of the Inter-American Coffee Agreement, they organized the division of the United States' market. The wartime rationing of shipping enabled them to enforce this accord and to prevent freeriding by smaller producers.

This chapter examines the postwar period. Changes in the domestic political structure of Brazil, it argues, freed the government to manipulate international markets to its advantage; and changes in the domestic political structure of Colombia freed its government to collude with Brazil. The weakening of federalism in Brazil and the end of party competition in Colombia enhanced their governments' ability to extract wealth from export agriculture. The chapter thus extends previous arguments about the domestic origins of trade policy.

The chapter focuses not only on the domestic but also on the global level. Forces unleashed by a postwar rise in coffee prices, it demonstrates, provoked a battle between northern consumers and southern producers. Equally as important, by promoting entry into coffee production, the price rise precipitated conflict among the southern producers themselves. The International Coffee Organization (ICO) represented the outcome of efforts by the dominant producers, Brazil and Colombia, to terminate free riding, restrict further entry, and thereby strengthen their ability to extract resources from the north.

The Great Price Rise

Faced with restricted access to international markets during the Second World War, farmers invested less in coffee production. As shown in figure 4.1, Brazil lost nearly one-quarter of its tree stock between 1939 and 1945. Much of the decline resulted from the frost of 1943; but, the figure suggests, farmers had not been renewing their capital stock prior to the frost and were reluctant to refurbish it afterwards.

Ocampo's research suggests that Colombia too emerged from the war with an aging, and relatively unproductive, capital stock. "By the middle of the

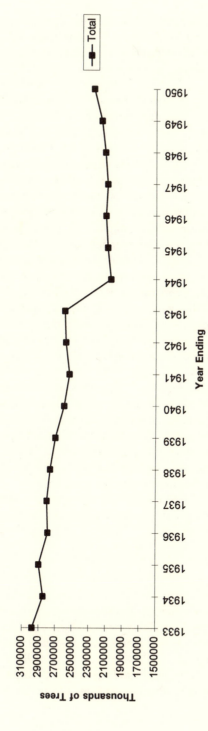

Figure 4.1. Brazil's Stock of Trees by Year. *Source:* Edmar Bacha and Robert Greenhill, *150 Years of Coffee* (Rio de Janeiro: Marcellino Martins and E. Johnston, 1992), Appendix, table 2.12.

1950s . . . 56% of the coffee farms" in Colombia, Ocampo writes, "contained trees averaging more than 15 years of age."[1] Productivity was declining at an average of 1.5 percent a year, Ocampo stresses; and "by the end of the period of study [1958], the coffee sector appears to have exhausted all its energies."[2]

Not only did Brazil and Colombia fail to renew their productive capabilities during World War II; they also reduced their inventories. Brazil's exports had to enter the Atlantic; but submarine warfare blocked shipments to the United States. The government therefore resumed the policy it adopted before the war: it physically destroyed its stocks, burning 10.3 million bags of coffee over the period 1939 to 1945.[3] Colombia, situated at the western end of the Caribbean, was less threatened by German submarines; and the FNC was able to fill the part of the market vacated by Brazil. The Federación therefore converted its stocks of coffee into stocks of cash, ridding itself of expensive inventories and accumulating liquid capital.[4]

Inventories also declined in the consuming nations. As seen in figure 4.2, consumption exceeded exports throughout the first several years of the war, leading to an erosion of stocks. When the war ended in 1945, the coffee market possessed limited supplies; but it experienced rapidly growing demand. If only to repel the challenges of Communist parties and left-wing alliances in the postwar elections, European governments, backed by massive infusions of capital from the United States, sought a rapid return to the level of prosperity enjoyed in the prewar period. As a consequence of its economic revival, Europe soon recovered its important position in world trade, including the international coffee market. France, it is true, gave privileged treatment to coffee from its African colonies; and England, short of dollars, favored imports from its colonies in the sterling zone. Nonetheless, the end of the war led to a sharp, outward shift in the demand for coffee from all origins.

The increased demand for stocks generated a rise in the price of coffee. As shown in figure 4.3, the price of coffee doubled between 1940 and 1947. Following the crisis in Berlin in 1949 and the invasion of South Korea in 1950, both governments and industries in the advanced industrial nations, fearing war, began to accumulate stocks of raw materials. Between 1947 and 1950, prices nearly doubled again.

Brazil

Within this economic environment, Brazil stood well prepared politically to implement an opportunistic marketing strategy, for it entered the postwar period with an institutional structure profoundly different from that which had prevailed in the Old Republic. Following the coup of 1937, Vargas abolished political parties and virtually eliminated the congress. Vargas also abolished the federal system, depriving Brazil's states of autonomous powers and ren-

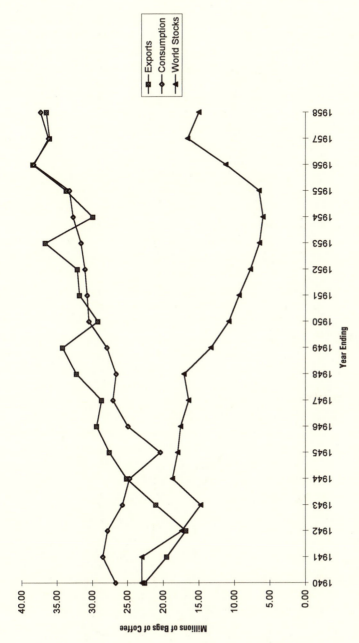

Figure 4.2. The Achievement of "Statistical Equilibrium." *Source:* Edmar Bacha and Robert Greenhill, *150 Years of Coffee* (Rio de Janeiro: Marcellino Martins and E. Johnston, 1992), Appendix, tables 1.2 and 1.6.

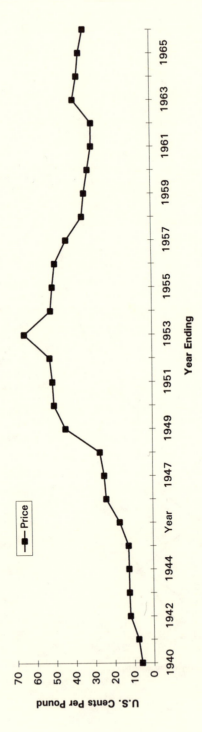

Figure 4.3. Postwar Rise in Average Coffee Price. *Source:* Edmar Bacha and Robert Greenhill, *150 Years of Coffee* (Rio de Janeiro: Marcellino Martins and E. Johnston, 1992), Appendix, table 1.8.

dering their administrations units of the central bureaucracy. Many of the institutional features that had defined the institutional structure of the Old Republic, and limited its capacity to act, came to an end in the Estado Nôvo.

In their place, Vargas created a new set of institutions: technocratic agencies that intervened in key economic sectors. The organization of markets, rather than the search for votes, characterized the Vargas regime. Technocrats and administrators took the place of party bosses; and rather than political elites competing for support from private interests, private interests instead competed for favor from bureaucratic elites—allocations of credit, access to markets, or favorable regulations. As stated by Schmitter, the national agencies "usually have virtually autonomous powers to set prices, wages, and quotas, distribute credit, and regulate foreign trade. . . . Their respective revenues are also virtually autonomous, resting on an obligatory tax on production or exports. The producers accepted this degree of state penetration . . . partly out of fear of official reprisal [and because these agencies] . . . 'are really cartels.'"[5]

Rather than mobilizing party workers to secure political support in Brazil's northeast, for example, as a president of the Old Republic would have, Vargas instead mobilized political support through the Instituto de Alcohol e Açucar.[6] So, too, with the coffee sector. Taken over in the 1920s by the beleaguered government of São Paulo, the coffee institute, called the Instituto Brasileiro do Café (IBC), was later assimilated by Vargas directly into the national government and administered national coffee policy.

The IBC managed the purchase, storage, and export of Brazil's coffee crop. On the basis of annual surveys of the stock of trees, their age distribution, the weather at the time of flowering, and the subsequent temperature and rainfall, the Instituto each year produced a "crop plan" that regulated the provision of credit, the supply of storage, and the movement of the harvest from the warehouses in the interior to the railways and thence to the coastal ports of Brazil. It set the loan rate for coffee financing and the national price of coffee; it thereby controlled the incentives for farmers to sell or retain their coffee on their farms and, if selling it, to offer it to the IBC (for subsequent storage) or to the commercial trade (for export).[7] Because of Brazil's market power, the IBC controlled the international price of coffee as well. In so doing, it also controlled Brazil's capacity to extract foreign exchange from international markets. For given Brazil's position in the international market and the price inelasticity of the demand for coffee, the lower the incentive to export, the higher the dollar price of coffee and the greater Brazil's earnings of foreign exchange.

Before implementing its annual crop plan, the IBC had first to secure its approval from the Superintendência de Moeda e do Crédito (SUMOC), or monetary council, chaired by the Minister of Finance.[8] As manager of the monetary system, SUMOC sought to ensure that the IBC's demand for credit to finance the stockpiling of coffee did not drive up the interest rate, resulting in higher unemployment, or in an emission of money that would exacerbate inflationary trends. SUMOC also structured the crop plan so as to control its impact on Brazil's foreign reserves. In doing this, its primary objective was to employ the coffee industry to increase the government's earnings of foreign exchange.

Prior to World War II, the coffee growers had, from time to time, gained control over the exchange rate and manipulated it to their advantage. In the Vargas era, the exchange rate was controlled by SUMOC, and the agency now harnessed the coffee industry to its purposes. The magnitude of the change was most dramatically signaled by SUMOC's creation of a multiple exchange rate. Under this system, the government and its agencies secured a highly discounted price for foreign exchange; the coffee sector received a highly unfavorable price.[9] Rather than the coffee growers securing the depreciation of the national currency, as they had in the Old Republic, they now were instead compelled to exchange dollars for cruzeiros at a rate reflecting a massively overvalued exchange rate. SUMOC thus subjected the coffee growers to a "confisco cambial," a tax on the earnings they gained in foreign markets.

The proceeds extracted from the coffee industry accrued to a special account, called the coffee account, located in the Central Bank. Under the direction of SUMOC, the funds were either retained for subsequent use by the coffee industry or on-lent to the Banco do Brasil for investment in projects or sectors given a higher priority by the government: the steel industry, the oil industry, the automobile industry, and so forth.[10]

The Brazil that emerged from the Vargas years thus differed profoundly from the Brazil of the Old Republic. Rather than the decentralization and division of powers characteristic of the Old Republic, the Estado Nôvo was highly centralized and dominated by the executive branch of government. Rather than coffee policy being made by party politicians, it was now made by technocrats. The coffee sector lay embedded within a regulatory agency that was controlled by the central government, not a state government accountable to a coffee-producing electorate. The agency was managed by financial technocrats. And they regulated prices and quantities in a way designed to maximize the nation's earnings of foreign exchange, a large portion of which they earned from exports of coffee and transferred into accounts credited to other sectors.

The Brazil that faced the coffee markets of the postwar period was thus endowed with a different set of political institutions than was the Brazil of the earlier periods. The Old Republic had found it difficult to behave as a unitary actor, exploiting Brazil's economic power in international markets. The decentralized structure of the Old Republic had made it difficult to organize coalitions in support of concerted economic strategies. With the centralization of power and the state's domination of the coffee industry, Brazil was better able to intervene. It aggressively did so in 1953, when a major frost left the market vulnerable to a "squeeze" by the major suppliers (figure 4.3).

Reporting in July to the Department of State in Washington, the United States' Consulate in São Paulo noted that "cold winds in Paraná on July 4, 5, and 6 of 1953 did not follow any previous pattern. . . . On July 4 a cold front moved from the south. This was apparently met by another cold front moving in from the Bolivian Andes. The two combined and turned eastward across North Paraná and Southern São Paulo. . . . On some ridges trees were frozen to the ground."[11] The frost of 1953 numbers among the most severe frosts ever to strike the coffee industry of Brazil. While causing less physical damage than the frosts of 1918 or 1975, its economic impact was fully as great, for it came at a time of rising demand and diminishing stocks of coffee (see figure 4.2).[12] Prices immediately soared, spiking sharply to the highest level hitherto attained in coffee markets.

Brazil rapidly responded to the opportunity created by the shortage of coffee.[13] Oswaldo Aranha, Minister of Finance, lowered the coffee exchange rate, offering fewer cruzeiros per "coffee dollar." The incentive to export coffee therefore declined, and the dollar price of coffee rose in world markets. Aranha also increased the price offered by the IBC from 56 cents to 90 cents a pound. As exporters could not earn profits selling coffee bought at this price, they abandoned the market to the IBC. The Instituto thereby gained control of the market; restricting exports, it drove prices to the highest level hitherto seen in the coffee market.[14]

Colombia

The government of Colombia had long sought to cooperate with Brazil in raising the price of coffee. When international forces—the punishment meted out by Brazil and the loss of European markets because of war—overpowered the resistance of the coffee growers, it was at last able to secure domestic assent to a change in international strategy.

The power of the growers, we argued, derived not from their power as an interest group but from their strategic location in the electoral system. They effectively occupied the midpoint of the electoral space; the national parties competed for their support; and, as a result, the growers could exact policy concessions. In the postwar period, the government was easily able to pursue a cooperative marketing strategy. A major reason, it would appear, was because of the end of party competition.

As revealed in the politics of the 1930s, political competition in Colombia arose within as well as between the two parties. Moderate factions were willing to make cross-party alliances and form governments of "national union." The militant factions within each party therefore feared political exclusion and often viewed their moderate colleagues as posing as great a threat as their partisan rivals. Tensions between moderates and militants produced major divisions in both the Liberal and Conservative parties.[15] Those within the Liberal Party proved significant; for in the election of 1946, the Liberals split, enabling a minority party, the Conservatives, with but 40 percent of the vote, to seize power for the first time since the 1920s.

In the 1940s, it was Jorge Eliécer Gaitán who filled the militant's role within the Liberal Party and Lleras Carmago who filled the role of the moderate. Gaitán's political base lay within the labor movement, elements of which he had organized and the collective interests of which he had long championed in the national political arena. While filling out the remainder of Alfonso López's second presidential term, Lleras Carmago viciously broke a series of postwar strikes by labor unions, causing a split in the ranks of the Liberal Party. In splitting, the Liberals enabled the Conservatives, led by Ospina Pérez, to come to power. Ospina then recruited Liberals to his cabinet, drawing them from Lleras's moderate faction. Gaitán and his militants remained outside of the government, serving as the opposition.

The opposition to Ospina found much to criticize. A change in party at the national level implied not only a change in policies; it implied as well radical changes in the opportunities and life chances of many citizens. As stated in *Semana*, Colombia's leading weekly:

> To lose power . . . meant that the mayor of the town would turn into a dangerous enemy, that the official of the branch of the Agrarian Bank would refuse the loan, that the new teacher would look with disfavor on one's child attending school, that the official of the Department of Health would first attend his fellow partisan . . . and that it was necessary to remain at a prudent distance from the local police.[16]

Labor militancy rose in Colombia in the postwar period just as it did elsewhere. The conflict between the government and the unions increased the tension between the government and Gaitán's militant faction. In an ever-mounting series of strikes and rallies, Gaitán mobilized his labor base in opposition to the government. Gaitán's appeal reached beyond his core supporters, however; for the wholesale dismissal of Liberal officeholders and the rising insecurity of Liberal citizens in municipalities now governed by Conservatives exacerbated political tensions. Such tensions inevitably sparked violent incidents; and Gaitán was able to exploit each in an effort to embarrass the government and to portray its Liberal members as disloyal to their party.

Skillfully picking apart Ospina's coalition, Gaitán undermined the power of the Conservative government. August 9, 1949, however, he was assassinated in downtown Bogotá. Militant supporters rioted, and the violence that swept out of Bogotá and into the countryside brought with it government reprisals.[17] Liberals working with the government could no longer command standing in their own party, as the state's security forces imprisoned or killed its members. The moderate Liberals therefore abandoned the Conservative government. And the government's political base soon narrowed further; after declaring Colombia to be in a state of siege, the government ruled by executive order, bypassing the Liberal congress. Citing the danger of open campaigning and the government's control of the ballot box, the Liberals withdrew from subsequent presidential elections. By 1952, Colombia had become, de facto, a one-party state.

There is little reason to extend this narrative. Let me only note that partisan conflict degenerated into increasingly authoritarian government; that the Conservative party, too, was riven by conflict; and that the rivalry between Ospina Pérez and Laureano Gómez reemerged with renewed vehemence, now that the Conservatives held power. The split created incentives for politicians to recruit allies within the military, with the result that the army intervened and a general, Rojas Pinilla, gained control of the government.[18] In 1953, one-party government, led by civilians, gave way to military dictatorship.

The coffee industry in postwar Colombia thus inhered within a political system differing greatly from that of the 1930s. Partisan competition between national parties had ended. The coffee growers and the FNC that represented them were therefore deprived of a major source of their power. As a consequence, they were less able to resist the policy dictates of the government, and, in particular, the government's determination to join with Brazil in defending the international price of coffee.

Resistance from the North

Changes in the domestic politics of Brazil and Colombia thus freed their governments to seek to shape international markets to their advantage. While facing fewer impediments at home, they did face challenges from abroad.

The postwar rise in coffee prices precipitated heated political conflict with northern consumers. In the late 1940s, the United States reimposed price controls; it thereby sought to use its market power to force down the price of coffee. Throughout the coffee-growing regions, farmers; merchant houses; workers and employees in the warehouses, railways, and ports; politicians and bureaucrats in the coffee-producing states—all found a common cause in the struggle to raise the price of coffee in the United States.[19] In São Paulo, for example, a wide range of interest groups petitioned Getúlio Vargas, president of the Republic, to seek an increase in the price at which they could sell their coffee in the United States. "The cost of living," they wrote, "has risen five fold over that prevailing before the war. Workers' salaries have increased in proportion and, even so, are insufficient to maintain the farm worker. . . . The rise in the prices of industrial goods and, consequently, of the profits of merchants—which derive from markups over the costs of these items—

would not be harmful if the price of [our] own product increased proportionately."[20]

Diplomats from Colombia and Brazil encountered little difficulty in recruiting supporters from the embassies of other producing nations in opposition to United States' policy; and their representatives in Washington united in support of a revision in the controlled price of coffee. The United States government resisted their entreaties, however. It had made the "5¢ cup of coffee" a symbol of economic prosperity in the postwar period.[21]

In the end, economic realities achieved what political pressures could not secure. When commercial houses could no longer profitably export coffee in Latin America for sale at the controlled price in the United States' market, coffee no longer became available at the controlled price and its price rose in the black market. The United States government then subsidized the roasters and traders, enabling them to supply the market at official prices.[22] The measure addressed the economics of the problem; trading in coffee resumed and the market once again functioned. But it further exacerbated the politics. To the producers in Latin America, it appeared that it was North American commercial houses that benefited from the change in policy, rather than themselves.[23]

The postwar struggle over the price of coffee was brought to a climax by Guy Gillette, a politically marginal U.S. senator from Iowa. Using his chairmanship of an obscure subcommittee, Gillette peppered the State Department with requests for information about the production and marketing of coffee in Latin America; the Commerce Department for information about the processing, warehousing, and retailing of coffee; and the Securities and Exchange Commission about the trading of coffee contracts in commodity markets. Representatives of Colombia and Brazil appeared before his subcommittee, as did business leaders and members of the coffee trade. Using the powers of his position, and his ability to attract the attention of the media, Gillette posed as the champion of the American consumer.

It is difficult to measure the impact of Gillette's campaign in the United States. Indicative, perhaps, is that he lost his seat in 1945 and, while reentering the Senate in 1948, remained but one term more. Indicative too, perhaps, is that his name remains misspelled in a leading biographical directory.[24] But it is not difficult to measure the impact of his investigations in Latin America. A reading of the minutes reveals that the Comité Nacional of the Federación Nacional de Cafeteros regarded Gillette as a major threat and discussed at length how best to counter his attack on rising coffee prices. In the minutes of March 25, 1950, for example, the Managing Director

read a cable . . . from the Minister of Foreign Relations and . . . Minister of Finance and Public Credit, presently in Washington, in which they reported on discussions with [the Colombian Ambassador to Washington] and the Ambassador of Brazil . . . concerning the urgent necessity to initiate a sweeping propaganda campaign by which to explain to the American public that the present coffee prices scarcely approximate a just level in relation to those for American products imported by the coffee producing nations.[25]

Even more powerful was the reaction in Brazil, where the press feasted off the reports emanating from Gillette's investigations. On December 5, 1949, *Correio de Manhã* carried on its front page statements attributed to Gillette saying that the price rise had cost the American consumer $650 million.[26] Reports in *O Globo* focused on speeches by public figures in Rio de Janeiro denouncing Gillette as "the champion of demagoguery, the chief disseminator of falsehoods, the great promoter and vehicle of injustices that are woven around coffee and the Latin American countries that produce it."[27] Newspaper commentators cast Gillette and his backers as agents of the large coffee-roasting firms, seeking to lower the price of raw materials so as to fatten the monopolistic profits of their firms.[28] One editorialist, writing in *O Journal* on December 22, 1949, asserted that "the illustrious American Senator would be indignant . . . if we asked him why an automobile that cost a thousand dollars . . . before the war now cost two thousand."[29] Gillette's actions, he emphasized, lent credibility to those who "speak of imperialism, colonizing capital, and other fantastic things."[30]

Brazil's subsequent intervention in the market led to a second major clash with the United States. It occurred at the time of the greatest price rise in the history of the coffee industry; the controversy therefore swept out of the chambers of commerce and into the corridors of power. Senator Gillette, up for reelection, reconvened his Senate subcommittee; the Federal Trade Commission (FTC) launched yet another investigation of coffee prices;[31] both deluged the United States' embassy in Brazil with inquiries; and American journalists intensively interrogated the United States' ambassador.[32] Even the Secretary of Agriculture and the President were drawn into the controversy, with Secretary Benson counseling consumers to switch to milk,[33] and President Eisenhower stating that he was "very interested in getting coffee back to a price where he thought it was reasonable."[34]

Getúlio Vargas had returned to power in 1951 as Brazil's elected president.[35] In 1953 Jânio Quadros defeated Adhemar de Barros for the governorship of São Paulo, thereby depriving Vargas of one element of his political base; in 1954, Vargas lost a second, when João Goulart, de facto head of the Partido Trabalhista Brasileiro (PTB, or Labor Party), was forced from his cabinet. The opposition União Democrática Nacional (UDN), led by Carlos Lacerda, had long opposed Goulart, whom it accused of cultivating close ties with Communists. When Goulart in 1954, as Minister of Labor, proposed a 100 percent increase in the minimum wage, the opposition viewed his proposal as an opening gambit in the forthcoming presidential elections. Lacerda, his party, and his chain of newspapers ripped into Goulart. Amidst the economic chaos caused by his wage hike, the political clamor raised by the opposition forced Goulart from Vargas's government.

Just as the coffee crisis was coming to a head, then, so too was the political crisis faced by Getúlio Vargas. When the president's personal bodyguard was implicated in an attempt to assassinate Lacerda, the military attempted to compel Vargas to resign. Instead, he committed suicide.

In a letter composed the morning of his death, Vargas referred to the forces "unleashed against me" and alluded to his struggles against "foreign enterprises" and "the underground campaign of . . . international groups . . . aligned with national groups" against the workers.[36] Stressing his efforts to create an energy industry independent of foreign corporations, he referred as well to coffee: "We tried to defend its price," he stated, and "the response was a violent pressure on our economy." "I have fought month by month," he went on, concluding: "I can give nothing more except my blood."[37]

Exercising its market power, Brazil had transformed the market into a political arena, polarizing relations between the industrial north and the agrarian south. The intervention produced political conflict and a political martyr. The price of coffee; the prices of industrial goods and manufactured products; the terms of trade between agriculture and industry, raw materials and industrial goods, north and south, and rich nations and poor; the role of multinational firms and foreign corporations; the disparity between prices generated in markets and prices that were just—the conflict over coffee prices in the postwar period focused attention on these issues, giving them currency and definition. In so doing, the politics of coffee also bequeathed a historical legacy: a compelling vision of the core issues in international trade and development.

Danger from the South

Opposition from consumers thus posed a threat to the implementation of an aggressive trade policy. More insidious and even, perhaps, more powerful was the reaction among producers. In the face of the great price rise, farmers invested in production for the market.

New sources of production arose within Brazil itself. Citing the decline in the stock of coffee trees that took place during the war, the United States' consulate in São Paulo noted:

> In 1945 or 1946, the trend was reversed. Prices of coffee and prospects for the future of the product were improved by the ending of the war and the lifting of ceiling prices in the United States. The rate of new planting increased and that of abandonment declined. An estimate of trees in July 1, 1949, . . . shows a total of 2,278 million trees, or 2 percent more than the 1942 total.[38]

Following the second wave of price increases in the early 1950s, planting in Brazil increased once again. Subsequent investigations confirmed a trend first noted in the war years: the entry of an important new coffee region in the state of Paraná. With costs of production averaging 26 cents a pound, in contrast to the costs in São Paulo of 35 cents, Paraná, with its virgin soils and newly constructed road system, represented a major new force in the world of coffee.[39]

Africa constituted a second new source of production. The end of the war marked a change in taste among North American consumers; they now demanded instant coffees. In so highly processed a form, arabicas lost their flavor advantage. And not only were robustas less costly than arabicas, but in the making of soluble coffee, robustas offered higher yields.[40] In response to the shift in demand, African producers planted more robusta coffee. As revealed in figure 4.4, total production in Africa reached 4 million bags by 1950, having doubled over the period of the war; following the peak of the coffee price rise of 1954, it more than doubled again.

The postwar rise in coffee prices began in 1945, accelerated in 1949, and boomed in 1953–54. Where farmers had been uprooting trees, they now stopped doing so; rather than replacing coffee with citrus or cattle, they now planted new stands of coffee. Those in established zones extended their coffee plots; others planted coffee in new regions, pushing the coffee frontier forward yet again, most notably into Paraná and portions of Africa. Entry thus threatened to undo the producers' gains in the postwar period.

The great postwar price rise peaked in 1954. Reaching their apogee in March and April, prices broke sharply downward in May, stabilizing only after the severe frosts in April of the following year. In 1956, coffee prices resumed their downward slide. Faced with entry from Central America and Africa, the price of mild coffees broke first (figure 4.5). As consumers switched to the higher quality coffees, now relatively inexpensive by comparison, the price for Brazil's unwashed arabicas also shifted downward. The price of robustas, nested at the bottom of the market, trended on, seemingly oblivious to the downward cascade. But in August 1958, it too broke downward, as it responded to the price of Brazil's higher quality coffees closing in from above.

The closing differentials in relative prices promoted a fall in the overall average price of coffee and galvanized the dominant producers into action. Early in 1954, the Managing Director of the Federación Nacional de Cafeteros (FNC) led a delegation to Brazil to study coffee production in São Paulo, collecting information about the new coffee-producing regions in Paraná and meeting with Brazilian policymakers.[41] At these meetings, the leaders of the FNC and Brazil agreed to coordinate their export policies so as to forestall the decline in coffee prices.[42] Other nations too had increased their production, they realized; and Colombia and Brazil therefore sought the cooperation of

Figure 4.4. Africa's Entry. *Source:* Edmar Bacha and Robert Greenhill, *150 Years of Coffee* (Rio de Janeiro: Marcellino Martins and E. Johnston, 1992), Appendix, table 1.8.

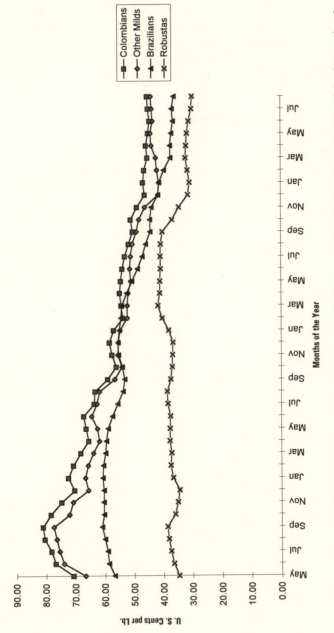

Figure 4.5. The Collapse of Coffee Prices: May 1958–August 1959. *Source*: Monthly data from the files of the International Coffee Organization.

other Latin American countries. At the 1954 meetings of the Inter-American Economic and Social Council of the Organization of American States, they pressed for the support of other delegations for a multinational agreement to restrict exports of coffee.[43] The dominant producers renewed their efforts at the subsequent meetings of the Economic Commission for Latin America.[44]

To promote these negotiations, the government of Colombia once again conferred official powers upon the FNC, appointing its Managing Director, Manuel Mejía, ambassador to Brazil.[45] Meeting with the Instituto Brasiliero do Café (IBC), the Minister of Finance, and the national president, he negotiated the basic elements of an accord, which Brazil and Colombia then presented to the other Latin American nations.[46] The result, in October 1957, was El Convenio de Mexico, an agreement that obligated producers to withhold a percentage of their coffees from the international market.

Under the terms of El Convenio de Mexico, each nation pledged to withhold coffee from export. The dominant producers, Brazil and Colombia, stood to benefit from a higher dollar price for coffee, but they incurred large costs as well. To fulfill its obligations under El Convenio de Mexico, the government of Brazil soon accumulated nearly 25 million bags of coffee (figure 4.6)—an amount equivalent to one-half of the world's total annual consumption. And the FNC of Colombia added over half a million bags per year to its inventories.[47] Both governments were compelled to run budget deficits in order to accumulate the stockpiles of coffee.[48]

The dominant producers thus incurred great costs in restricting exports. The benefits they reaped depended upon the behavior of the competitive fringe. El Convenio de Mexico and its successors applied only to the Western Hemisphere, however; African producers remained outside the agreement and, as shown in figure 4.4, rapidly increased their exports of coffee. The producers of other milds had joined El Convenio de Mexico; but, as shown in table 4.1, they free rode. While Brazil and Colombia withheld a large fraction of their exportable production from world markets, El Salvador, Guatemala, and Costa Rica exported all they produced and sometimes more, selling previously accumulated stocks at higher prices and serving as centers for the re-export of coffee shipped from the dominant producers.

Clearly, under El Convenio de Mexico, the sacrifices made by Colombia and Brazil were being undercut. The dominant producers were incurring costs but reaping few benefits. They therefore either had to abandon their interventionist strategies or develop a more effective international agreement.

A primary reason for the failure of the producers' agreement was that Brazil, its leader, lacked the ability credibly to threaten new entrants. In the 1930s, Brazil had punished Colombia for failing to collude in its marketing strategy. But Colombia was the second-largest producer of coffee. The costs incurred by Brazil therefore generated major benefits, resulting from Colombia's retention of coffee exports. In the 1950s, however, the competitive

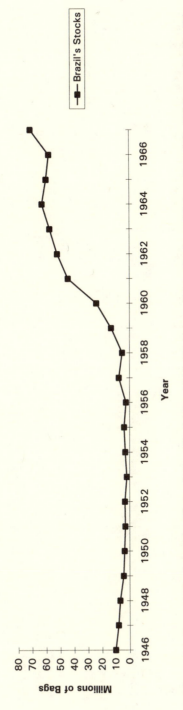

Figure 4.6. Beyond "Statistical Equilibrium": Brazil's Stocks, 1946–67. *Source:* Edmar Bacha and Robert Greenhill, *150 Years of Coffee* (Rio de Janeiro: Marcellino Martins and E. Johnston, 1992), Appendix, table 1.2.

TABLE 4.1

Adherence to Quotas under El Convenio de Mexico

Sources	1958					1959				
	Exportable Production	Exports	Addition to Stocks	Exports as Percent EP	Percent Total Exports	Exportable Production	Exports	Addition to Stocks	Exports as Percent EP	Percent Total Exports
World Total	46.20	36.50	9.70	79.00	100.00	52.00	42.60	9.40	81.92	100.00
Total Western Hemisphere	35.90	26.40	9.50	73.54	72.33	40.20	31.60	8.60	78.61	74.18
of which										
Brazil	20.80	12.90	7.90	62.02	35.54	26.00	17.70	8.30	68.08	41.55
Colombia	7.00	5.40	1.60	77.14	14.79	6.90	6.40	0.50	92.75	15.02
Mexico	1.50	1.30	0.20	86.67	3.56	1.20	1.20	0.00	100.00	2.82
El Salvador	1.30	1.40	-0.10	107.69	3.84	1.40	1.30	0.10	92.86	3.05
Guatemala	1.20	1.20	0.00	100.00	3.29	1.20	1.40	-0.20	116.67	3.29
Costa Rica	0.70	0.80	-0.10	114.29	2.19	0.80	0.70	0.10	87.50	1.64
Other	3.40	3.40	0.00	100.00	9.32	2.70	2.90	-0.20	107.41	6.81
Total Africa	8.90	8.80	0.10	98.88	24.11	10.40	9.70	0.70	93.27	22.77
of which										
Ivory Coast	1.80	1.20	0.60	66.67	3.29	2.40	2.00	0.40	83.33	4.69
Angola	1.30	1.30	0.00	100.00	3.56	1.40	1.50	-0.10	107.14	3.52
Uganda	1.40	1.30	0.10	92.86	3.56	1.50	1.50	0.00	100.00	3.52
Kenya	0.40	0.40	0.00	100.00	1.10	0.40	0.40	0.00	100.00	0.94
Tanganyika	0.40	0.40	0.00	100.00	1.10	0.40	0.30	0.10	75.00	0.70
Others	3.60	3.40	0.20	94.44	9.32	4.30	4.00	0.30	93.02	9.39
Total Asia and Oceana	1.40	1.40	0.00	100.00	3.84	1.30	1.30	0.00	100.00	3.05

TABLE 4.1 (Continued)

Sources	1960					1961				
	Exportable Production	Exports	Addition to Stocks	Exports as Percent EP	Percent Total Exports	Exportable Production	Exports	Addition to Stocks	Exports as Percent EP	Percent Total Exports
World Total	66.40	42.50	23.90	64.01	100.00	52.40	43.70	8.70	83.40	100.00
Total Western Hemisphere	52.80	30.60	22.20	57.95	72.00	37.00	30.50	6.50	82.43	69.79
of which										
Brazil	37.00	16.80	20.20	45.41	39.53	22.00	17.00	5.00	77.27	38.90
Colombia	7.00	5.90	1.10	84.29	13.88	6.70	5.60	1.10	83.58	12.81
Mexico	1.50	1.40	0.10	93.33	3.29	1.40	1.50	-0.10	107.14	3.43
El Salvador	1.50	1.20	0.30	80.00	2.82	1.30	1.40	-0.10	107.69	3.20
Guatemala	1.40	1.30	0.10	92.86	3.06	1.30	1.30	0.00	100.00	2.97
Costa Rica	0.80	0.80	0.00	100.00	1.88	1.00	0.80	0.20	80.00	1.83
Other	3.60	3.20	0.40	88.89	7.53	3.30	2.90	0.40	87.88	6.64
Total Africa	11.90	10.70	1.20	89.92	25.18	13.30	11.30	2.00	84.96	25.86
of which										
Ivory Coast	2.50	2.40	0.10	96.00	5.65	3.20	2.60	0.60	81.25	5.95
Angola	1.80	1.40	0.40	77.78	3.29	2.70	2.00	0.70	74.07	4.58
Uganda	1.90	1.90	0.00	100.00	4.47	1.90	1.80	0.10	94.74	4.12
Kenya	0.40	0.40	0.00	100.00	0.94	0.50	0.50	0.00	100.00	1.14
Tanganyika	0.40	0.40	0.00	100.00	0.94	0.50	0.40	0.10	80.00	0.92
Others	4.90	4.20	0.70	85.71	9.88	4.50	4.00	0.50	88.89	9.15
Total Asia and Oceana	1.70	1.40	0.30	82.35	3.29	2.10	1.70	0.40	80.95	3.89

Source: J.W.T. Rowe, *The World's Coffee* (London: Her Majesty's Stationery Office, 1963), p. 21.

Notes: EP stands for exportable production; the units are millions of 60-kg bags.

fringe was made up of a host of small producers (see table 4.1). Should Brazil
have dumped its 50–60 million bags on the market, it would have incurred
losses from the resultant fall in price. The future gains resulting from the
withdrawal of small amounts of coffee would have been slight. In the 1950s, it
therefore made little sense for Brazil to punish violations by the free riders,
now made up of producers that were small.

Adding to Brazil's impotence was its desperate need for foreign exchange. The
government of Brazil committed to a program of rapid economic development. It
needed foreign exchange to finance imports of capital equipment. Politically,
moreover, Brazil's government was insecure. Brazil's economic aspirations and
political instability at home rendered it impatient abroad. Only the promise of
large future gains could offset the losses that would result immediately from
implementing a punishment strategy; for, being impatient, Brazil would heavily
discount those future gains while placing a high value on current losses.

Brazil's impatience therefore made it less willing to inflict costly punishments. The other producers, knowing that, often cheated on the terms of the
international accord. Brazil threatened, and threatened often, to punish non-
cooperators. But the competitive fringe discounted those threats. They were
not credible. In the phrases of the Comité Nacional, Brazil could not "force
them [to comply], by coercing them internally or externally."[49] The Comité
Nacional therefore advocated another approach: to return to the method employed in the Inter-American Coffee Agreement, wherein export constraints
were enforced not by the producers but by a third party. The third party would
be the bureaucracies of the consuming nations themselves, and the alliance
between producers and consumers would be known as the International Coffee Organization (ICO).[50]

Discussion

In seeking to understand the creation of the ICO, I have applied both game
theoretic and systemic theories of international politics. The game theoretic
approach helps to account for the demand for the new regime. The formation
of a stable oligopoly, created and enforced by producers in noncooperative
settings, game theorists demonstrate, requires the use of threats that are credible. The international arena constitutes a noncooperative setting; there is no
international government and therefore no possibility of enforcing agreements. And, as we have seen, Brazil's threats were not credible. Noncooperative game theory thus provides insight into the failure of the producers' accord, El Covenio de Mexico, and thus into the demand for the creation of a
new political body, based upon third-party enforcement.

Game theory offers one approach to the study of international politics; but it
requires the analysis of domestic politics for its completion, for it assumes
that states are capable of strategic behavior. But, as we have seen, their ability

to act strategically in the international arena results from a preliminary domestic political struggle.[51] Systemic theories, too, provide insight into international politics; but they, too, force us to the study of domestic politics. In the postwar period, Brazil indeed behaved as systemic theorists would have it: Brazil adopted a trade strategy that enabled it to exploit its position of economic power in the international marketplace. Explaining Brazil's behavior required, however, the marshaling of facts that normally remain excluded from systemic explanations. Brazil's ability to act as an economic "hegemon" represented the result of a domestic political transformation, in which state institutions were centralized, federal structures dismantled, and the Congress and political parties reduced in political significance.

We are thus driven back to domestic politics. In returning there, we will learn how the government of Brazil continued to marginalize the coffee sector, even after the postwar return to a federal and democratic form of government. We shall learn how changes in political institutions in Colombia also led to the political emasculation of its coffee industry. Such changes in domestic political relations facilitated the creation of global institutions that promoted and defended cooperative marketing strategies. Once again, however, we shall also see the significance of reciprocal forces originating in the external, that is, international, environment. We shall see that the creation of collusive economic relations abroad fortified and enriched governments at home; the launching of the ICO represented the international corollary of an expansion of political power by Third World governments and of their control over their economies. Forces at the international level helped to restructure domestic political relations, altering the relationships between governments, industry, and export agriculture.[52] Causality thus runs from the domestic to the international, and back again.

The Return to Domestic Politics

In the postwar period, Brazil underwent a return to electoral democracy. It returned to a federal structure of government, with a division of powers at the national level. Despite this return to a decentralized structure of political institutions, Brazil nonetheless remained steadfast in its coffee policies. While raising the price of coffee abroad, the government taxed the resulting profits at home, if only by grossly overvaluing the exchange rate for coffee.

In the prewar period of decentralized political institutions in Brazil, the coffee sector was able to defend its interests by bundling coffee policy with exchange-rate policy. It thereby created a coalition that spanned state delegations and branches of government. In the postwar period, however, this political tactic no longer worked. In effect, it was finessed by the developmental policies of the national government, which reduced the value of this package of policies to potential coalitional members. The coffee interests, and their political allies in São Paulo, therefore remained isolated and politically vulnerable.

This argument can best be advanced by examining the presidency of Juscelino Kubitschek.[53] As revealed in his campaign document, *Directrizes Gerals do Plano Nacional de Desenvolvimento*, Kubitschek viewed Brazil as an "undeveloped and semi-colonial country," kept in a state of "economic and cultural dependency on Europe and the United States."[54] The remedy, he argued, lay in national economic mobilization. He asserted that the state should invest directly in power, energy, transportation, and heavy industry; and it should provide the credit and tariff protection necessary to promote private investment in manufacturing, thereby reducing dependence on imports and promoting development.

Drawing on the technocratic capabilities bequeathed by the Estado Nôvo, Kubitschek placed the Banco Nacional do Desenvolvimento (BNDE) directly under the office of the president.[55] In doing so, Kubitschek further augmented the power of technocrats. Backed by the president, the BNDE was able to recruit the very finest of Latin America's economists, many through the Comisión Económica para América Latina (CEPAL, the United Nations Economic Commission for Latin America). The BNDE developed plans for a wide variety of projects, subjected them to engineering and financial analysis, and mobilized the financing for those that fulfilled its requirements. The agency provided the technical and professional core, and the president the political muscle, to mobilize the resources necessary to make "50 Years Progress in Five," in the words of the slogan.

The impetus for Kubitschek's program derived in part from the skill with which he articulated the political visions of his generation: one shaped by the postwar clashes between Brazil and the United States over the price of coffee; by the struggle to establish a domestic oil and steel industry; and by the suicide, and suicide letter, of Getúlio Vargas. It came as well from his ability to impart that vision not only through his own speeches but also through the Instituto Superior de Estudos Brasileiros (ISEB), which, in the words of Thomas Skidmore, "became a mecca for research . . . on Brazil's problems as conceived from the broad position of developmentalist-nationalism. The institute published a stream of books and lectures offering a rationale for industrialization and explaining the cause and effect of underdevelopment in every sector of the country's society and economy."[56] The ISEB not only promoted research into Brazil's economic development but also, by running short courses, seminars, and training sessions, created a cadre of intellectuals trained in, and committed to, the government's development program.

Ideological commitment, shaped by historical experiences and formal training, thus imparted direction and energy to Kubitschek's policies. But so too did his political base. The Kubitschek/Goulart government represented an alliance of the Social Democratic Party (Partido Social Democrático, or PSD) and the Brazilian Labor Party (Partido Tabalhista Brasileiro, or PTB), the two parties created by Vargas at the end of the Second World War. Both were based upon elements of the public bureaucracy: the PSD on the departments administering the state and local governments and the PTB upon the Ministry of Labor and its state-sponsored trade unions. With the organization of elections at the municipal, state, and national levels, bureaucrats and administrators moved, via the parties that they themselves had created, from administrative to elective office. As stated by Ben Ross Schneider, "the largest mass movement from appointed office to legislative seat came when Vargas created the PSD and PTB out of the officials he had appointed to local government and the labor administration. Thus the core elected coalition . . . had served as appointees of the Estado Nôvo."[57] Given the origins of the parties in power, it is therefore not surprising that they responded to Kubitschek's developmentalist slogans. Statist in background, they were statist by inclination and naturally viewed economic development as a problem in public administration. That the channeling of economic resources through the government would also enhance their political popularity and personal fortunes only intensified their commitment to Kubitschek's programs.

Given the ideological foundations and partisan base of the Kubitschek government, it is therefore not surprising either that Brazil joined Colombia in promoting El Convenio de Mexico. Doing so enabled the government to restrict exports, to raise the dollar price of coffee, and, by maintaining the "confisco cambial"—the differential between the exchange rate offered coffee and other traded goods—to accumulate foreign exchange, which it then plowed into industry and development projects sponsored by the Kubitschek government.

The coffee producers vigorously contested Kubitschek's policies. They petitioned for redress, dispatched delegations to the state and national governments, and organized mass demonstrations. The most dramatic took place in October 1958, when a caravan of over two thousand set out from Rio de Janeiro. The demonstrators demanded a higher domestic price for coffee; protested the *confisco cambial* (the confiscatory exchange rate placed on coffee); and called for free and unlimited exports of coffee. The *confisco cambial,* they argued, simply paid for cheap imports of oil; and the restrictions on exports simply benefited "the African countries" whose robusta coffees replaced those of Brazil in the market.[58]

The growers received support from Jânio Quadros, governor of São Paulo and an opponent of the president and the party in power. In a series of stirring denunciations, he condemned the government's policies. São Paulo, Quadros stated, remained "the center of coffee production"; and coffee, he proclaimed, was now "threatened with extinction" by the reintroduction of the quota of sacrifice, the reduction in the domestic price, and the *confisco cambial.*[59]

Even though backed by the powerful Quadros, governor of the state of São Paulo, the protests failed to change the government's policy. In the Old Republic, the governor of São Paulo had been able to influence national policy by recruiting allies from other states, thereby putting together a coalition broad enough to generate majorities in congress. The instrument for doing so had been the depreciation of the currency, which increased the local currency earnings of the exporters throughout Brazil and the competitive advantage of import substituting firms. In the modern era, Quadros could not forge such a coalition, for this tactic had been finessed by Kubitschek's industrial policy.

The Kubitschek government aggressively protected the domestic market. As stated by Fishlow:

> [T]he strategy was to [promote] import substitution. . . . Through . . . exemptions from duty on intermediate inputs and capital goods after 1957 when an *ad-valorem* tariff was instituted, attraction of foreign capital, and the internal channeling of credit, production was initiated in automobiles and other consumer durables, and substantially extended in chemicals, electrical machinery, and metallurgy.[60]

Through the overvaluation of the exchange rate, the government cheapened imports of capital equipment; by providing public sector credits, it subsidized industrial investment; and by protecting their products, it increased the earnings of import substituting firms. The government's protectionist and interventionist measures thus underpinned the profits of urban industry. While targeting such measures on heavy industries and the production of consumer durables, the government extended its protection to other forms of manufacturing as well. Imports were licensed, and for an item to be imported, the applicant had first to demonstrate that domestic firms lacked the capacity to manufacture it.[61]

The policy of industrial development provided a specific and powerful counter to any attempt by the coffee growers to build an intersectoral coalition in opposition to the government's policies, for it nullified the capacity to use the issue of the exchange rate to build political alliance. By protecting the products of domestic manufacturing firms from foreign competition, but enabling imports of capital equipment to enter duty free, the government enabled the firms to lower their costs and increase their profits by purchasing capital equipment with a currency whose value was artificially appreciated. The structure of protection thus rendered overvaluation a source of profits for industry.

Economic historians, writing on Brazil in the prewar period, emphasize the role of the exchange rate; development economists, writing on Brazil in the postwar era, emphasize the role of effective protection. Treating the two policies in separation, the scholars fail to see how the one was used to defend the coffee industry in the first period and the other to marginalize it in the second.

Colombia

Upon entering the international agreement, the government of Colombia also sought to restrain exports of coffee and thereby raise the price of coffee in international markets. The result was a tumultuous political struggle, as the government and the coffee industry battled to seize the benefits and to avoid the costs generated by the international accord.

The coffee boom took place during the military dictatorship of Rojas Pinilla. The military government imposed a windfall tax and spent a major portion of the resultant revenues on industrial projects, the steel industry, and the military itself, purchasing equipment, building bases, and constructing a modern military hospital. Not only did the government mishandle the boom in coffee prices; it mishandled as well the subsequent bust. Imports rose just as export earnings declined, and the government responded by imposing tariffs and quantitative restrictions, demanding advanced deposits for the purchase of imports, and accumulating growing arrears in payments to foreign creditors.[62]

Rising prices eroded popular support for the military regime. So too did mounting evidence that those who had imposed the control regime profited from the management of it. Rojas Pinilla's accumulation of ranches and cattle herds; the running of a railway spur and paved road to his estate in Melgar; his family's favored access to loans and contracts—all induced cynicism, resentment, and political opposition to his government.[63] The government's growing authoritarianism accelerated the erosion of its political support in Colombia. Pledged to end political violence and to return the government to civilian rule, the regime appeared instead to promote violence and to resist a return to democratic politics. The increased erosion of political rights provoked widespread demands for the end of military government.[64]

Implemented by the military, the overthrow of Rojas in 1957 was led by civilians and, in particular, by the heads of the two great parties. The origins of military rule, they realized, lay in partisan conflict; the origin of partisan violence, they reasoned, lay in fear of permanent exclusion. To reduce the fear of exclusion, the leaders of the Liberal and Conservative parties, having overthrown Rojas, agreed to a new political rule: the national presidency would alternate between the two parties. In presidential elections, the leaders of one party would propose a candidate, whose nomination would then be confirmed by the leaders of the other, and who would then run as the candidate of the so-called National Front: the combined electoral forces of the two giant parties. Within the executive, moreover, posts would be evenly divided between the two parties: the cabinet and the councils of the governors and mayors. So too the judiciary. Regardless of vote, legislative seats would also be evenly divided between the two parties, and a two-thirds majority would be required for legislation to pass.[65]

With no prospect of decisive or permanent victory, there was therefore little prospect of permanent exclusion; and there was therefore less incentive for Conservative or Liberal militants to view elections as a form of political conquest or to resist defeat by force of arms. Given the change in political expectations, the Liberal and Conservative parties could unite in seeking a return to civilian government and in a manner that reduced the likelihood of civilians behaving in ways that would once again draw the military into politics.

The overthrow of Rojas Pinilla thus signaled the end of military rule. But it did not restore party competition. The changes therefore reduced the ability of those who, like the coffee growers, had been able to extract policy benefits by exploiting the structure of party competition.

It was the National Front that committed Colombia's coffee industry to El Convenio de Mexico. To generate the benefit of a higher world price for coffee, the government committed Colombia to withholding 20 percent of Colombia's output from international markets. The government imposed physical constraints on the export of coffee, called a "retention" tax: for every one hundred bags exported, at first ten, then fifteen, and shortly afterwards seventeen bags had to be surrendered, gratis, to the Federación. In addition, the government imposed a special exchange rate. When it devalued the peso in 1957, the National Front failed to devalue the exchange rate for coffee to the same extent as for other commodities. Exporters had to exchange their dollars for pesos at the Central Bank at the rate below that at which the government was able to sell their dollars in the open market; the government pocketed the difference, thereby imposing an additional tax on coffee exports.[66] And the government increased the export tax to 15 percent ad valorem, extending it to 1966.[67]

One result of the government's policies was a decline in coffee exports. As noted by the United States' Embassy, "In early April [1958] . . . it was predicted that [Colombia's] exports for the second quarter April–June might not even reach 1 million bags. . . . These . . . predictions appear to have been well founded, since shipments from 1 April through June 14 total only 770, 158 bags" for a projected annual total of 4 million bags, whereas Colombia had shipped nearly 5 million bags the year before.[68] Another result was a fivefold increase in the "tax bite" on coffee exports. As illustrated in table 4.2, whereas government taxes imposed a 5 percent differential between the external and the domestic price of coffee in Caldas in 1957, the differential increased to over 20 percent in 1958.

The coffee producers naturally opposed the government's attempts to tax them. The issue first arose within the Comité Nacional, and split it, with the representatives of the producers attacking those of the government. In March 1958, the coffee representatives resolved that the taxes proposed by the government represented "discriminatory and unequal treatment";[69] the government's delegation voted against it, thus ensuring its defeat.[70] The departmental committees, however, contained no representatives of the government. And, led by that of Caldas, the biggest of these committees, they rebelled against the new policies—and against the Comité Nacional itself.

The leaders of the Caldas committee dispatched telegram after telegram, opposing the measures taken by the government and the Comité Nacional. By accepting a "coffee" exchange rate and retention tax, the FNC "had renounced its role as a defender of the coffee producers," they claimed, and had aban-

TABLE 4.2

Impact of Changes in Taxes on Price Differentials, Local and International Prices, Caldas (Percentages)

Period	Internal Price	Taxes and Contributions	Total
1932–33	72.80	0.60	100
1934–35	71.10	6.70	100
1936–37	69.50	4.40	100
1938–39	69.10	3.00	100
1940–41	65.20	13.20	100
1942–43	60.40	20.50	100
1944–45	80.00	2.80	100
1946–47	81.00	1.30	100
1948–49	81.80	0.90	100
1950–51	79.80	0.50	100
1952–53	80.80	8.60	100
1954–55	85.80	3.40	100
1956–57	79.50	4.80	100
1958	64.30	20.20	100

Source: Mariano Arango, *El Café en Colombia, 1930–38* (Bogotá: Carlos Valencia Editores, 1982), table 1.4.

doned the "democratic ideal" of equal treatment under the law, and agreed to an exceptional form of taxation.[71] The Caldas committee formed delegations, exchanged correspondence, and filed joint petitions with that from Antioquia. It met with delegations from the Asociación Nacional de Industriales (ANDI) and the Federación Nacional de Comerciantes (FENALCO), the organizations that represented industrial and commercial interests, respectively, in an effort to elicit their backing.[72] It marshaled support from municipal governments and chambers of commerce throughout the coffee zones.[73] Taking advantage of the return to civilian rule, it developed lists of candidates for elections to the national legislature.[74] And when the leader of the Caldas committee, Londoño Londoño, won a seat in the Chamber of Deputies, it urged him "in the name of the . . . coffee growers to take up your position in the Chamber, so that from so elevated a position you can assume our defense against the arbitrary and discriminatory treatment by the government."[75]

The climax of Caldas's rebellion came at the Twenty-first Congress of the Federación Nacional de Cafeteros. Londoño Londoño opened the meetings with a detailed analysis of the taxes imposed upon the coffee sector and of the uses to which they were put. The total tax burden for 1958, he claimed, was 907 million pesos (see table 4.3), over half of which was transferred to other sectors. With the fall in coffee prices and the burden of government taxes, the coffee growers were in crisis: "This is an industry that has lost 40 percent of

Table 4.3
The Government's Use of Coffee Funds, According
to Londoño Londoño

Revenues and Expenditures	
Revenues from Coffee Industry	
Export Tax	385,967,547
Reintegro	100,414,446
Exchange Rate Differential	102,171,675
Retention Tax	240,994,667
Pasillo y Ripio	77,609,691
Correction	73
Total	907,158,099
Expenditures	
Outside Coffee Sector	
Payment of External Debt	384,646,365
Other Transfers	100,414,449
Total	485,060,814
Within Coffee Sector	
Accumulation of Stocks	343,166,352
Expenditures of Departmental Committees	77,609,691
Administrative Expenses	1,321,242
Total	422,097,285

Source: Adapted from Acta 5a, sesión vespertina, octubre 5 de 1959,
pp. 4–5, Federación Nacional de Cafeteros, XXI Congreso Nacional de
Cafeteros, *Actas, Acuerdos, Resoluciones, 1959.*

its value," he proclaimed.[76] The fall in price from 75 cents to 80 cents and
thence to 40 cents a pound, he went on to argue, profoundly disrupted "the
economy of a department like Caldas."[77] The government had to defend the
price of coffee; but the government had to do so by placing funds behind that
defense, not by extracting funds from the coffee sector.

The Caldas delegation returned again and again to the issue of taxation,
stressing over and over that the benefits of the international agreement were
being reaped by the government and the costs born by the coffee growers.
Why should the coffee growers be asked to pay taxes to pay off debts incurred
by a greedy military government, desirous of new planes and ships and other
expensive weapons; or the debts of the merchants and manufacturers, who
had imported goods from abroad?[78] In disgust and indignation, they branded
the Comité Nacional an official body, called for the formation of a private
organization free of government, and resigned from the FNC.

Struggles over the allocation of the costs of an international accord thus
split the Comité Nacional, divided it from the Coffee Congress, and split the

Congress itself. But Caldas could produce no other crop as profitably as it could produce coffee; even when taxed, Caldas's producers would remain in production and the government would continue to collect revenues from exports of coffee. Caldas's leaders sought to threaten the government politically. They left the FNC, but, given the structure of national political institutions, they had nowhere else to turn. They could not transfer their organization, votes, or political support to the opposition, for the National Front constituted a politically united front. The threat to defect therefore posed few dangers to the government. In the absence of electoral competition, the coffee growers could not pivot, and thereby extract policy concessions from the government, as they had in the past. Weeks passed, and quietly the Caldas delegation returned to the FNC, assuming once again positions in an organization that, in their own words, represented the interests of the government.

Conclusion

Changes in the domestic political structure of Colombia and Brazil freed their governments to collude at the international level. Changes in the structure of political institutions strengthened their governments' capacity to capture, subdue, and prey upon their coffee industries. Interest groups thus do not determine policies. Rather, policies are the result of political processes in which groups gain, or lose, power, depending upon the structure of domestic political institutions.

This chapter has also shown that changes in the international economic environment affect domestic politics. In Colombia, the movement toward an international accord in coffee provoked a fundamental restructuring of the relation between the government and export agriculture. And in both Colombia and Brazil, the achievement of an international accord in the coffee market strengthened the hands of the governments, enabling them to alter their coffee policies and to extract resources from export agriculture. Once locked into a collusive marketing strategy, the governments of Colombia and Brazil used the very instruments that gave them control over international prices to extract resources from exporters. The measures they took to gain control over global prices strengthened their power to tax the coffee sector.

5

The Supply of an Institution: United States' Entry

IN SEEKING to explain the creation of the International Coffee Organization, I have approached it as a cartel. It represents, I have argued, an attempt by the producers of raw materials to raise prices to consumers, and, given inelastic demand, thereby to redistribute income to their advantage.

Systemic theories provide one justification for such an interpretation. Kenneth Waltz, for example, invoking market structure analogies, attributes the behavior of states to the distribution of capabilities. As he states, "In defining a system's structure . . . the economic analogy will help. . . . The structure of a market is defined by the number of firms competing. . . . If few firms dominate the market, competition is said to be ologopolistic."[1] Viewed from a systemic perspective, the creation of the ICO represents the stabilization of such an oligopoly. Either in the guise of international relations or the new trade theory, game theoretic approaches provide a second justification, as they model strategic interaction among nations as imperfect competition among firms.[2] Both approaches suggest that the creation of the ICO can be treated as the use of political power to limit entry, enabling dominant producers to set prices in international markets.

The behavior of Brazil exposed one deficiency in this argument: because such approaches placed insufficient emphasis on politics at the domestic level, neither could adequately account for Brazil's shift from a price-taking competitor to a price-making hegemon in international markets. The case of the United States exposes another, which cuts even deeper. Put directly: the United States provided third-party enforcement for the cartel; but the United States was a consumer, not a producer, of coffee.[3] What kind of cartel could the ICO be, if it was enforced by consumers?

Recognizing the force of this question compels us to retreat to, and then to abandon, a series of analytic positions. The behavior of the United States was economically irrational: by enforcing the ICO, it raised the price of goods that it consumed. In an effort to salvage the premise of rationality, we are driven in search of political benefits that would compensate for the economic costs of the United States' policy choices. We are therefore driven back to systemic theory, and to a consideration of the impact of alliance politics and bipolarity in the international distribution of power.[4] The economic costs of participation in the ICO, we learn, were paid as part of the price of fighting communism in Latin America.

But the case materials drive us from this position as well. They force us to

realize that such an interpretation—one that invokes a trade-off between political and economic objectives—is misconceived. The communist threat
reached its apogee in 1962 with the stationing of Soviet missiles in Cuba. At
the very height of the cold war, the U.S. Congress blocked the implementation of the coffee agreement, postponing its implementation for nearly three
years!

In this chapter, then, we confront a series of explanations that fail. Seeking
to find a theory that fits the case and the broader narrative within which it is
lodged, we are forced to reconceptualize the facts that lie before us. We are
compelled to dig deeper in our search for the roots of the ICO.

The United States Joins

Following the collapse of coffee prices in the mid-1950s, the governments of
Colombia and Brazil sought to form an alliance among producing nations to
withhold coffee from the international market and thereby drive up its price.
As described in previous chapters and as revealed in table 4.1, the arrangements failed. Colombia and Brazil therefore sought to re-create the system of
marketing controls that had prevailed during World War II, in which the customs authorities of the advanced industrial nations would enforce restrictions
on the supply of coffee to consumer markets and thereby police free riding.

The United States constituted the single largest market for coffee, accounting for over 50 percent of the world's imports; and for Africa it was the most
rapidly growing. Whereas Africa's total exports had risen by 170 percent over
the 1950s, exports to the United States had risen more than 200 percent.
African exporters could ill afford to lose access to the United States' market.
United States' interests in the developing nations focused on Latin America;
those of Europe focused on Africa. The interests of the African nations therefore strongly shaped those of Europe. France, Britain, Belgium, and Portugal
clung to the last remnants of their colonial empires, and each feared the impact of the collapse of coffee prices on their colonies. In addition, the Eu-
ropeans were producers as well as consumers of coffee; they owned plantations in the Congo, Angola, the Ivory Coast, and East Africa. For economic
as well as political reasons, then, the European governments feared Africa's
exclusion from the United States' market.

The dominant producers of coffee, Colombia and Brazil, thus viewed the
participation of the United States as a key to the formation of a global agreement: one limiting free riding by the competitive fringe, including the African
producers of robusta coffees. They recognized that the participation of the
United States could not be based on economic interests, however.[5] The solution lay in making it in the political interests of the United States to incur the
economic costs of paying higher coffee prices. As stated by the Comité Nacio-

nal of the Federación Nacional de Cafeteros in Colombia, "We can seek a restructuring of the producer accord using a political appeal, emphasizing to the United States the necessity of protecting and aiding the Latin American nations by means of a coffee pact and of sustaining the price of coffee so as to avoid the imminent danger of economic ruin among the producing nations."[6]

Colombia

Backed by the White House, Secretary of State George Marshall, in 1947, began the negotiation of a series of regional security pacts aimed at stopping the spread of communism. The first was to be created in Latin America. The Department of State therefore organized a meeting of the Foreign Ministers of the Latin American nations for August of 1948 in Bogotá.

The founding of the Organization of American States (OAS) inevitably became entangled in Colombia's domestic politics. The leading Liberal critic of the Conservative government, Jorge Eliécer Gaitán, had long been a militant critic of United States' corporations in Colombia; when he pressed for a position in the Colombian delegation to the OAS meetings, President Ospina Pérez denied his request. Gaitán thereupon broadened his attacks on the Conservative government to include attacks upon the Bogotá conference, characterizing it as further evidence of the government's subordination to the "giant of the north." Gaitán intensified his attacks when Ospina Pérez appointed Laureano Gómez, the Liberal's principal enemy, to the Colombian delegation and, indeed, nominated him as president of the conference. Just as the foreign dignitaries assembled in Bogotá, Gaitán was assassinated. The subsequent insurrection engulfed the inaugural conference of the Organization of American States.[7]

The riots in Bogotá confirmed the deepest suspicions of those in charge of United States' national security policy that Latin America had become a target of international communism.[8] The events in Bogotá placed Colombia on the front lines of the cold war.

The United States sought to integrate Latin America into its global alliances by forging multinational institutions. In 1954, for example, Secretary of State John Foster Dulles secured the so-called Declaration of Caracas from the Tenth Inter-American Conference—one branding the existence of a communist-dominated regime as a threat to inter-American security—and used it, months later, to justify the overthrow of Jacobo Arbenz, president of Guatemala.[9] The Latin American nations, for their part, used such conferences to extract economic concessions from the United States. In exchange for their support for the Declaration of Caracas, for example, they secured a pledge from Dulles to convene a special Economic Conference of the Inter-American Economic and Social Council of the Organization of American

States, where they debated a report outlining the transfer of capital necessary to promote international development—and negotiated the first of the coffee agreements.[10]

The external relations of the United States are managed by the executive branch. The policies that result are in part a function of the way in which the President, as chief executive, parcels out policy decisions among the units of the bureaucracy.[11] The Tenth Inter-American Conference had dealt with the security of the Western Hemisphere; the United States' delegation was therefore led by Secretary of State Dulles. The meeting of the Inter-American Economic and Social Council was defined as an economic conference, however; and the United States' delegation to the conference was therefore led by the Secretary of the Treasury, George Humphrey, who viewed commodity agreements as restraints of trade and violations of free-market policies.[12] So long as the President continued to define policy toward Latin America as a branch of economic policy, the Treasury Department retained jurisdiction. Acting on its preference for the free operation of markets, it would continue to veto United States' participation in an international coffee agreement.

In their efforts to promote an international coffee accord, Colombia and Brazil soon found the United States' government better configured, as it were, for their purposes. For the views of the White House soon changed. Following the hostile receptions for Vice President Richard Nixon during a state visit to Venezuela, the Eisenhower Administration concluded that communists had penetrated more deeply into the Western Hemisphere than had hitherto been realized. The White House therefore gave the Department of State greater control over Latin America policy and weakened the hold of the Treasury Department. International economic policy should not be based exclusively on market principles, it acknowledged, but rather with a view to countering political challenges from the Left. Backed by the White House, Assistant Secretary of State Thomas Mann began actively exploring the conditions under which the United States could support the creation of an agency to regulate international trade in coffee.[13]

It was the Cuban revolution that decisively shaped the executive branch's conception of the United States' interests in Latin America, however. John F. Kennedy became President following a campaign that focused on the threat of communism globally and of Castro in the Western Hemisphere. Given the priority placed on the fight against communism, particularly in Latin America, the Kennedy Administration vested control over Latin American policy in the hands of the President's security specialists. The United States Agency for International Development (USAID) was merged with the Department of State in Washington, and its mission directors were subordinated to its ambassadors in the field. And the team that formed about Thomas Mann in the Department of State became a virtual adjunct of the White House.

In the 1960s, the fear of "Castroism" defined United States' policy toward

Latin America as part of the struggle against international communism. The dominant producers of coffee could exploit the political fears of North American security specialists to secure economic objectives. In particular, they now gained political leverage in their campaign for a coffee agreement. Patterns of political conflict within Brazil exacerbated the fears of the United States, enabling Brazil to join Colombia in eliciting support for such an agreement.

Brazil

When Vargas created political parties in Brazil, he based the Brazilian Labor Party (PTB) on a labor movement that had been organized and superintended by his government. In appealing to workers and intellectuals, the Partido Trabalhista Brasileiro confronted a political rival: the Communist Party. With Vargas's return to power in the election of 1951, the PTB became a governing party. When the United States entered the Korean War, the Communist Party sought to disrupt Brazil's relations with the United States. It became therefore an active opponent of Vargas, and in seeking to overthrow his government, it focused on undermining the PTB, forcing it, and any government of which it was a part, to move to the Left.

João Goulart served as the head of the PTB and as vice president for both Juscelino Kubitschek and Jânio Quadros, his successor. In each government in which Goulart served, he became the focus of partisan challenges. Some, of course, came from the Right; Carlos Lacerda rose to prominence on the strength of his criticism of the PTB. Others came from the Left, as militants continued to seek to move Brazil to the Left by undermining the appeal of the governing parties among workers, peasants, and intellectuals.

Those charged with promoting United States' security interests in Brazil remained deeply troubled by Goulart and his impact upon Brazilian politics. They abhorred his penchant for competing with the Left by championing its causes—land reform, the nationalization of foreign firms, the unionization of noncommissioned ranks in the military forces—and by co-opting its leadership, as by placing members of the Communist Party in influential positions within the government-sponsored wings of the union movement. And they were confronted by an incontestable political fact: given Goulart's tactic of competing on the Left, any government in which he held office would be driven in directions contrary to their conception of the United States' interests.[14]

The security agencies adopted a number of tactics to counter the impact of Goulart. One was to locate and to cultivate alternative politicians; another was to channel and to manipulate development assistance so as to strengthen the political position of the United States' allies. The United States' support for Carlos Lacerda, Goulart's sworn enemy, best illustrates the use of such tactics. When Goulart at last became Brazil's president, Lacerda held the governorship of Guanabara. Declaring the state an "island of sanity," the United States channeled a disproportionate amount of its development assistance into Lacerda's domain.[15] Less dramatically, in an earlier period, the United States had backed Jânio Quadros. Quadros had appeared to offer an important alternative to the PTB. He appeared able to appeal to its constituency; he had, after all, twice defeated Adhemar de Barros in São Paulo. And yet he also had appeared to appeal to the professional and middle classes; he had been endorsed by Lacerda's Uniãon Democrática Nacional (UDN,) the conservative party that opposed the PTB. As stated by Peter Flynn, the United States' government therefore had fastened on to Quadros and determined "that everything possible should be done to help . . . the outstandingly successful candidate of the middle classes."[16]

To back Quadros, the Kennedy Administration targeted Brazil for a large portion of the funds distributed under the Alliance for Progress. In addition, it backed efforts to stabilize the international price of coffee.

As governor of São Paulo, Quadros had criticized the magnitude of the costs borne by the coffee farmers, as the national government sought singlehandedly to raise the international price of coffee. As president of Brazil, he, of course, viewed with greater favor policies designed to increase the government's command over foreign exchange. An international accord responded to both of his interests; it promised to maximize Brazil's earnings of foreign exchange on the one hand, while, on the other, transferring a major portion of the costs from Brazil's producers, concentrated in São Paulo, to producers in other nations. By backing a coffee agreement, the United States could thus back the government of Jânio Quadros, and so "stabilize" the politics of Brazil.

The Domestic Origins of United States' Policy

In response to the question, Why would consumer nations join an agreement that, like the ICO, would raise producer prices? we can thus answer: for security reasons. The United States was willing to trade economic costs for political benefits.[17] That a consuming nation should join a cartel is not surprising, this response contends, for state actors sacrifice economic interests out of a regard for the defense of the national security.

This response seeks to elude the contradiction created by treating the ICO as an economic phenomenon. It does so by redefining the United States' policy choices as the result of a trade-off between political and economic values. It redefines the problem as one in political economy.

The contradiction posed by the ICO resists so facile a solution, however. While the pursuit of security interests may explain the support of particular agencies for United States' participation in the ICO, it does not explain its actual behavior. Endorsed by the President and the State Department at the height of the cold war—a war that had threatened to become hot once the nuclear threat entered Latin America—the policy was not in fact implemented until nearly three years later. There is thus a severe discrepancy between the urgency of the impulse and the desultory character of the response. Put another way: the pursuit of security interests may have been necessary for the United States' entry into the ICO, but it clearly was not sufficient.

To explain the United States' behavior in the global arena, we have first to examine its domestic politics. In particular, we have to comprehend the significance of its political institutions, which rendered the executive branch's support of policies a necessary—but not sufficient—force in securing the United States' participation in the coffee agreement.

The Delay

The U.S. executive branch regarded an international coffee agreement as an important, indeed critical, component of policies promoting the security of the United States. Through the Alliance for Progress, the United States had pledged $20 billion in development assistance; for, in the words of President Kennedy, "If the only alternatives for the people of Latin America are the status quo and communism, they will inevitably choose communism."[18] But such expenditures would be wasted, were prices to collapse in coffee markets. "A drop of one cent a pound for . . . coffee," the President noted, "costs Latin American producers $50 million in export proceeds—enough to seriously undercut what we are seeking to accomplish by the Alliance for Progress."[19] As Thomas Mann, the Administration's leading maker of policy toward Latin America, bluntly phrased the Administration's position: "The agreement is the key to the Alliance for Progress."[20]

The executive branch signaled its commitment to an agreement in public statements at international conferences, most notably the one at Punta del Este that unveiled the Alliance for Progress; in public ceremonies at home, the most publicized being a White House reception for ambassadors representing the Latin American nations; and in statements and testimony before Congress. Despite the efforts expended by the executive branch, Congress responded reluctantly to its appeals for legislative action. Diplomats from the State Department signed the International Coffee Agreement on September 28, 1962; the President submitted it for ratification by the Senate on the fourth of October. But hearings did not commence until March 1963, and the treaty was not formally ratified until December 20, 1963, a year and a quarter after first being signed. Negotiations with the House of Representatives imposed further delays. Influential members of the House were unwilling to leave policy-making to the executive branch and Senate; the treaty, they insisted, required implementing legislation: legislation that would empower the customs authorities to regulate shipments of coffee. Deferring to the power of the House, the executive branch introduced such legislation in the House in October 1963; the bill was passed by the House and submitted to the Senate in November. In the Senate, it was amended by the Finance Committee and passed as amended in July 1964. A conference committee agreed to the Senate version of the bill, which was then returned to the House in August 1964—where it was defeated! Only in the next Congress did the enabling legislation finally receive a majority of votes in both houses.

Despite the heated state of the cold war in the early 1960s, when the ICO was proposed, the United States therefore did not begin to enforce its provisions until three years later. The delay resulted from the need of the executive branch to secure the support of the legislative branch of the government.

The United States did eventually join and enforce the International Coffee Organization, then; but it did not do so because it was a unitary actor, willing to incur economic costs in order to secure political benefits. The international policy of the United States was the result of a domestic political process in which majorities had to be forged within and across different branches of government. Not only did this requirement influence the timing of the policy; it also influenced its content. The policy was implemented in such a way that it would safeguard the electoral interests of both houses of Congress.[21]

The U.S. Congress

Technically, the agreement on coffee represented an international treaty. It therefore required ratification by the Senate. But the executive branch feared the power of the House. Even though the House could not block a treaty, it could block other legislation, and the Kennedy and Johnson Administrations therefore sought to accommodate the political interests of its members. A major reason for the United States' delay in implementing the terms of the ICO and for the form in which it eventually did so was the determination by the executive branch to seek implementing legislation from the House that would offer its members credible safeguards against the political dangers of a rise in coffee prices.

From the executive branch's point of view, the Senate posed few political difficulties. The treaty fell within the jurisdiction of the Committee on Foreign Relations, where, by and large, it received a sympathetic hearing. Chaired by William Fulbright, the committee numbered among its members such noted internationalists as Hubert Humphrey, Wayne Morse,[22] Michael Mansfield, and Jacob Javits, for example. The committee had just completed a study of Brazil that depicted shortages of foreign exchange as a major source of economic and political instability.[23] The committee supported the administration's position, with Hubert Humphrey intemperately—and characteristically—arguing that "this is a matter of life or death, a matter of Castroism versus freedom. . . . Castroism will spread like a plague throughout Latin America unless something is done about the prices of raw materials produced there."[24]

Far more problematic was the House of Representatives. While the coffee agreement was sponsored in the Senate by the Committee on Foreign Relations, whose members shared the executive branch's vision of its role in security policy, the agreement fell within the purview of the Ways and Means Committee in the House. Ways and Means possessed a domestic agenda and, in particular, focused on economic issues. With the Democratic Party controlling both Congress and the executive branch, Wilbur Mills, the chairman of Ways and Means, was predisposed to cooperate with the executive branch; but he was far less willing than his counterparts in the Senate to inflict economic costs upon domestic consumers in order to secure political benefits abroad.

It must be remembered that many leaders of Congress in the 1960s had been members of Congress in the 1940s. They had experienced the price rises of the postwar period, the militant response of labor, and the political polarization that resulted. They had witnessed the ability of political nonentities, like Senator Guy Gillette, to become prominent nationally by capitalizing on the issue of inflation. In that era, the government's defense of "a 5¢ cup of coffee" symbolized its defense of the economic welfare of the common man. Members of the House therefore treated with the deepest skepticism any legislation that might lead to higher prices, even any motivated by the imperative of national security and the struggle against communism.

Fearing to give power to the bureaucracy that would result in price rises for which Congress might be held accountable, the chairman of Ways and Means therefore created a special arrangement for delegating power to the executive: the House would grant authority to the President to implement the agreement, but while the agreement lasted for five years, the enabling legislation would last for two, or the duration of but one Congress. The necessity for renewal gave the members of Congress the chance to monitor the performance of the agreement, and the renewal's short duration gave its members the chance to terminate the United States' participation, should it start to cause political problems. Under the terms of the legislation, incumbents thereby reduced their political risks. By offering such terms, the executive branch could assuage the political fears of Congress.

The executive branch's respect for the power of the House therefore led to a delay in implementation, while it forged the legislation necessary to secure its support. Moderate frosts in 1962 and 1963 resulted in higher coffee prices; taking counsel from its congressional leadership, the executive branch further postponed legislative action. The ambassadors of the coffee-producing nations refrained from pressuring Congress, fearing that "their actions would be cited as arguments in favor of opposing passage of the bill"—an assessment fervently endorsed by the Department of State[25]—and the congressional leadership continued to delay debate on the bill. When August arrived, they could do so no longer; the members of Congress were anxious to depart from Washington to compete in the 1964 elections.

Unfortunately for the coffee-producing nations, the Democratic House had just passed a bill reducing quotas for imports of beef. The Democrats' candidate for President, Lyndon Johnson, came from Texas, a beef-producing state, and the Republicans sought to make the bill a campaign issue. Like the legislation on beef, that for coffee imposed import quotas. When the enabling legislation came to the floor, sixty liberal Democrats, seeking to deprive the Republicans of further political ammunition, refrained from voting on the coffee bill. The bill was defeated, with 183 voting for it and 193 voting against it.[26]

As the Democrats won the election of 1964 in a landslide, the Johnson Administration held a far greater majority of the votes in the subsequent Congress. Legislation that had been defeated in the Eighty-seventh Congress easily passed in the Eighty-eighth, including that for the coffee agreement.

Even though cast as a centerpiece of the United States' fight against communism in the Western Hemisphere; even though offered as a tool in the fight against Castro; even though proposed at the height of the cold war and the bipolar struggle for global domination—the United States' entry into the coffee agreement had been rejected, delayed, and then implemented in terms that can only be explained by the electoral interests of the members of Congress. The United States' policy toward the world coffee market is thus best understood as a by-product of political struggles as structured by domestic political institutions.

The Role of Business

In the end, Congress did pass the enabling legislation, and the executive branch, through its customs authorities, began regulating the inflow of coffee into the United States' market. The competitive fringe no longer cut their prices in an effort to free ride off of the efforts of the dominant producers; and the dominant producers no longer retaliated, cutting their prices in response. Average prices therefore stopped their fall, and the agreement began effectively to regulate the prices of coffee in international markets. Members of Congress of course remained deeply concerned about the price of coffee. Why, then, did they let the agreement proceed?

One reason, as already mentioned, was that the Democratic landslide of 1964 gave the executive branch a larger political majority in Congress. Nonetheless, the interests of the members of Congress were not those of the Department of State, and the former continued cautiously to assess the political dangers arising from the possible upward revision in coffee prices. In doing so, they sought information about the possible impact of the agreement on coffee prices.

Coffee is not grown in the United States;[27] unlike sugar, cotton, or wheat, for example, no bureaucracy superintends the production of the commodity, thereby acquiring expertise about the economics of production, consumption, or the behavior of markets. The executive branch possesses few experts on coffee. When specialists in diplomacy or security affairs sought information about the coffee market, they therefore turned, by necessity, to private industry. In particular, they turned to executives in the roasting companies that purchased coffee from abroad for processing and marketing in the United States.

Historically, coffee consumption everywhere has grown at the rate of growth of population plus real per capita income. Demand therefore grows slowly, and in the United States in recent years the rate of growth has declined, as younger and wealthier consumers have switched to the consumption of cola products.[28] The largest firms in the industry, General Foods and Procter and Gamble, are regarded as being well managed, dynamic, and expansionary and have access to large amounts of capital.[29] With large firms competing in a mature market, the rivalry among them is intense. Competition takes the form of the introduction of new forms of coffee: soluble coffee in the 1950s, freeze-dried in the 1960s, and decaffeinated in the 1970s, for example. It takes the form of introducing new brands, such as Taster's Choice, Brim, International Coffee, High Point, and Mellow Point. It also takes the form of penetrating regional markets. Historically, General Foods' Maxwell House tended to dominate markets in the East: Procter and Gamble's Folgers, markets in the Midwest. Folgers, however, invested heavily in advertising and promotional campaigns to capture selected markets east of the Mississippi.[30] General Foods, for its part, retaliated, cutting its prices and concentrating its advertising in the "home base" from which Folgers had launched its expansion.[31]

Though intense, this rivalry between the firms is not competitive, in the strict meaning of the term. At the time that the United States sought to enter the International Coffee Organization, the top four firms accounted for roughly 60 percent of the domestic sales of coffee (table 5.1). As revealed by Gallop and Roberts, authors of an economic study of the United States' coffee market, the roasting firms behave as though they realize that they are locked into interdependent relationships, and therefore take into account the impact of their choices upon the behavior of their rivals.[32] Gallop and Roberts grouped over 160 roasting firms by size, assigning one large firm (General Foods, one must presume) to a category of its own; the five next largest firms

TABLE 5.1
Characteristics of Six Leading Firms

Firms	Market Share (Percentages)		Percentage of Sales from Coffee	
	1955	1961	1968	1970
General Foods	21	34	36	28
Procter and Gamble	9	12	15	5 to 15
Standard Brands	6	6	5	less than 10
Hills Brothers	8	6	9	greater than 90
Nestlé	4	3	4	20 to 30
A & P	NA	NA	7	less than 10
Totals	48	61	69	

Source: Stephen D. Krasner, "Business Government Relations: The Case of the International Coffee Agreement," *International Organization* 27, 4 (Autumn 1973):503.

Notes: NA = not available; all totals exclude A & P.

to a second group; and the remaining 150 or so, each with less than 1 percent of the market, to a third. They then calculated the reaction functions of firms in each category. The small firms, they found, behaved as if taking into account the behavior of larger firms; and the leading firms chose levels of production as if anticipating the behavior of firms in every size class. "This behavior," they concluded, was consistent with "dominant firm leadership" in a market characterized by imperfect competition.[33]

Being locked in strategic interrelationships with other roasters, the large firms thus possess incentives not only to compete but also to cooperate. In the marketplace, cooperation can take the form of refraining from entering into a particular market or from cutting prices in an effort to increase market share. In the political realm, it can take the form of providing public goods, as by seeking to influence public policies toward the industry. When policymakers sought advice about policy toward the coffee market, then, it is not surprising that it was the large firms that took the initiative in providing it.

Government bureaucrats had worked closely with the private businessmen during the Second World War. This was true in many industries, including coffee. Drawn onto the trade advisory committee of the Inter-American Coffee Board, executives in the large roasting firms had provided the information about government regulations in the ports of Latin America; about the paperwork and documents necessary for the purchase, insurance, and transportation of coffee; about the stocks necessary to accommodate seasonal fluctuations in demand and shortfalls due to frost, strikes, and other contingencies; about the types of coffee, their use in home, restaurant, and workplace, their origins and the time of year they entered international trade; and about the relationship between spot and futures markets and the use of the latter in the management of risk.[34] In search of the expertise with which to reconstruct controls over the coffee market in the postwar period, the U.S. Department of State therefore drew once again on the expertise of the large roasting firms.

When the executive branch turned to the coffee industry, it turned to the National Coffee Association (NCA)—an organization that represented the interests of importers, roasters, and distributors of coffee. As control over the making of policy toward international commodities moved from the Treasury Department, with its commitment to free trade, to the State Department, with its preoccupation with national security, the NCA organized a Foreign Affairs Committee to monitor and advise the government as it prepared to intervene in coffee markets. The committee intensified the association's efforts to educate the bureaucracy about the economic and commercial realities of these markets. It communicated by letter,[35] by dispatching delegations to the Department of State,[36] and by hosting State Department representatives at business conferences.[37] And, at the department's invitation, the Foreign Affairs Committee of the NCA participated in the Coffee Study Group, a committee organized by the Department of State to develop the regulations that constituted the framework for the International Coffee Agreement.[38] As communicated to Bruchey in his interviews with officials in the State Department:

> The State Department recognized that the NCA was in a unique position to provide information and expertise in the development of a regulatory system, and that its cooperation would be desirable, if not required, for administering US participation in an agreement. The State Department and other government bureaucracies had relatively few commodity experts, and readily acknowledged their appreciation of business assistance in developing, implementing, and operating the I[nternational] C[offee] A[greement].[39]

When congressmen sought information about the possible impact of an agreement on the price of coffee, they turned for advice to the bureaucracy; the bureaucracy, in turn, turned to the industry. Alternatively, Congress itself turned directly to the private sector. But when Congress did so, it too turned to the National Coffee Association and its Foreign Affairs Committee, the same source of information employed by the Administration's own experts.[40] The Foreign Affairs Committee of the National Coffee Association drew its membership from the large roasting firms (table 5.2). These firms included General Foods, producer of Maxwell House, Yuban, and other coffees, and by far the largest firm in the market; Procter and Gamble, maker of Folgers; and Standard Brands, Hills Brothers, and A&P, the largest of the regional and "own brand" firms. The Congress and the bureaucrats thus drew their information, advice, and expertise from the representatives of the large firms that dominated the United States' coffee market.

In the postwar period, members of Congress had mounted highly publicized investigations into the causes of rising coffee prices; siding with the

TABLE 5.2
Members of the Foreign Affairs Committee

Year	Six Largest Roasters	Six Largest Green Coffee Firms	Small Firms
1960	3	0	3
1961	3	0	4
1962	3	1	3
1963	4	1	1

Source: Stephen D. Krasner, "The Politics of Primary Commodities: A Study of Coffee, 1900–1970." Ph.D diss., Harvard University, 1971, p. 255.

United States' consumer against foreign cartels had proved to be good politics. Congress was now being asked to empower the government bureaucracy to work with foreign producers to "stabilize" the price of coffee. But members of Congress had reason to fear that political challengers could exploit this issue against them. Had industry experts testified that the agreement possessed the potential to harm the United States' consumer, their testimony could have triggered the fears of incumbents, leading to a blockage of the agreement. Indeed, the roasters later proved their ability to do so: the same Wilbur Mills who sponsored the enabling legislation in 1963 caused the suspension of the agreement in 1969, when the large roasters briefly turned against it.[41] Congress appreciated the importance of the agreement to foreign policy but feared its repercussions domestically. Should experts forecast that their empowerment of the bureaucracy to regulate the international trade in coffee would generate price rises, thus threatening incumbents' chances in the next election, Congress would have withheld that power. As stated by Bruchey, "It can be seen in retrospect that consumer protection sentiment, whether principled or simply expedient, expressed in Congressional debates, amendments, and in the actual defeat of the first coffee bill in 1964, could have been considerably amplified under hypothetically different circumstances, for example, if the National Coffee Association had chosen to oppose the Coffee agreement."[42]

Conclusion

By entering into an agreement with the dominant producers, the United States provided the policeman necessary to constrain exports to the world's largest market for coffee; members of the competitive fringe therefore joined the agreement, for fear of being excluded from that market—and of having to sell at prices reflecting the impact of supplies diverted from the United States to the smaller markets elsewhere in the world. With the United States' entry into—indeed, sponsorship of—an international agreement to regulate global trade in coffee, the global market was transformed into a politically regulated market, governed by an international agency.

The founding of the ICO poses a paradox: the organization was designed to raise the price of coffee, but it relied for its enforcement on the United States, which is a consumer nation. The paradox calls into question economic explanations of the ICO and forces the abandonment of any straightforword use of economic models of cooperation, such as those derived from game theory. It motivates a move from economic reasoning to explanations based upon *political* economy. Clearly security interests motivated those in the United States who supported the agreement; the power of such interests is highlighted by the obvious parallel between the International Coffee Agreement, launched as part of the response to the penetration of communism into the Western Hemisphere, and the Inter-American Coffee Agreement, launched in response to the threat of nazism. The participation of the United States could thus be seen as reflecting its willingness to pay economic costs—the costs of a higher price for coffee—for political benefits—the benefits of enhanced security.

This reformulation amounts to a rejection of the conceptual framework that defined the initial paradox. The framework is reductionist: it reduces the behavior of nations to purely economic terms. The problem posed by the ICO is a *political*-economic problem, however. It must therefore be analyzed by taking into account a wider range of interests than those that prevail in the marketplace, and especially the transcendent interest of nations in defending their international security.

But attempts to explain the behavior of the United States by citing the political benefits secured in compensation for the economic costs do not suffice, for the staggering and uncertain policy response was not commensurate with the magnitude of the security threat. Nor did the nature of the threat help to explain the terms and conditions under which the policy was implemented. Rather, the international policy of the United States is better understood by examining the domestic political process and, in particular, the power of the Congress and the need for its members to secure periodic reelection.

Congress did not cooperate with the executive branch because their interests coincided or because Congress deferred to the transcendent importance of national security. Congress, after all, initially rejected the executive's policy. The security interests explanation thus cannot be salvaged so readily. Rather, Congress cooperated with the executive branch because it was able to structure the implementing legislation in a form that reduced the political risks of doing so, and because it extracted information from the executive branch and from the experts in the private sector that underscored the large magnitude of the benefits to the national security and the small level of the risks to the reelection of its members.

Table 5.3 schematically presents the conditions for the United States' entry

TABLE 5.3
Necessary and Sufficient Conditions for Passage of Executive's Policy

Condition	Executive Branch	Congress
Necessary Condition	+	0
Sufficient Condition	+	+

Notes: + = supports; 0 = does not object.

into the international coffee agreement. While the backing of the executive branch may provide a necessary condition for the United States' entry into the international coffee accord, such a backing is not sufficient to explain that choice of policy, for policy is the result of a domestic political process. As suggested by table 5.3, Congress possesses the power to block the executive branch. Rather than policy being made through a process of command and control, as might be expected in matters of national security or cold-war geo-politics, in the area of the coffee agreement, policy was instead made in a process that more clearly resembled the "iron triangle" model of domestic politics: one in which the executive branch structured its programs to serve the interests of organized groups, thereby eliciting the support of Congress.[43]

The focus on international security thus resolves the initial paradox. It does so by transforming the problem from one of pure economics to one of political economy. But an appreciation of the significance of Congress provokes a further reformulation: one in which foreign economic policy is viewed from the perspective of national, rather than international, politics. It also highlights the central role of the roasting firms, a subject to which I return in the next chapter.

6

The Functioning of an Institution: The International Coffee Organization

STUDENTS of international relations have long studied the sources of political order. Among the literatures devoted to this theme, that on regimes is the most relevant. Students of regimes focus on international agreements on posts and telecommunications, shipping, fishing, banking, trade, travel, and a host of other subjects.[1] The number and significance of these agreements, they stress, suggests that students of international relations must focus on cooperation, as well as conflict, in the relations between states. Indeed, they must focus on more than nation-states themselves.[2] Populated by nation-states, the international arena is also populated with organizations.

The International Coffee Organization (ICO) was not one-off but long-lived, for over two decades. It possessed a professional staff and organization. It was based upon "rules and decision-making procedures" that enabled nation-states to enforce and maintain agreements regarding the coffee market.[3] It monitored and regulated international trade in one of the most valuable commodities exported from the tropics. The ICO constituted an international regime.

Within the literature on regimes, two major approaches stand out.[4] One emphasizes efficiency. Keohane, for example, explores the reduction in transactions costs that regimes provide and notes their capacity to enhance the ability of states to secure welfare-enhancing agreements. By lowering the costs of monitoring, reducing the costs of getting information, and providing procedures for arriving at agreements, he argues, regimes provide "ways to overcome the deficiencies that make it impossible to consummate . . . mutually beneficial agreements."[5] A second approach emphasizes distribution. Regimes, it is held, do not merely make possible welfare-enhancing trades; they also structure exchanges such that those with power can secure benefits from others.[6]

The one approach stresses collective benefits and cooperation; the other, distribution and coercion. The approaches were once treated as rivals, in part because they echoed the tiresome debates between liberal and realist theories of international politics. More recently, however, they have been viewed as complements, in large part because of the impact of game theoretic modes of reasoning. Based upon a single play of the prisoner's dilemma game, the logic of collective action suggests that if a large producer stands to secure a sufficient portion of the collective gains, that producer will then be willing to incur the costs of providing the regime that guarantees them.[7] Distributive advantages thus operate in the service of the provision of collective benefits, providing incentives for large actors to provide public goods. The implication of single-shot prisoner's dilemmas finds support in the folk theorem of repeated play, wherein coercive punishments can support strategy choices that underpin efficient equilibria.[8] Coercion and efficiency, distribution and cooperation: game theoretic reasoning suggests that rather than representing alternatives, these phenomena complement each other, helping to explain the sources of cooperation.

As we shall see, the study of the ICO contributes to the elaboration of these arguments. It also encourages us to deepen our understanding of regimes by making greater use of game theory. In this chapter, I use the logic of subgame perfection[9] to suggest how the rules of a regime become self-enforcing. I argue that once they do so, they enable agents to make promises that are credible. The result is that transactions become rule-governed.[10] Rather than merely supporting spot exchanges, a regime can then support intertemporal commitments, in which present costs are incurred for the sake of future benefits. Behavior that might be too risky in the absence of institutionalized guarantees might be chosen by rational agents in their presence. I offer insight into the way in which the ICO became rule-governed, constraining and modifying the conduct of its members. I show how it became an institution.[11]

Institutional Rules

In seeking to transform the international market into an international organization, the dominant producers shed one kind of risk—that arising from market competition—only to encounter another—the possibility of political predation.[12] For should they succeed in creating an organization, it might well be turned against them. And their consumer allies, who provided the enforcement necessary to regulate the market, faced the prospect of economic predation were the ICO to be used to radically raise the price of coffee. In shifting from an unregulated to a regulated market, the dominant producers and their consumer allies therefore sought to contrive rules that provided assurances against these risks. The need for such assurances helps to explain the structure of the organization that they formed.

Voting Rules

In the context of the International Coffee Agreement, prices were no longer set purely by market forces; they were set by economic forces that were politically constrained. Within the regulated environment, allocations were not made purely in response to supply and demand and the subsequent formation of prices; rather, they resulted from a political process. Brazil and Colombia sought to create a political organization that would be powerful enough to constrain coffee shipments, and thus enable them to limit their own exports without fear of exploitation by free riders. But they also sought to structure the rules so that they need not fear that small producers would use the power of the organization to engage in political predation.

Their first line of defense lay in the allocation of votes, the basic "currency" of the "political market" created by the International Coffee Agreement (ICA). Under the terms of the agreement, a total number of votes—1,000— was divided among the producer nations of the ICO. Twelve percent of the votes were divided equally among the producing nations; the remainder, proportionately to the producer's "weight" in the coffee market.[13] Figures from 1964 illustrate the impact of this rule: with 12 percent of the 1,000 votes allocated among the 24 members, each producer received a "basic" allocation of five votes. Colombia, with nearly 14 percent of the market, received an additional 122 (880 $\times$ .1386) and Brazil, with 41.6 percent of the market, received an additional 366 (880 $\times$ .416). In the making and unmaking of political majorities, the larger producers were thus better endowed with votes than were the smaller.[14]

The so-called economic clauses—the clauses mandating the setting and adjustment of quotas, so as to regulate prices—constituted the core of the agreement. The drafters prescribed that all decisions regarding the economic clauses require a two-thirds majority. Given the weighting of the votes, the implication was clear: were the small producers of Africa and Latin America to oppose the wishes of the dominant producers, the former could not prevail. The dominant producers possessed one-third of the votes, sufficient to prevent a majority of sufficient size to form, given the rules.

The weighting of votes also assured the dominant producers of membership in key committees of the International Coffee Organization. The most important was the Executive Board, which consisted of seven members. In selecting the board, each nation was required to cast all its votes for a single candidate; the seven candidates receiving the highest number of votes secured membership on the board. Under the rules, simply by voting for themselves, Brazil and Colombia could guarantee themselves seats on the Executive Board. And with weighted voting, they could control nearly 60 percent of the votes on the board and so dominate the administration of the agreement.

The finance committee superintended the budget of the International Coffee Organization; a committee on statistics superintended the gathering and dissemination of data; a third committee monitored the collection of certificates of origin, and thus of adherence to the quota; a fourth monitored retentions and stocks; a fifth, internal administration. The Executive Board selected the members of these committees. Dominating the board, Colombia and Brazil controlled appointments to other committees as well.

The representatives of the dominant producers were intensely aware of the significance of the voting rules and of their influence upon the conduct of member nations. In seeking to convince the headquarters in Bogotá that the agreement would prove hospitable to Colombia, the Federación's delegate to the ICO assured his superiors of his ability to guarantee Colombia's representation on key committees. In so doing he provided an illustration, demonstrating that, given the rules for voting, Colombia was assured of election. I quote directly from his memorandum:

(a) Total number of votes   1,000

(b) Votes of Brazil   292

(c) Number of posts   8

(d) Number of votes that
    would ensure a post $(a - b)/(c - 1)$*
(e) Votes of Colombia   114

What is required is that $e > d$:
$$= e > (a - b)/(c - 1)$$
$$= 114 > 708/7$$
$$= 114 > 101$$
Therefore, Colombia is assured of election.
    *Excluding Brazil[15]

Given its assurance of election, Colombia was assured as well of access to the political power to safeguard its interests within the regulatory agency, the delegate counseled; and Colombia therefore could confidently and assuredly participate in the affairs of the organization.

The dominant producers realized that the rules would affect the behavior of the smaller nations; once credibly in place, the smaller nations would have to alter their behavior in ways useful to the dominant producers. In the last stages of negotiating the agreement, Colombia's delegate reported, "Brazil and Colombia deliberated over the matter of voting and drew attention to the important fact . . . that a single small nation will have no influence."[16] The implication was obvious: such a nation "will find itself in a very precarious position if it chooses to operate alone."[17] Empowered by the political rules, he argued, the dominant producers should be able to transform economic competitors into political clients, seeking favorable alliances within those in control of the organization.

Monitoring Quantities

The agreement sought to defend coffee prices by limiting coffee exports. Member nations chose a market price; knowing the demand for coffee, they set quotas so as to supply international markets with an amount of coffee that would secure that price. The significance of the rules is revealed in their impact upon the construction of key instruments for monitoring the quantities exported and the prices at which they were sold.

As discussed above, during the price rise caused by frosts in Brazil in 1962 and 1963, the United States' Congress was reluctant to pass the legislation necessary to secure implementation of the agreement; the members of Congress feared being blamed for the price rise. As a consequence, United States' customs authorities lacked the power to require the documentation necessary for the implementation of the agreement. The United States consumed over 50 percent of the world's coffee; other nations, such as Canada and (to a lesser degree) Mexico and Japan, imported their coffee through the United States; and should those other nations desire to evade the restrictions imposed by the agreement, they could increase their purchases in United States' markets. The failure of the system in the United States thus meant the failure of the system worldwide.

Following the United States' adoption of implementing legislation in 1965, further loopholes remained. Imports from nonmembers did not require certificates of origin. Uganda and Tanzania exported through the port of Mombasa, located in Kenya, which was a nonmember nation at the time; both therefore could ship coffee to Europe and the United States unaccompanied by certificates of origin. Any producer could export to ports in nonmember countries; merchants in New York or London could purchase this coffee and import it without having to remit certificates to the secretariat of the ICO.[18] Should a nation ship a volume of exports that exceeded its quota through this means, then, its performance would not be recorded, even were its coffee eventually to be consumed by another member nation.

An analogous problem arose in the so-called "new markets," to which producers could also ship coffee without certificates of origin. Such shipments should not count against quotas, it was argued, as they were not being made to traditional markets but rather to markets in which coffee had not yet become a staple of consumption. The problem, of course, was that the coffee could be reexported from the "new" market to the "traditional" market, without it being credited against the producer's quota. This possibility soon became a reality, especially in Africa. Investigations revealed, for example, that the West African nation of Guinea had exported over 100,000 bags of coffee to Europe using its own certificates of origin—coffee that had in fact originated in Angola and the Ivory Coast, enabling those two countries to increase their market shares beyond those allowed them by their quotas.[19]

Participation in the International Coffee Agreement resulted from strategic calculations. Nations would participate if they knew that others too were restricting their exports. To determine whether their costly efforts to limit exports were being undercut by others, producers needed to be able to measure the extent of compliance. In response to the problems experienced in initial efforts to enforce the accord, the ICO Executive Board therefore required certificates of origin to be collected from *all* imports of coffee, be they from member or nonmember nations. In 1967, they required that a member's shipments to new markets also bear certificates of origin and be counted against its quota. By the rules governing the certificates of origin, the customs authorities of member nations were required to collect certificates of origin from each shipment and return them to the Secretariat of the ICO, which then kept a tally on the quantities of coffee exported by each producer.[20] The magnitude of the quotas was increased accordingly, the primary objective being not to limit exports to new markets per se but rather to ensure that when such exports were made they were publicly recorded, thereby strengthening the incentives of competitors to bear the costs of cooperation.

Monitoring Prices

The monitoring of quantities through certificates of origin represented a means to an end: the raising of market prices. Members of the agreement chose a target price and then chose quotas that, given the demand for coffee, would generate that price. As changes in the price triggered increases, or decreases, in quotas, the indicator price constituted another important instrument in the operation of the agreement. In principle, the construction of the indicator price was straightforward: it would be but the weighted average of the prices of the different coffees. In practice, its construction generated conflict among the member nations.

Debate centered on the weights to be assigned the coffees whose prices would be combined into the price indicator. It also centered on the accuracy of the data concerning the quantities sold and therefore the weight that a particular coffee should bear in the overall measure. Repeatedly, doubts were raised about the actual volumes traded, and thus whether the movement in the relative prices should be taken seriously—that is, allowed to trigger changes in the right to ship coffee in the international market.

Debates also focused on the choice of market in which price quotations were to be secured. Dominant producers, such as Colombia, sought to build a market that would institutionalize a small price differential between their coffee and that of their chief rivals, the producers of the "other milds." German consumers tend to purchase higher quality coffees than do those in the United States; they tend to pay higher prices for superior coffees. Colombia therefore preferred the use of price quotations taken from the Hamburg market. The producers of the other milds preferred to use prices quoted on the New York market, where consumers purchased a higher proportion of lower quality coffees.[21]

Controversy centered not only on factors affecting the level of prices but also on those affecting their variability. Coffees that were "thinly" traded experienced large price movements; if they were included in the composite price, changes in their prices could trigger costly changes in the level of exports. Producers therefore feared the inclusion of thinly traded coffees in the construction of indicator prices; they worried that their inclusion might create opportunities for consumers or speculators to manipulate the indicator price. Conflicts thus arose as to whether Ambritz BB or AA should be used in the robusta price indicator, when the latter fell to less than 20 percent of Angola's exports.[22]

The International Coffee Agreement operated in reaction to systematically collected information. The content and properties of this information—the means of the prices and their variability, for example—were of great significance for the member nations. The manner in which the information was collected, constructed, and used therefore constituted a controversial issue for the organization. The indicator price signaled whether quotas should be maintained, increased, or cut. And reports about shipments of coffee, collected by means of certificates of origin, were used to enforce quotas. Such information signaled to a member nation whether others were abiding by the agreement, and thus whether they ought to continue to cooperate as well.

In debates over those issues, the voting rules enhanced the ability of the large to insure themselves against the claims of the small. The small producers queried and contested estimates and raised numerous and contentious objections.[23] The large, by contrast, remained detached. Indeed, they were willing to delegate these issues to technocrats in the Secretariat.[24] Because they controlled over one-third of the votes, the large producers possessed the power to block unfavorable responses to movements in the data. Nothing in the data could therefore trigger a response of the institution in a way that would be systematically biased against their interests. Because the small producers could not be certain of that, they remained vigilant and contested the estimates in a partisan manner, while those who dominated the organization affected an air of being apolitical about an issue charged with distributive implications.[25]

Bicameralism

The dominant producers sought an agreement that would imbed the international market within a political organization, and so transform the competitive fringe's choice of economic strategy. In the context of the assurances provided by that transformation, they would then themselves be willing to engage in costly behavior that would yield the collective benefit of the higher price of coffee. To secure this behavioral transformation, the dominant producers needed the cooperation of the United States. But the United States too faced risks in entering the agreement. It too, therefore, sought rules and structures that would insure it against exploitation.

Bicameralism constituted its first line of defense. The Executive Board and all committees were divided into an equal number of producer and consumer

TABLE 6.1
Coffee Shipments Arriving in New York, 15 February–10 March 1966

From	Origin	Number of Bags
Hamburg	Various African countries	4,877
Casablanca	Liberia	14,787
Marseilles	Ivory Coast	1,268
Tangier	Liberia	78,667
Rotterdam	Various African countries	16,386
Antwerp	Indonesia	69,489
Trieste	Guinea	33,592
Antwerp	Various African countries	1,001
Total		220,067

Source: Acta No. 9 de la sesión del día 10 de marzo de 1966, Comité Nacional, *Actas, vol. 1, enero–abril 1966.*

representatives. In addition, votes in the Council, in which all members were represented, were divided equally, with the consumers securing the same number of votes, 1000, as the producers. Lastly, in all matters affecting the prices and quantities of coffee—in all matters falling within the preview of the economic clauses—not only did decisions require two-thirds majorities, but they also required *distributed* majorities. To intervene in the market, the organization required two-thirds of the votes of the producers *and* two-thirds of the votes of the consumers. For a proposal to secure passage, it required a two-third majority from each house of the two-chambered organization.

The structure of the agreement thus provided a means whereby the consumers could check the producers, were the latter to attempt to impose changes that violated their interests. The United States held 400—or 40 percent—of the consumer votes. It therefore held veto power. Single-handedly, it could use its 400 votes to block any economic measure. When combined with two other rules—bicameralism and the need for distributed majorities—weighted voting thus insured the dominant consumer, the United States, against the political imposition of unfavorable changes in the prices or quantities of coffee.[26]

The Effect of Consumer Cooperation

Table 6.1 documents the arrival of one-quarter of a million bags of coffee, originally exported from member countries but shipped from nonmember nations in an effort to elude the quota system. Taken from deliberations held by the Comité Nacional of the FNC, table 6.1 documents the ability of the coffee producers to use the customs authorities of the producing nations to monitor shipments.

The cooperation of the consumers helped not only to monitor but also to police the evasion of quotas. In some instances, consumer enforcement produced dramatic effects. An example is provided by Aruba/Curaçao, a notorious entrepot for shipments of "tourist" coffee from Central America to ports in the Gulf Coast and in the western United States.[27] In the words of the Colombian envoy in Aruba, following the intervention of United States' customs authorities on "the 25th of March, not a single sack of contraband coffee has arrived in this island, for the United States has put into practice the requirement of a certificate of origin. The government of Aruba has decried in the local press the suffering brought to the people of Aruba as a result. In the ports, all movement has been paralyzed."[28]

More representative, however, were the incessant reports of illicit shipments of coffee through the ports of Europe, especially the free ports of Hamburg, Rotterdam, and Trieste. Merchants and governments in Europe argued that coffee held in the free ports constituted coffee in transit; if resting in a free port, they contended, a shipment had not yet been imported into a member nation and its certificates of origin therefore need not be remitted to the ICO. The docks and the warehouses of the free ports could hold thousands of tons of coffee. A producing nation could export coffee in excess of its quota, store the excess in the free ports, and thereby elude the monitors of the agreement.

The information provided by the port authorities revealed that the tendency of the smaller producers was to employ the free ports to evade quota constraints. Investigators repeatedly documented Ivory Coast's evasion of its quota, for example, and gathered detailed information about the methods used. In one scam, agents in the Congo Republic would ship a consignment of, say, 100,000 bags on a ship destined for Le Havre. In fact, exporters in Congo would dispatch only 10,000 bags; but the ship would then stop at Abidjan, a port of the Ivory Coast, where it would take on an additional 90,000 bags of coffee from that country. The entire 100,000-bag shipment would then be sold in the free ports and credited to the Congo Republic, enabling Ivory Coast to exceed the limitations of its quota.[29] Rather than denying their wrongdoing, the small countries sought to justify it in terms of "special circumstances"—a special need for foreign exchange due to war, earthquake, or some other act of God—and sought exonerations from the quota constraints, as allowed by Article 34.

Cooperation among the producers thus remained problematic. The willingness of one producer to abide by the constraints laid down by the ICO depended upon that producer's perception that others would also adhere to them. Information of high quality constituted a necessary requirement for such assurances. That enforcement remained in the hands of "third parties"—in the hands of the consumers, rather than the producers themselves—blunted the knife-edged nature of the pact; nonetheless, cooperation, once achieved, could quickly unravel. The result was constant tension within the ICO, as individual producers who cooperated with the agreement poured over the reports on coffee shipments, seeing if they were being cast in the role of the sucker.

Sources of Cooperation

The threat of evasion was real; by shipping "tourist coffee," producers evaded quota restrictions. And yet, as documented at the outset of this study, the agreement appears to have worked. While causing tensions among the producing nations, illegal shipments were not sufficiently great to trigger the breakdown of the agreement. We are thus led once again to inquire into the sources of its stability.

Brazil's Undershipments

Some have argued that Brazil, on its own, bore the costs of the agreement, withholding coffee from the market, undershipping its quota, and thereby underpinning the price of coffee. This argument was advanced with particular force within Brazil itself, where critics accused the government of adhering to an agreement that resulted in the loss of market share to other suppliers.[30] There is some merit to this argument; Brazil did in fact tend to undership its quota. But the fact that Brazil did so should be seen as evidence of the effectiveness of the agreement, rather than of its weakness. For policymakers in Brazil had sufficient confidence in the capacity of the ICO to restrict shipments by others that they were willing, in the context of the agreement, to make sacrifices that would have made little sense had other producers been able to increase their exports and thereby exploit Brazil's costly efforts to raise market prices.

The differentials in price thus did not result from Brazil's actions alone. Brazil restrained exports because it knew that others would—with some slippage, of course—restrain their exports as well. Why, then, did the producers cooperate?

Central Enforcement

A possible source of cooperation might have been fear of punishment. The rules of the agreement, and in particular Article 36, specified penalties for overshipments of quotas. Producers could ask for exonerations from their quotas. And the ICO could give them, but on conditions set out in Article 36: that excess shipments in one year be deducted from the quota for the next; that excess shipments in a second year be penalized by a doubling of the deductions in the next; and that a third violation lead to the loss of voting rights and the possibility of expulsion from the International Coffee Organization.

The rules were thus designed to deter the small producers from evading their quotas. But the evidence is clear that the rules were leniently applied. In the coffee year 1963–64, for example,[31] the Executive Board authorized an exoneration of 160,000 bags in El Salvador's quota; El Salvador used that exoneration—and exceeded it by another 300,000 bags! In the coffee year 1964–65, El Salvador came back for a further exoneration, this time of 225,000 bags. And in 1966–67, it exceeded its quota by nearly 780,000 bags (or by nearly 60 percent)—the highest figure registered until then in the life of the agreement. As noted in the report of the Colombian delegation to the ICO: "In December 1967, the Council [of the ICO] approved resolution number 154 by which El Salvador was sanctioned for violations of the quota. Total applicable deductions in this case were 2,017,928 bags. Nonetheless, for practical reasons, only 329,481 were deducted."[32]

The rules were clear. So too was the fact of their violation. But, once the rules were violated, the punishments were not applied. The ICO remained a confederation of independent nations. It lacked the most distinctive attribute of a single state: the capacity to use coercion. As noted by the Colombian delegation: "One of the weakest instruments of the agreement is that of sanctions. . . . [I]t is not easy to create or to administer sanctions at the international level since it is difficult to apply them to sovereign states."[33]

When rules were violated, then, punishment was not implemented. Nonetheless, even at the height of the flood of "tourist coffee," promoted by smuggling through the free ports and exonerations for overshipment, quota violations amounted to a total of 2 million bags, or less than 5 percent of the authorized total exports by member nations.[34]

Leadership

If no central authority provided penalties enforcing adherence to quotas, perhaps such penalties were applied by dominant powers.

The United States constituted one such power. The United States' government was intensely aware that the success of its broader development assistance programs in Latin America would be strongly affected by the success of the International Coffee Agreement. If the agreement was successful, the magnitude of the transfer of resources to Latin America through the coffee market would equal or exceed that through international development programs; if unsuccessful, the losses in income resulting from the fall in the coffee price could undermine the impact of those programs. The United States therefore ran the development-assistance and coffee-support programs in tandem. As part of its aid programs in the early 1960s, for example, the United

States established a $12 million fund for Mexico, Guatemala, El Salvador, Costa Rica, Honduras, and Nicaragua to build warehouses and to finance retentions of coffee.[35] Blocking shipments that violated the rules of the ICO on the one hand, the United States invested resources on the other that enhanced the ability of producers to withhold shipments from the international market.

From time to time, the United States followed a second tactic. It signaled to the "competitive fringe" that should they not adhere to the coffee agreement, they would not be eligible for benefits from the Alliance for Progress.[36]

While the United States used its aid program to offer inducements and sanctions, little evidence suggests that these measures affected the behavior of nations in the coffee market. Rather, the evidence suggests that such blandishments lacked credibility. Political leaders in Latin America knew that the United States needed allies in the cold war; they knew that the U.S. State Department feared alienating governments in the region by canceling their aid programs. In addition, they knew that the State Department feared political reactions at home; the actions could easily and credibly be portrayed as a use of "American" tax dollars to assist producers in exploiting "American" consumers by raising coffee prices.[37]

Brazil constituted the second major power. Brazil had accumulated enormous stocks, the quantity of which exceeded in the early 1960s the annual world consumption of coffee.[38] At the meetings of the International Coffee Organization in 1984, which I attended, Brazil's intentions and capabilities constituted a central preoccupation. How many bags did Brazil really have in stock? In what condition were these coffees? Where were they located? In the interior? On the coast? Or in warehouses in Europe? How willing really was Brazil to unload these stocks on the market? How could the smaller countries push the limits of the agreement without provoking retaliation by this giant?

Brazil's capacity to punish, its capacity to revert to a competitive marketing strategy, thus constitutes a possible source of stability in the agreement. For, given its economic power, Brazil stood in a position to punish other nations should they fail to cooperate, thereby making continued cooperation more attractive than the short-run gains to be secured from violating the quotas set by the ICO.[39]

It is tempting to invoke the economic power of Brazil to account for the maintenance of the agreement. But while such an approach accounts for some forms of cooperation, it fails to account for others. Because Brazil was a large actor in the coffee market, it could influence coffee prices; precisely for the same reason, however, Brazil would incur large costs, were it to sell its crop at prices made lower by the dumping of its stocks on the market. Its threat to dump thus was credible only at times when the agreement was being negotiated, but not once it was in place.

When the agreement was being renegotiated, which it was every five years, then Brazil's threat to dump was taken very seriously. Brazil would incur high costs from reverting to a competitive marketing strategy. But its costs from not doing so would be great as well; for in the absence of an agreement, it would face unconstrained shipments by *all* other coffee producers. When the agreement was on the verge of lapsing, then, Brazil's threats were regarded as credible. Thus the observation of Colombia's diplomat at the time of the negotiation of the original agreement; Brazil's stocks, he wrote,

> have been the most forceful argument for pressuring Central Americans with their suaves and France and Portugal with the coffees of Africa into entry and strengthening a coffee agreement.[40]

> • • • • • • • • • • • • • •

> The coffee [is available] at no cost of production. That is a permanent threat to other producers.[41]

The files of the Federación Nacional de Cafeteros record Brazil's renewal of this warning each time the agreement or its quotas came up for renewal.[42] The threats caused grave concern in the minds of Brazil's biggest trade rival.

But when the agreement had been ratified and was in place, Brazil's threats lost credibility. Brazil might locate and document an infraction of the rules by another producer, but it could not credibly threaten to punish an *individual* free rider. The benefits of forcing, say, El Salvador to reduce its exports by 300,000 bags would fail to compensate for the costs incurred by dumping, rendering Brazil's threats incredible against such single acts of noncooperation.

The International Coffee Organization was an alliance among independent nations. It lacked a powerful executive branch, capable of punishing transgressors. As illustrated by the cases of Ivory Coast and El Salvador, while the ICO was capable of detecting violations of its rules, it was incapable of punishing them. Although it was a pact among independent nations, the International Coffee Agreement was not a pact among equals. Major economic powers, such as the United States among the consuming nations and Brazil among the producers, loomed as economic giants among the Lilliputian states of Central America and Africa. And yet, the very size of the major economic powers undermined the credibility of their threats to punish small transgressors. So large were their interests that the costs they would incur from imposing punishments would outweigh the benefits they might procure by modifying the opportunistic behavior of a small free rider.

And yet, the agreement appears to have worked. To reiterate: From where did the incentives come?

Refinements in the Rules

At its inception, the ICO used one indicator price, which recorded the weighted average of prices for all kinds of coffee. When quantities increased, the indicator price would fall, and its fall would trigger a reduction in quotas. But the design of the indicator price promoted free riding.

Consider the African producers of robusta coffees, which were weighted at 33 percent of the indicator price. Given that their coffees had but a small weight in the indicator, the private effects of their export decisions differed from the social. Should the producers of robusta increase their exports, while Brazil did not, then they would lower the price of their own coffee; the widening differential between the price of their coffee and that of Brazil's would encourage roasters to substitute African for Brazilian coffee in their blends. Cheating would thus yield private benefits. It would also produce social costs: a lowering of the average price of all coffees. But—and this was the key—the magnitude of this social cost would be less than that of the private benefits. For robustas constituted but one-third of the coffees used in calculating the indicator price. The producers of robusta coffee could therefore secure reductions in their price relative to those for Brazil's without producing proportionately large movements in the average price of *all* coffees.

In the context of the prices prevailing in November 1965, for example, the average price of coffee stood at 41.65 cents; only by falling below 38 cents would the indicator trigger quota cuts. Robustas could thus fall by more than 10 cents a pound before generating the 3.65 cents fall in the indicator necessary to trigger a reduction in quotas.[43] The African producers of robusta coffees thus faced weak incentives to abide by their quotas.

In an effort to strengthen the ICO, the organizers of the agreement therefore changed the rules. They developed separate price indicators for each of the four kinds of coffee. Under this new system, a fall in the indicator price of a specific kind of coffee could trigger a cut in the quota for that particular kind of coffee. Price indicators are constructed from weighted averages; and a particular nation, such as the Ivory Coast, had roughly twice the weight in the new robusta price indicator than it did in the old, composite indicator. As a consequence, increases in exports became more visible, and such increases more rapidly triggered cutbacks in quotas, reducing the private benefits of defection.

The single-indicator price possessed several defects: It led to disparities between the private and the social impact of marketing decisions. It promoted externalities. And it made it difficult to monitor noncompliant behavior. The first two defects weakened incentives to abide by the quota system. The last increased the costs of policing. The movement toward a system of multiple or selective indicator prices—one for each group of coffees—thus reduced both the costs of monitoring and the incentives to evade.

While the incentives to free ride were weakened, they were not extinguished, however. The indicators for Colombian and Brazilian coffees, in both instances, were virtually constructed from the sales of a single country's coffee.[44] Such, however, was not the case for the indicator price for other milds and robusta coffees, or those produced by the competitive fringe. These indicators were constructed from sales of coffee by a multitude of small producers. The change in the system of indicator prices thus may have strengthened the incentives to cooperate, by rendering cheating more visible and less rewarding. But, because the actions of small nations still made but a small impact on their respective price indicators, the change in rules did not extinguish the incentives to free ride. And yet: the agreement appears to have worked.

The Role of the Roasters

Thus far we have taken the agreement on its face: We have analyzed it as a pact among nation states. To better comprehend the reasons for its effectiveness, however, we need to look at the industrial structure that underlay its legal formalisms. It is time to turn once again to the role of the large coffee roasters.

Even a casual reading of the commercial press and the minutes of organizations in the Latin American coffee industry yields an appreciation of the prominence of the executives of the large roasting firms. The arrival of, say, George Robbins, head of the coffee division of General Foods, amounted to a state visit, with formal receptions, ceremonial dinners, and extensive coverage by the national press, on the political, economic, and society pages. And Robbins did visit, regularly touring the great coffee centers: Rio, Santos, São Paulo, Manizales, and Bogotá.[45]

One of the most significant of his visits took place in Bogotá in July 1963. The treaty, it will be recalled, had been ratified by the United States' Senate in December 1962. General Foods had participated in the trade advisory committee that had helped to draft the accord in Washington and in the delegation that helped to negotiate its ratification by member nations. And its executives participated in the delegation representing the United States at meetings of the ICO. In the meetings in Bogotá in July 1963, Robbins, formerly a member of the United States' delegation, entered into direct commercial negotiations with the Managing Director of the Federación Nacional de Cafeteros (FNC). He was proposing a deal. And the Comité Nacional convened a series of secret sessions to deliberate his proposal.[46]

In the early 1960s, General Foods was purchasing 1,800,000 bags of Colombia's coffee annually, or nearly one-quarter of Colombia's total production and nearly two-thirds of its exports to the United States. It now offered to increase its annual purchases by 500,000 bags, with a commitment to continue at this increased level for each of the next three years. In exchange, General Foods wanted a reduction of 2 cents a pound in the price charged for the additional bags purchased, over and above its usual discount of 10 percent. And it offered to launch a new brand of coffee, to be called Yuban, that would feature "pure Colombian" coffee.

The leaders of Colombia's coffee industry treated General Food's offer with great caution. They had long sought to build consumer loyalty to Colombian coffee in the United States and had paid for the services of a leading advertising firm to promote it. General Food's offer to feature a "pure Colombian" label would, they felt, inspire emulation by other roasters, and so contribute to their marketing campaign. Possible liabilities counterbalanced such advantages, however. One was the danger of becoming even more dependent on General Foods; another was the danger of being seen by other producers as cutting the price of coffee, just at the time of the launching of an accord to stabilize prices.[47] In the end, the Comité Nacional decided to go ahead with the deal. The reason, I think, is because it strengthened, not weakened, the international agreement.

Shortly after the launching of postwar efforts to build an accord, the dominant producers signed bulk contracts with the large coffee-roasting firms. Colombia appears to have signed its first such contract with General Foods in 1959; Brazil, in May 1960.[48] The evidence suggests that similar contracts were signed with other major roasters: Nestlé, Rotfus, and Procter and Gamble. The contracts committed the roasters to the purchase of fixed amounts of coffee per quarter—450,000 bags, in the case of General Foods in the early 1960s—in exchange for discounts in the price of coffee. Under the terms of the contract, the discount was applied to the costs of future purchases. Because the discount was not paid immediately, but rather rebated in the subsequent periods, the market for coffee was transformed from a spot market. Under the terms of the bulk contracts, the producers and roasters entered into long-term relationships.

Financial costs and benefits constitute a significant component of the exchange between the dominant producers and the large roasting firms, of course. The 2 cents per pound price reduction in the purchase of Colombian coffee, noted above, enabled General Foods to pay nearly $2 million less for its 1,500,000 bags of coffee and Colombia to generate a 17 percent increase in its sales in the North American market. But Colombia got even more out of the bargain. As part of its relationship with General Foods, it also secured political services.

General Foods and the other large roasters were not just purchasers and processors of coffee; they were also lobbyists and members of national delegations. They testified before Congress on behalf of United States intervention and they provided the executive branch with the information necessary to maintain and to regulate the coffee trade. From Colombia's point of view, the discount in the price of coffee to General Foods thus bought compensating advantages: help by a large roaster in securing the United States' enforcement of the international coffee agreement, thereby checking opportunistic behavior by the competitive fringe—and raising the average price of coffee.

General Foods and the other large roasters who signed bulk contracts in turn received major economic advantages. The large roasters operated in the national market. Because of their payments for advertising, distribution, and promotion, their purchase of raw materials constituted a comparatively small portion of their costs. For the small, regional roasters with whom they competed, however—Chock Full O'Nuts in Baltimore and Atlanta or Breakfast Cheer in Pittsburgh—the price of raw materials constituted a relatively larger percentage of total costs.[49] By structuring the regulation of the market to increase the price of raw materials, and by securing rebates from the dominant producers of those raw materials, the larger roasters were able to increase the costs of raw materials to their competitors. They thereby achieved a cost advantage.[50]

The use of the agreement to secure a competitive advantage did not require access to capital, as would, say, a protracted price war; nor did it require immediate sacrifices for the prospect of uncertain future gains; nor did it require complex signaling, so as to render threats credible. The large producers needed only to incur the costs of providing expert testimony, such that if the government regulated at all, it then regulated effectively—in a way that prevented cheating by the competitive fringe. Coupled with rebates from the producers seeking to organize an effective agreement, the effective policing of quotas served to drive up the price of coffee—but only to competitors. The coffee market lay embedded within domestic political institutions and international diplomatic relationships. Within that political context, political service by the large roasters constituted economic competition by other means.

The bulk contracts thus built a relationship in which commercial advantages were exchanged for costly efforts, at lobbying and advising, to help to enforce the agreement. Thus the head of the Federación Nacional de Cafeteros reported:

> In the late afternoon I received a visit from a representative of Folgers with whom we have on-going negotiations concerning closer ties with Colombian coffee. We are considering a three year [commercial] program.
>
>   The matter of the agreement also arose, and, after discussion, he made it clear that they had decided that they would support the agreement in the [Foreign Affairs Committee] of the National Coffee Association.[51]

The economic and the political thus became one.

By offering long-term contracts, with deferred rebates, the dominant producers created positive incentives for the large roasters to secure the cooperation of the consuming nations in efforts to regulate the international trade in coffee. And while the threat of a dominant producer, such as Brazil, to sanction another nation, such as El Salvador, may not have been credible, the threat of a dominant producer to sanction a firm, such as Folgers, was. The reasons lie in the behavior of the market and the location of the dominant producers within it. When a large roaster, like General Foods, helped the United States' government to police illicit shipments of Central American coffees, it drove up the price of those coffees. The differential between the price of Colombian and other mild coffees then declined. Given differentials between the quality of Colombian and other mild coffees, buyers switched to Colombian coffee. Not only did the closure of the differential produce higher average prices, thus serving the collective purposes of the agreement; not only did it reward the dominant producers, thus serving the private purposes of the agreement; but also, as more buyers turned to Colombian coffee, Colombia's dependence on any given buyer of its coffee declined, thus reducing the costs to Colombia of canceling its contract with any given firm. The very actions that enforced the agreement thus generated the conditions that helped to sustain it; they did so by making threats credible. The agreement thus became self-enforcing. It became an equilibrium.

This argument suggests that when the international agreement was working, it was supported by the threats of large producers to punish the large roasting firms. Insofar as these threats were credible, of course, they would not have to be applied, rendering a direct test of my argument impossible. I was, however, able to gain insight into the expectations of one chief executive as to what would happen were he to stray off the equilibrium path and to fail to provide political services in support of the ICO. Procter and Gamble, the second largest roaster of coffee in the United States, cultivates a reputation for a strong commitment to "all American" values: patriotism, capitalism, and competitive markets. In a telephone interview,[52] I once questioned the head of its coffee division about the agreement, and he indicated that he did not support it and that "the free market would be O.K." "We may in fact testify in Congress against it," he added. "How about Brazilian reprisals?" I asked. "Would they be likely to punish you by canceling your contracts?" There was a long pause before the executive replied, "Don't even breathe that possibility to anyone else. I will have to explain to our Chief Executive that the Brazilians may force us on board. I would be less than honest if I didn't say this to him. The Brazilians price coffee so attractively to us—we go with that contract and buy big and use it. We buy all we can get. But then they can put the screws on us." The CEO of Procter and Gamble preached the virtues of the free market; the head of Folgers, its coffee division, had to deal with the realities of the coffee market. I take the latter's comments as confirmation of his beliefs as to what would happen were his company to violate the terms of its relationship with the organizers of the accord. He believed that his company would be punished.

Further Refinements

In a series of brilliant papers, Delfim Netto, an economist at the University of São Paulo, calculated the relationship between the demand for Brazilian coffees and their prices relative to the coffees produced by the competitive fringe.[53] In 1964, the military, with the backing of the United States, over-

threw the government of João Goulart; and when Costa e Silva succeeded
Costello Branco as military president of Brazil, the new president made Del-
fim Netto his Minister of Finance. As head of Brazil's monetary council, the
Minister of Finance dictates coffee policy; indeed, so completely did Delfim
Netto dominate the making of coffee policy that at one point this former
scholar installed his favorite coauthor, Albert de Andrade, as president of the
Instituto Brasileiro do Café (IBC).

Delfim Netto introduced two changes into the contracts Brazil signed with
the large roasting firms. First, the contracts no longer quoted a number; they
quoted a function. Rather than offering a price, Brazil posted a price formula.
The price of Brazilian coffee became a weighted average of the price of other
milds and robusta coffees, the weights being derived from the cross-elasticities
of demand that Delfim and Albert de Andrade had calculated in their earlier
research. Secondly, the IBC now publicized the conditions of its contracts; the
terms of the "special contracts" with the large roasters, formerly clouded in
secrecy, now became public knowledge. Delfim Netto left one important feature unchanged, however: the contracts remained long-term.

Delfim's innovations thus made Brazil's strategy and payoffs common
knowledge to all actors in the industry. By quoting a price formula rather than
a price, Brazil in effect proclaimed that were the producers of other milds or
robusta coffees to lower their prices, the price of Brazilian coffees would
automatically follow. Knowing that—and Brazil took care to ensure that the
formula was publicly known—members of the competitive fringe would be
less inclined to engage in actions that would reduce their prices. While it
cannot be proved, it would appear that the changes Delfim Netto introduced
thus strengthened incentives to abide by the international accord.

Conclusion

The International Coffee Agreement was a pact among nations. It created a
public body, the International Coffee Organization (ICO), to regulate the international market in coffee. While possessing fixed rules of procedure, a bicam-
eral legislature, a committee system, and staff, the ICO could not sanction its
member units. It was not a state; rather, it was a pact among sovereign nations. And yet, when its economic clauses were in place, the ICO appears to
have effectively regulated the international coffee market. It appears to have
shaped the behavior of nation-states.

The explanation, we have argued, lies in viewing the ICO not as a coalition
of states but rather as a coalition among bureaucrats, politicians, and industrialists who mobilized the power of states to regulate an international market.
The state actors felt politically insecure. In the consuming nations, they were
driven by a need for security in their global struggles with other advanced

industrial societies. In the producing nations, they confronted domestic political instability and a desperate need for foreign exchange. The managers of firms found in political insecurity economic opportunity; for additional profits, they performed services that enhanced the political interests of those in power. For the politicians in the south, the firms promoted public policies in the north that raised the value of exports. For the bureaucrats in the north, they helped to deliver clients in the south, and a passive U.S. Congress. By maneuvering domestically, these subnational actors were able to mobilize the power of states to create an international regime capable of imposing political constraints on markets and regulating coffee prices.

The result was the creation of a market in which political rules took the place of market processes. In the introduction, I presented evidence that these rules were effective. In concluding this chapter, I present further evidence, documenting their power to influence the choices of nations.

The Operation of the Rules

The best documented example of the impact of the rules came from the negotiations that took place in the assignment of quotas in 1982.[54] Quotas had been suspended when prices rose above the target range because of shortages resulting from the Brazilian frost of 1975. As prices returned to the level at which the ICO would seek to defend them, Brazil proposed a new set of quotas. Under this proposal, Brazil would secure over 33 percent of the market, a share that they had held in the 1960s but long since lost, particularly after the frost of 1975. The primary victim of Brazil's proposal would have been Colombia, who would be constrained to less than a 19 percent share of the market, after having captured over 22 percent of it following the frost. Colombia therefore set out to block Brazil's proposal by crafting one of its own.

Several features of the resultant political maneuvering are significant. One is that the rules proved to be so regular that they can be formalized. A second is that the rules appear to have counted: they shared the choices of states. Thirdly, the rules appear to have safeguarded the interest of the larger producers.

We begin with the first: that the rules were sufficiently well defined that they can be formalized. Article 13 of the International Coffee Agreement governed the allocation of votes. Under Article 13, the proportion of total exports for the period 1976–77 to 1979–80 accounted for by a given producer, i—call them P_{1i}, where the subscript 1 stands for the time period above, i for the producer, and P for *export performance*—determined the proportion of the *votes* controlled by that producer—call that proportion W_i. This rule can be represented as:

$$(1) \quad W_i = f(P_{1i})$$

Article 30 of the agreement governed the allocation of quotas. Claims for quotas, this article stated, were to be based on average exports over one of two three-year periods: 1968–69 to 1971–72 *or* 1976–77 to 1979–80.[55] Claims for quotas were to be transformed into actual quotas only when voted upon, however; quotas were set by a (distributed) two-thirds majority vote of the member nations. Article 30 can therefore also be represented in the form of a function, wherein the *quota* assigned to a particular nation, i, (q_i) is a function of *past export performance* (P_{2i}, where the subscript 2 refers to the time period noted in this paragraph, rather than that used in the allocation of votes, as discussed above) and of *votes* (W_i). Thus:

$$(2) \quad q_i = g(P_{2i}, W_i)$$

We have noted a second feature: that the rules appear to have counted; that is, to have influenced actual conduct. Rule-governed environments produce opportunities for sophisticated behavior. In the presence of voting rules, actors can behave strategically. In majority-rule environments, they can convert endowments of votes into political power by converting coalitions into political majorities. Given a set of rules that defines a winning majority, the Shapley value of an actor provides a measure of that actor's power: the percentage of all coalitions among members of the group which that actor, given its allocation of votes, can convert into a winning majority.[56] Once again, the reasoning can be formalized:

$$(3) \quad S_i = h(W_i)$$

where S_i stands for the *Shapley value* of nation i and W_i for its endowment of votes, as noted above.

The rules that governed the assignment of the quotas by the ICO thus can be formalized as a system of equations:

Equation	Justification
(1) $W_i = f(P_{1i})$	Article 13
(2) $q_i = g(P_{2i}, W_i)$	Article 30
(3) $S_i = h(W_i)$	Behavioral assumptions

In effect, this system constitutes a formal model of how quotas (q_i) would be assigned under the rules of the ICO, were actors making sophisticated use of the powers conferred upon them by those rules. The advantage of the formalization is that it suggests a way of measuring the impact of the rules. We can estimate the parameters of the variables in these equations, and thus the impact of the rules of the agreement. The constant terms, P_1, and P_2 provide instruments to eliminate the correlation between S_i and q_i produced through their association with export performance.[57]

Equation 4 presents the results for the allocation of the quota proposed by Colombia:

$$(4) \quad q_i = -0.2279 + 0.8281P_{2i} + 0.2175S_i$$
$$ (0.1214) \quad (0.0674) \quad\quad (0.0746)$$

The figures in parentheses represent standard errors of the estimated parameters. The standard errors of the estimated coefficient relating Colombia's Shapley value to its quota is one-third the value of the parameter itself, and is therefore statistically significant.

These results can be interpreted as suggesting that Colombia took cognizance of the rules and their effect on the distribution of power and allocated quota entitlements so as to accommodate the voting power of particular nations. Indeed, documentary evidence underscores that the Colombian delegation counted votes and crafted its proposal accordingly.[58] The rules thus appear to have shaped the behavior of member nations and, in particular, the allocation of rights to export in international markets.

I have argued that the rules of the agreement were designed to safeguard the interests of the large producers. By creating the ICO, the dominant producers created a governance structure that enabled them to reduce the risks of opportunistic behavior—risks that undermined their capacity to incur costs with the certainty that they, and others, would reap the benefit of higher coffee prices. The results of the estimates also provide a test of this argument. The Shapley value provides a measure of the ability of a nation to convert coalitions into winning coalitions, i.e. into ones that command electoral majorities. Under the rules of the agreement, bigger producers were endowed with greater numbers of votes; intuitively, they should therefore have possessed more power. Equation 5 provides the test we seek. As seen in equation 5, the relationship between the voting strength of a nation and its Shapley value is indeed non-linear; it is quadratic, such that as the number of votes controlled by a nation increased, its Shapley value rose more than proportionately.

$$(5) \quad S_i = 0.8227 \, W_i + 0.0152 W_i^2$$
$$ (0.0031) \quad\quad (0.0018)$$

The lesson is clear: controlling more votes, larger nations gained more "Shapley power" (as shown in equation 5) and therefore could extract greater quotas (as shown in equation 4). The rules they constructed thus safeguarded their interests. The ICO offered the large producers the assurance that were they to restrict exports, they need not fear predation by the smaller exporters.

The values of the parameters estimated from the model provide a further measure of the economic significance of the political rules put in place by the ICO. They suggest, for example, that had Kenya possessed but one vote more in 1982, it could have increased its quota such that it could have earned an additional U.S. $168.5 million each year throughout the 1980s. We can thus see how the rules of this government of coffee affected the wealth of nations.

The ICO was rule-governed. Its rules became self-enforcing. They affected the strategic choices and the economic fortunes of states. The rules were so precise that they can be formally modeled and the model tested against data generated by the political choices and economic behavior of states. Where the rules of an organization are so precise that they can be formalized, and where the tests of the resultant model suggest that the rules in fact shape the conduct of actors, then I, for one, am willing to call that organization an institution.

7

Conclusion

IN THE EARLY 1960s, nations of the world created a political regime to regulate the international market in coffee. The evidence suggests that it worked, raising and stabilizing the price of one of the most valuable products shipped from the tropics. The International Coffee Organization lasted for over two decades. This book has explored its creation, maintenance, and impact. It will also explore its demise.

The demand for this regime arose among the coffee exporters. It was articulated most forcefully by the dominant producers, Colombia and Brazil, who sought to create an international defense against free riding by smaller producers. For reasons explained in this study, the dominant producers could not credibly threaten free riders; the ICO required third-party enforcement, which was provided, ironically, by the consumers. Once credible constraints against free riding were in place, the dominant producers were willing to withhold coffee shipments and to bear the costs of price formation.

Under the ICO, "anarchy"—or at least market competition—thus appears to have given way to "cooperation"—or at least collusion in the marketplace. International behavior appears to have become rule governed; the rules of the ICO appear to have constrained the allocation of coffee exports and determined the level of market prices. Abiding by the rules appears to have become, in equilibrium, a rational act; the rules appear to have become self-enforcing. The ICO thus appears to have become an institution.

In analyzing the creation and maintenance of the ICO, I have sought to make use of several literatures. One is that on international regimes. The ICO, I have argued, became a regime, and, indeed, even an institution, because actors at the subnational level found ways of making it in the interests of others to abide by its rules, for fear of threats of penalties should they defect. The threats were subgame perfect, and therefore credible; they were profitable, if acted upon.

Systemic theories offered a second source of insights. Clearly, Brazil stood as an economic hegemon in the coffee market; its dominance cast it as the leader of efforts to provide the collective good of higher coffee prices. And, clearly too, the United States constituted a political hegemon, whose security interests inspired efforts to provide a global economic infrastructure, including the coffee agreement. Systemic theories thus capture the broad outlines of the story of the ICO; but they fail to capture critical features of it. While a systemic approach explains the support for the agreement among the major powers in the coffee industry, it does not explain the failure of such support. In particular, it does not explain why Brazil repeatedly failed to intervene in the market, nor the uncertain backing of the United States. Nor do systemic approaches address the domestic political transformation required for concerted and strategic action at the global level: the changes in relationships between bureaucrats, politicians, and economic interests that made possible the domestic arrangements necessary to forge an international organization.

Game theoretic approaches to international relations provided a third relevant literature. Ironically, perhaps, they did best in explaining the *failure* of efforts at collusion, rather than their success. Consideration of the magnitude of costs and benefits of punishments for noncooperation, and the rate at which they were discounted by an insecure and financially starved Brazil, help to explain the inability of producers to organize. But this literature fails to explain the *success* of the efforts to form the agreement. "Cartelization" was achieved by third-party enforcement; but enforcement was provided by consumers! The approach thus founders on a contradiction between its premise of individual rationality and its economic vision of the ICO.

As with the systemic approaches to the study of international behavior, game theoretic approaches too thus prove unsatisfactory. Game theory is economic in its origins; the ICO, political-economic in its nature. The game theoretic approach assumes unitary actors; the ICO constitutes an international alliance between subnational actors: some political—bureaucrats, security specialists, and politicians—and others economic—coffee growers and large processing firms. These subnational actors mobilized the power of states to create an alliance capable of intervening in global markets in ways that served their interests.

In the case of each literature, then, we were driven from the international to the domestic level in search of explanations. We therefore sought theoretical approaches that would enable us to address the domestic politics of the nations that participated in the international accord. The first was dependency theory; the second, neoclassical trade theory. Both offer interest-based theories of economic policy-making.

Forged to explain the underdevelopment of Latin America, dependency theory focused heavily on the case of Brazil. In particular, it argued, Brazil remained undeveloped in large part because of the political domination of export agriculture and agriculture's imposition of public policies that retarded the growth of industry. Brazilian scholars have challenged this interpretation, and I subscribe to their criticisms. My contribution lies in the grounds upon which I dissent. The basic weakness of the dependency approach, I have argued, is its failure to note the importance of political institutions. Given the institutional barriers put in place by the constitutional structure of Brazil, the coffee growers had first to bundle coffee policy with exchange rate policy in order to capture political power. The structure of Brazil's institutions, I argued, thus helped to explain both its seeming reluctance to capitalize upon its potential power in international markets and the nature of the economic policies that the government adopted, once it decided to do so.

Dependency theory focused on the global level as well as on the domestic level of politics. A basic divide, it argued, runs between the advanced industrial nations of the north and the providers of raw materials in the south. By promoting an alliance among coffee producers, the ICO empowered tropical producers to reverse the decline in their terms of trade. Viewed through the lens of dependency theory, the ICO therefore represented an attempt by the coffee producers to escape the subordinate position to which they had been consigned by the division of labor in international markets.

I have countered that this interpretation fails to recognize the significant conflicts that exist among the southern nations themselves: the ultimate reversal of price falls at the global level resulted from an anterior political struggle between the coffee giants in Latin America and the smaller producers in Africa and Central America. It also fails to recognize the commonality of interests between north and south that undergirded the ICO: the ICO was successful, it appears, because northern firms could align with southern governments and redistribute resources from the consumers of coffee. The lines of conflict so neatly drawn by the dependency theorists thus fragment in the coffee market. The case of coffee thus exposes deficiencies in the international, as well as the domestic, components of the dependency perspective.

I therefore considered a neoclassical alternative to dependency theory and in particular, the neoclassical theories of Frieden and Rogowski.[1] Their approaches, too, seek to explain political outcomes in terms of economic forces. But they too fail.

Neoclassical trade theory takes the structure of relative prices in international markets as given. Shifts in these prices resulting from exogenous shocks produce shifts in the return to domestic factors of production. External shocks therefore inspire redistributive struggles between domestic interests, animating policy choices by governments. The sequence thus runs from the international market to domestic policy choices, with economic interests providing the causal linkages.

The case of coffee challenges this formulation. Clearly, for Brazil, the international market price constituted an exogenous factor only some of the time; at others, international prices resulted from Brazil's own policy choices. Moreover, the active agency was not always the coffee industry. Following the government's takeover of the coffee institute, Brazil's intervention in international markets was organized and implemented by the state. And after the early years of Vargas, the state set international prices by adopting policies that were adverse to the interests of most growers. The causal path thus runs from state policy to the behavior of international markets and to the welfare of domestic interests—a sequence that deviates strikingly from that traced out by Frieden and Rogowski.

There are other differences, and these too pose challenges to the neoclassical approach. For Frieden, it is fixed and specific factors that provide the economic impetus to politics. These factors earn rents, which are defined as the differentials between the return a factor can achieve in a particular economic activity and the return that it could secure in its next best use. The ready movement of the coffee frontier in Brazil and the rapid shifting of land, labor, and capital out of the production of coffee and into the production of livestock, soy beans, sugar, citrus, and other commodities suggests that in Brazil the factors of production employed in the coffee industry were not highly specialized. What rents there were most likely resulted from public policy rather than from natural advantage. Price distortions, barriers to entry, subsidies: such governmental interventions created rents in the coffee sector, just as they did in the sugar industry, the grain industry, and other portions of the Brazilian economy.[2] The Brazilian evidence thus suggests that rather than quasi rents creating public policy, public policy created quasi rents.[3] Again, it would appear, the causal sequence runs in the wrong direction. It runs from the political to the economic, rather than the other way around.

The facts encountered in this study of the coffee market thus lead us to question two of the dominant approaches to the study of politics in open economies: the one Marxist, the other neoclassical. They lead us to consider a possible alternative: the new trade theory.[4] In contrast to neoclassical approaches, the new trade theory recognizes that even at the global level markets are not "perfect." Particular firms or industries or nations can loom large even in global markets, and so possess the power to influence prices. In this context, domestic policies that otherwise might be inefficient might in fact be chosen by rational actors, for they might yield competitive advantages in the strategic pursuit of profits in external markets. Strategic trade theory thus provides grounds for understanding the reversal of the causal sequence that bedevils the neoclassical accounts. The internal patterns of intervention in the Brazilian coffee industry, which create barriers to entry and generate rents, can be viewed as a prelude to the competitive struggle abroad—one in which Brazil was a price maker, not a price taker, as neoclassical theory would have it. The approach also helps to correct for deficiencies in the dependency account. Brazil and Colombia might be "tropical" nations; but, given the structure of the coffee market, the new trade theory would emphasize, they are nonetheless powerful. Given Brazil and Colombia's market power, they therefore could be expected to structure conditions in the marketplace to their advantage. Rather than constituting disconfirming data, their efforts to restrict the exports of fellow tropical producers of coffee were precisely the kinds of behavior that the new trade theory would expect.

The new trade theory thus provides a perspective that corrects for deficiencies in both the neoclassical and dependency accounts. Yet it too requires reformulation.

As revealed in this study, neither a "Brazil" nor a "Colombia" entered the global coffee market; planters and peasants did, each of whom was small within that market. There are few scale economies in coffee production. Brazil and Colombia therefore became large actors not as a result of economic transformations but rather as a consequence of political decisions, in which a multitude of small producers were compelled to market in concert. *The imperfect international market for coffee was thus a political creation.* It followed a domestic political struggle in which interests were aggregated in ways that were shaped by the structure of political institutions. In our attempt to understand trade policy, we are therefore driven yet again to the domestic level of analysis and to the study of politicians and the political institutions that structure their choices.

Dependency theory, neoclassical theory, and the new trade theory: all provide interest-based theories of politics. Classes, factory owners, producers, and firms: these constitute the agents that animate policy choices. Others have offered alternative interest-based theories. Nelson, for example, reviewed endogenous tariff theories, most of which are based upon the demand for protection from factors, industries, or firms.[5] Gourevitch studied the clash of interests precipitated by international recessions and developed from it a comparative theory of the politics of advanced industrial states.[6] While giving greater primacy to the strategic calculations of political elites, Katzenstein, Cameron, and others have accounted for the trade policies of small, open economies in part in terms of the structure of political bargaining among economic interests.[7] An increasing number of scholars have taken explicit account of the role of political institutions: Judith Goodstein, Wendy Hansen, Mark Hansen, Ronald Rogowski, and Beth Simmons, for example.[8]

The results of this study add impetus to this trend; they suggest the value of an institutionally based, rather than an interest-based, approach to the study of politics in open economies. The results do *not* support the kind of institutional analysis that has been all too common in comparative politics, however. They do *not* support, for example, an equation of federalism and the division of powers with one sort of policy and centralized government with another. Rather than citing macro-level institutional facts, the study instead underscores the power of micro-level incentives. It emphasizes the costs that institutions impose upon interests seeking to gain control over policy, and the incentives that institutions create for politicians to cater to particular interests. And it equates the power of interests with the degree to which they can strategically pivot in the creation or overthrow of governments, given the institutions that structure the competition for power.

Compare, for example, the fate of the coffee industry in São Paulo and Colombia in the 1920s. In São Paulo, the emergence of party competition devastated the power of the coffee industry; in Colombia, it magnified it. When party competition emerged at the state level, São Paulo's political leadership became divided; its delegation lost bargaining power at the national level; and the coffee industry lost its ability to project its power nationally. In Colombia, by contrast, when party competition reemerged in the 1920s, it magnified the power of the coffee growers. Given the structure of the political space in Colombia, and the position of the coffee industry within it, the growers could make or break national governments. Party competition rendered the coffee industry politically pivotal in Colombia; it weakened the ability of the coffee growers to be so in Brazil.

It is not simply the structure of political institutions that counts, then. Rather, it is the game of politics that the structure defines. Political institutions create, or deny, strategic opportunities. Within the game they define, they help to determine the power of particular interests. They do so by rendering them, or preventing them from becoming, politically pivotal.

The point is both substantive and methodological. It is substantive insofar as it emphasizes the significance of institutions; it is methodological insofar as it conceives of institutions as defining political games in which interests compete for influence over public policy. The distinction is critical, for it is the methodology, not the substance, that is general. In making comparisons, then, it is not the institutions themselves that should be compared; it is the game that they define and the strategic possibilities that they offer. In this sense, it is perfectly legitimate to compare one set of institutions in the case of Brazil with another in the case of Colombia. Brazil's federal system can be compared to Colombia's party system, for the two kinds of institutions belong to a common class, as defined by the research problem: the class of determinants of the strategic possibilities open to the coffee industry and thus their ability to influence the trade policies of their governments.[9]

Clearly, international politics cannot be studied without taking recourse to domestic political facts. Clearly, too, the manner in which domestic polities articulate with the international economy varies; thus our effort to explain and account for variation in the terms under which coffee industries gained access to international markets. Political institutions shaped the terms of this incorporation. We are thus driven to an open-economy form of domestic political analysis, and one that stresses the significance of institutions.

Institutions are important for another reason: the terms of export agriculture's incorporation into the world economy often register in the nature of the economic institutions that surround it. The Federación Nacional de Cafeteros constituted an economic institution, provisioning growers with public goods, constructing reputations for quality, policing free riding, and curtailing externalities in the production and marketing of coffee. The Federación thus constituted an economic institution, helping producers to transcend incentives that undermined the efficiency of their industry. It provided an economic governance structure that organized the industry in ways that enabled it to maximize its export earnings.

The existence of this institution, which underpinned the private economy, did *not* imply an absence of politics, however. To the contrary; depolitization was a political act. The Federación remained private because Colombia's politicians found it in their interests to allow economic agents to organize the nation's resources in ways that maximized the private incomes of coffee growers. The coffee growers of Colombia were fortunate in being endowed with a game of politics that gave them strategic opportunities. They exploited their position to make it in the interests of politicians to delegate to them control over the coffee industry. The private economy is the creation of politics.

Methodology

In a sense, the history of the coffee organization constitutes a narrative. It constitutes a story, with a beginning, a middle, and, as we shall see, an end. It is saturated with detail. But it constitutes a single case, and therefore poses a challenge to scientific understanding.

Some, such as King, Keohane, and Verba, have counseled us to pick our cases with care, so that we might efficiently extract the information available and do so with a minimum of bias.[10] However sympathetic and illuminating, this counsel is of little use when it is the case itself that is of interest. The collapse of the Soviet Union, the American Civil War, the outbreak of World War I—these events happened but once, leaving little opportunity to use principles of case selection to gain scientific understanding. So too the history of coffee.

The tactic I have adopted is to bring theory to bear upon narrative.[11] I have attempted, for example, to apply the theory of cartel formation to the facts of the ICO. The theory illuminated the case, and the case highlighted the properties—and, more importantly, the limitations—of the theory. Indeed, it was by precipitating the theory's demise that the case proved most informative, driving us to a basic reconceptualization of the reality that we confronted and to a deeper understanding of how an international market came to be regulated by a political agency.

It is relatively easy to recognize the failure of a theory; case studies have long been employed to disconfirm.[12] How, then, can we be confident of theories that appear at first to work? How, in a sense, can we come to rest, gaining enough confidence in a theory that we accept its interpretation of our narrative? In this study, I have employed several methods. In closing, I describe them.

Out-of-Sample Comparisons

One way to answer these questions is to move outside of the original sample. As seen in map 1.1, coffee production girds the globe. The multitude of producers offers opportunities for testing the interpretations offered for this narrative. On the basis of the Colombia case, for example, I have argued that small farmers tend to be politically weak but that party competition can provide incentives for politicians to offer them favorable terms for incorporation into international markets. To test this interpretation, we can turn to Uganda.

The British government developed the initial framework for Uganda's industry when it created a so-called Coffee Control to purchase coffee for sale to the Ministry of Food during World War II. Dominated by local processors and government agents, Coffee Control operated as a monopsony in the robusta market. As prices rose toward their peak in the mid-1950s, the government reconstituted the agency, renaming it the Coffee Industry Board. Created by the government, not by the producers, the Board was governed by bureaucrats, not by representatives of the coffee growers themselves. And while it organized the provision of public goods, such as research and technical services, it also served as a means for extracting resources from the coffee industry.

As a monopsonist, the Coffee Industry Board set local prices; it placed a wedge between the world and domestic price and extracted the difference in the form of a Coffee Price Assistance Fund. Through this fund, the Board accumulated public revenues, some of which it returned to the coffee industry in the form of price supports but much of which it lent to the government at low rates of interest.[13] As noted by Van Zwanenberg and King, "The Uganda government had discovered a cheap and easy method of taxation."[14]

With the collapse of colonial rule in East Africa, however, political parties began to compete for the votes of peasant farmers. The United People's Congress (UPC) aligned with the Kabaka Yekka (KY) party of Buganda and formed the first African government in Uganda; in seeking power, it sought votes in the south, the primary coffee-growing region. The UPC-dominated coalition relaxed the stringent pricing policies that had been adopted by the colonial government. As noted by Van Zwanenberg and King: "The new government appears to have very rapidly used up the funds by paying high prices to peasant producers. . . . The Uganda peasants had suddenly become of political significance."[15]

As in many other African countries, however, the government moved to single-party rule. Under Milton Obote, the UPC adopted socialist programs, providing the party militants with the economic power with which to elicit political deference to his regime; among the targets of these programs stood Uganda's rich coffee industry. All coffee, once harvested, had to be sold to the state.[16] Illustrative of the resultant policy bias was the way in which the government set coffee prices. The Cabinet, made up of leaders of the ruling party, met in secret session. It first deducted from the estimated world price the costs of the Coffee Marketing Board; then those of the cooperatives; and then the revenue needs of the government, and especially its needs for foreign exchange. The residual constituted the price the government paid to the farmers.[17] Under Obote and his successor, Idi Amin, the government of Uganda paid farmers on average 30 percent of the international price of coffee.[18]

The case of Uganda appears indeed to suggest that governments can dominate peasants, should they wish to do so. If the aspirants for office must win votes to achieve power, however, then the government will indulge, not penalize, peasant producers. When they no longer must compete for votes, they adopt policies that violate growers' interests. One way of testing hypotheses extracted from case studies is thus to move outside of the original sample. The case of Uganda lends support to the interpretation inferred from the original data set.

Disaggregation

Another tactic is to disaggregate.[19] Rather than seeking new cases, we can work with the same set of cases but subdivide them into multiple samples. This technique generates additional observations, thus enabling us to move from case studies to statistical analysis. I illustrate by returning to the case of Colombia.

Studying the Colombian politics of the 1930s, I inferred the impact of party competition upon the influence of the coffee growers on government policy. As a first check, I turned to the 1950s, which lay outside the original sample. But I can go further. Subdividing the history of Colombian politics into annual slices, I can generate a larger number of observations. The number of cases thus becomes such that I can test my ideas statistically. The danger with this strategy is that the observations may not be independent; in this case, being drawn from the same history, they may be serially correlated. I use several techniques to guard against this danger.

Table 7.1 presents the list of variables and the sources from which they were taken; tables 7.2–7.3 present the results of the analysis. In general, they suggest that international agreements enabled the government to tax the coffee industry, but that the nature and beneficiaries of the tax depended on the existence of party competition. Where there was party competition, the tax was retained within the coffee sector; when there was not, the revenues were transferred to the government or to import-substituting manufacturing firms.

Equation 1 (see table 7.2) exhibits the results from a regression in which taxes and export earnings are measured in current units (pesos in the case of taxes and dollars in the case of coffee revenues). Both variables are nonsta-

TABLE 7.1

Variables, Definitions, Units, and Sources

Variable	Definition	Units	Sources
TOTAX	Total taxes extracted from coffee sector	Thousands of Colombian pesos	Federación Nacional de Cafeteros, *Informe(s) del Gerente* (Bogotá: FNC, various years).
DTOTAX	First difference of total tax: $DTOTAX_t = TOTAX_t - TOTAX_{t-1}$	Thousands of Colombian pesos	Federación Nacional de Cafeteros, *Informe(s) del Gerente* (Bogotá: FNC, various years).
RTOTAX	Total tax in real units; base year 1985	Real value in U.S. dollars: TOTAX divided by 1,000, divided by conversion factors (pesos per dollar), and divided by U.S. consumer price index (1985 = 100)	Conversion factor: end-of-period market rate, International Monetary Fund, *International Financial Statistics* (Washington, D.C.: IMF, various issues). CPI 1939–50: Bureau of Statistics, *Historical Statistics of the United States: Colonial Times to 1970* (Washington, D.C.: U.S. Department of Commerce, Bureau of Statistics, 1975). CPI 1951–90: International Monetary Fund, *International Financial Statistics Yearbook* (Washington, D.C.: IMF, various issues).
INTL	International dummy	0 if no agreement or treaty; 1 if an agreement (but no treaty); 2 if a treaty)	Consult sources listed in the text.
NONCIV	Military government dummy	0 if a civilian government; 1 if a military government	Consult sources listed in the text.
PRTCOMP	Party competiton dummy	0 if no party competition; 1 if party competition	Consult sources listed in the text.
FROSTS	Dummy for supply shocks: droughts or frosts in Brazil	0 for years in which there were no frosts or droughts; 1 for years in which there were	Consult sources listed in the text
PQ	Total export revenues from coffee	Log of New York price of Manizales coffee in U.S. cents per pound times the log of quantity exported	Price, 1940–46: FAO, "The World Coffee Economy," *Commodity Bulletin Series* (Rome: FAO, 1961). 1947–84: ICO, *Informe(s) del Gerente General* (Bogotá: Federación Nacional de Cafeteros, various years). CPI: 1939–50. Bureau of Statistics. *Historical Statistics of the United States, Colonial Times to 1970* (Washington, D.C.: U.S. Department of Commerce, Bureau of Statistics, 1975). 1951–90: International Monetary Fund, *International Financial Statistics Yearbook* (Washington, D.C.: IMF, various issues).
RPQ	Real value of total export revenues from coffee	Log of real prices in cents per pound (deflated by U.S. consumer price in-	Price, 1940–46: FAO, "The World Coffee Economy," *Commodity Bulletin Series* (Rome: FAO, 1961). 1947–84: ICO, *Quarterly Statistical Bulletin on Coffee*

TABLE 7.1 (*Continued*)

Variable	Definition	Units	Sources
		dex) times log of quantities exported	(London: ICO, various years). Quantity: Federación Nacional de Cafeteros, *Inform(s) del Gerente General* (Bogotá: FNC, various years).
PCTRET	Percentage of total taxes from coffee retained within the coffee sector	Percentages	Federación Nacional de Cafeteros, *Informe(s) del Gerente General* (Bogotá: FNC, various years).

TABLE 7.2

The Impact of International Agreements on the Taxation of Exports: Colombian Taxes on Coffee, 1940–74

Variable	Equation 1	Equation 2
Dependent variable	DTOTAX	RTOTAX
Intercept	−248565**	0.0804
	(−2.573)	(0.353)
Independent Variables		
LL3 FROST	321573**	0.7235*
	(−2.168)	(1.943)
LL4 FROST	383751**	1.2822***
	(2.596)	(3.337)
DPQ	174278***	
	(2.969)	
DRPQ	—	0.1501
		(1.149)
INTL	265583***	1.5500***
	(4.343)	(10.13)
Adjusted R^2	0.467	0.786
$F_{14,26}$	7.571	28.544
DW	1.897	0.873

Notes: LL stands for lag; D for first difference; and *DW* for the Durbin-Watson statistic: *t* statistics appear in parentheses; for definitions and sources, see table 7.1.

*Significant at .10 level; **significant at .05 level; ***significant at the 0.1 level.

tionary, however, resulting in serial correlation. They are stationary in their first differences, however. As the Breusch-Godfrey test[20] suggested that the dependent variable is correlated with its own lagged value, we are compelled to explore the relationships among first differences (Equation 1).[21] Of particular interest is the coefficient of the variable INTL, which takes on the value of 0 when there is no international agreement (as in the late 1940s and early

TABLE 7.3
The Impact of Domestic Variables

Variable	Equation 1	Equation 2
Dependent Variable	PCTRET	PCTRET
Intercept	19.190***	30.197***
	(2.793)	(4.112)
Independent Variables		
LPCTRET	0.2773	0.227
	(1.563)	(1.350)
LL2PCTRET	0.1215	0.128
	(0.721)	(0.809)
FROSTS	−9.795	−8.226
	(−1.121)	(−0.996)
PRTCOMP	12.288*	
	(1.714)	
NONCIV		−20.483***
		(−2.642)
Adjusted R^2	0.197	0.289
$F_{4,28}$	2.957	4.259

Notes: L stands for lag; t statistics appear in parentheses; for definitions and sources, see table 7.1.

*Significant at .10 level; **significant at .05 level; ***significant at the 0.1 level.

1950s); a 1 when an agreement is in place but not enforced (as during El Convenio de Mexico or in periods when the ICO was in place but its economic clauses were not operative); and a 2 when an agreement is in place and when the agreement's economic clauses are being enforced. The estimated coefficient is positive and highly significant, suggesting that international agreements increase the level of taxes collected by the government. Equation 1 accounts for nearly one-half of the variance in the dependent variable.

Equation 2 (table 7.2) re-estimates the model, while employing real values of the measures of tax revenues and export earnings. The real value of total taxes is stationary. The real value of export earnings is not, save in first differences; it therefore enters the equation in difference terms. Equation 2 accounts for nearly 80 percent of the variation in the dependent variable. Once again, the coefficient for the variable measuring the existence (and strength) of international accords is of special interest. It is positive and highly significant, again suggesting that international agreements increase the level of the taxes collected by governments.

As emphasized in table 1.2, however, the taxes can take many forms. Of greatest concern is whether they result in transfers of resources from the coffee industry (as in Policy III), or whether the resources are retained within the industry (as in Policy V).

The coffee industry of Colombia has been subject to a series of different taxes, and these have been clearly earmarked. The proceeds from some, such as the *cuota de retención* and the *pasilla y ripia*, are assigned to the industry itself; revenues from others, such as the *impuestos ad valorem*, accrue to the government. Summing the taxes accumulated from the *cuota de retención* and the *pasilla y ripia* and dividing by the total of all taxes paid by the coffee industry thus provides a measure (named PCTRET, for "percent retained") of the extent to which the proceeds from taxes are retained within the coffee sector.

The variable PCTRET is nonstationary. Applying the Breusch-Godfrey test suggests that while nonstationary, it is not autocorrelated in equations including its own lagged value. To avoid loss of variability from the use of differencing, we therefore employed an autoregressive specification. The variable PRTCOMP takes a value 1 when party competition prevails in Colombia and a 0 when it does not. The sign and significance of the coefficient of this variable in Equation 1 (table 7.3) suggests that in years in which the government faced a partisan challenge at the polls, it favored the use of taxes whose proceeds were earmarked for retention within the coffee industry.[22]

Because of ambiguities in dating the end and the revival of party competition and the sensitivity of the results to the dates chosen, Equation 2 makes use of an alternative measure: the variable NONCIV takes on the value 1 during periods of military government and 0 in other years. The value and significance of the coefficient of this variable strongly reinforce the conclusions drawn from Equation 1. They suggest that the coffee sector found in civilian institutions, such as political parties and electoral competition, a defense of its economic interests (see table 7.3). Under civilian regimes, the coffee industry was able to retain taxes levied from exports within the sector itself.

Our strategy has thus been to bring analysis to bear upon narrative; it has been to use theory to "interrogate" case studies. Where an interpretation fails, the case study has generated information; it has suggested how existing theories may be wrong and indicated the modifications necessary to correct them. When a theory seems to fit the facts of the narrative, then we have gone in search of additional cases. We seek in particular observations drawn from outside of the original sample, which can thus serve as checks of the interpretations we have drawn from the cases within it. And, by disaggregation, we have sought to multiply the number of observations, such that we can employ statistical methods to evaluate our hypotheses.

Comparative Statics

This study has advanced an explanation of the International Coffee Organization. The use of comparative statics provides a third means for testing explanations. Given a conception of the factors that produce a particular outcome, we can look for instances where a particular causal factor takes on a different value while observing whether the outcome itself varies in the manner sug-gested by our theory. We illustrate this method by testing our explanation of the ICO against the data generated by its demise.

As noted in the introduction, the ICO collapsed in 1989. However, this study has also suggested that the ICO appears to have been successful and sought reasons why it should have been so. It is important to note, then, that the ICO appears to have broken up in part precisely because it *was* successful.[23] The political rules and administrative regulations that it imposed had so effectively constrained the market that powerful economic interests that had once supported the organization now turned against it. The factors that account for the creation and maintenance of the organization thus also account for its demise.

The ICO, I have argued, represented or constituted a coalition among firms and bureaucrats who used their states to regulate international markets. Key to the ability of the producers to secure third-party enforcement was the willing-ness of coffee roasters and security specialists in the United States to elicit the enforcement of the agreement. The constraints imposed by the ICO, because they were binding, allocated resources in the coffee market in a way that alienated these key interests.

The ICO secured higher coffee prices by enforcing quotas and constraining exports. The quotas resulted from a rule-governed political process in which coalitions were formed to secure the majorities necessary to approve them. The allocation of votes was a function of past exports performance. For politi-cal reasons, then, quotas were stable: the quotas, once chosen, resulted in a record of exports that sustained the allocation of votes that had generated it in the first place. Quotas were stable for a second reason: they were costly to negotiate. The dominant producers maintained skilled diplomats in London who were paid ambassador-level salaries to marshal and maintain such major-ities. When quotas were to be set, negotiators spent weeks cultivating dele-gates; and when votes were to be taken, they labored for days at a time to secure the requisite majorities. Throughout the process, they faced the pos-sible breakdown of negotiations and the costly return to market competition. Neither Brazil nor Colombia, then, welcomed the prospect of the renegotia-tion of quotas.

Quotas, once chosen, thus tended to remain in place. The result was that the mix of coffees supplied by the producers remained invariant. The mix of coffees demanded by consumers did not, however. In the United States, con-sumers switched from soluble coffees, which intensively employed robustas, to ground coffees, which had a higher percentage of arabicas. Coffee roasters, responding to changes in consumer preference, employed a greater percentage of washed arabicas, as opposed to Brazilian coffees, in their blends. In seek-ing to respond to changes in consumer preferences, however, the roasters confronted the constraints imposed by the ICO. Under the ICO, the supply of coffee was set by votes, not by market forces; and the increased demand for mild coffees failed to elicit an increase in supply.

Because the ICO worked, it resulted not only in a fixed proportion of coffees of different types but also large price differentials between member and nonmember markets. This rigidity also promoted disaffection with the agreement. As the differential increased, so too did the fears of the large roasting firms, who worried that competitors would secure low-cost coffee, illicitly importing it from nonmember countries. The cooperation of the large firms remained knife-edged: each was willing to cooperate only so long as it was certain of the cooperation of others. Insofar as the agreement worked, then, incentives to elude the administrative barriers strengthened; so too did the readiness of key actors to abandon the agreement.

In the 1980s, two changes appear to have tipped the balance. One was the large-scale movement of European roasters to Berlin, attracted by favorable tax policies. The other was the entry of a European firm, Nestlé, into the North American market.[24] The large United States' roasters now faced a competitor with possible access to cheap coffee, purchased in the nonmember markets of Eastern Europe.

In response to the constraints imposed by the ICO on the mix of coffees available in the market and on the price of coffee in member markets relative to those outside of the agreement, the Foreign Affairs Committee of the National Coffee Association switched from a supporter to a critic of the ICO. In February 1980, it resolved:

That the interests of the United States' coffee . . . industry are best accommodated by free and unrestricted trade of coffee. Two severe weaknesses in the operation of the current agreement were:
1. *The sale of coffee to non-members . . . at prices substantially below the price at which . . . coffee is offered to members of the Agreement.* This practice has created a so-called "two-tier" market which is not only economically unfair to member states, but also encourages various illegal or clandestine diversions of coffee. . . .
2. *The inflexibility of the quota system in making coffee of the origins or types required by consumers available to the market.*[25]

The U.S. Department of State constituted a second key element in the domestic coalition underpinning the ICO. The State Department had sought to promote economic development in Brazil, and thereby stabilize its politics. By the 1980s, the Left no longer posed a political threat in Brazil; and in a variety of industrial and agricultural markets, Brazil more closely resembled a mature economic rival than a struggling developing nation. The State Department instead saw the primary threats to hemispheric security as originating in Central America. Given the rigidity of the ICO's quotas, the administration could not alter the pattern of coffee exports so as to reward its friends or punish its enemies in that region. Nor could it increase coffee imports from Mexico, whose reformist government it sought to fortify. Another key element of the ICO's support coalition, the Department of State, therefore came to regard the agreement as a liability rather than as an asset.

In our model of United States policy-making, we viewed presidential leadership in structural terms. Executives influence outcomes by assigning policies to bureaucratic jurisdictions and by structuring bureaucracies, I argued.

The Reagan White House placed a strong priority on the promotion of market forces. To secure that objective, it channeled all trade policy through the Economic Policy Council, a Cabinet-level body dominated by the Treasury Department and one committed to the reduction of government intervention. In addition, the Secretary of State, George Shultz, required that policies toward commodity agreements be vetted by the Division of Economic Affairs within the State Department, which he staffed with former colleagues from the department of economics of the University of Chicago. The White House thus structured the policy process so that the ICO was assigned to jurisdictions that were governed by agents who placed a high priority on the economic costs to consumers and a low priority on its political benefits to producing nations.[26]

To safeguard its economic objectives, the U.S. executive branch took one further step. When the agreement came up for renewal, the Secretary of State inserted a trusted economist within the ranks of the delegation and dictated instructions requiring that it achieve unanimity before reaching decisions.[27] Because of its indecisive conduct, Brazil's and Colombia's representatives inferred that the United States' delegation had received vague and contradictory instructions.[28] Rather, it had been structured precisely to prevent it from reaching an agreement that would violate the principle of free markets.

The structure of policy-making in the United States required that the executive branch push for the agreement, and that it secure the consent of Congress. Essential to the latter was the backing of the coffee-roasting firms. Given the structural realities, when the United States' delegation did succeed in reaching a negotiating position, it united about one requiring an increase in the supply of washed arabicas. It demanded an increase in Central America's share in the coffee market.

The ICO was a political organization. It arrived at quota allocations by casting votes. Within the political framework of the ICO, the reallocation of the quota called for by the United States was not feasible. The United States' demand could not receive a majority. Knowing that, other delegations therefore viewed the United States' position as an attack on the organization. As stated in the Colombian delegation's report to headquarters, the United States' representative

> ingenuously chided us for not accepting his offer nor accepting the proposal of the
> other milds. With all simplicity he intimated that to save the accord we ought to
> abandon Brazil [and] Africa.

> $\cdot \quad \cdot \quad \cdot \quad \cdot \quad \cdot \quad \cdot \quad \cdot \quad \cdot \quad \cdot \quad \cdot \quad \cdot \quad \cdot \quad \cdot$

> Nothing could be further removed from the political realities. In practical terms,
> [the reallocation of the quotas] requires a substantial diminution of the quota of

Brazil and the principal exports of Africa. . . . That is, the defeat of the proposal is guaranteed.[29]

.   .   .   .

We are thus left with the impression that the United States seeks the breakdown of negotiations, so as to neutralize the agreement and to obtain a free market.[30]

The domestic political coalition that supported the ICO within the United States had collapsed. And in 1989, so too did the negotiations for its renewal. The ICO no longer existed; it no longer regulated the international market for coffee.

The collapse of the ICO marks the end of this narrative. The institution did not endure. But the explanations advanced for its creation and maintenance appear to have survived the test posed by its demise. The reasons for its failure lay in those for its success. Changes in the value of explanatory variables impacted decisively, and in ways expected, upon the politics of the coffee market.

*Appendix*_____

Economists have long studied coffee markets.[1] Coffee demand is deeply understood, with aggregate statistics and consumer surveys documenting:

• High inelasticity with respect to price: Estimates lie in the range of −0.40 to −0.20, with most clustering at the lower level. A 10 percent increase in price, if taking place in the normal range of prices, thus leads to a small (2–4 percent) decrease in the quantity demanded. Because the restriction in quantity is less than proportionate to the increase in price, demand is said to be price inelastic. Only at times of extraordinarily high prices—such as those attained in the mid-1950s or mid-1970s, for example—has coffee demand appeared elastic with respect to price.

• Coffee's properties as a normal good: Through most ranges of income, coffee consumption increases as incomes rise. At the highest income levels, however, consumption of coffee appears to decline, as consumers shift to the consumption of alternative sources of caffeine, such as cola drinks.

• The "vegetal" growth of coffee demand over time: The major determinants of aggregate demand appear to be the number and per capita incomes of consumers. To the extent that these variables grow, so too does the consumption of coffee.

Economists have also probed the economics of coffee production,[2] concluding that:

• In the short run—periods of a year or less—coffee production is price-elastic. In the short run, coffee output increases proportionately with price. Price increases influence the level of resources devoted to the fertilization of coffee trees, the amount of labor devoted to their care, and the intensity with which they are harvested.

• In the longer run—periods of one to three years—coffee production is price-inelastic. The increase in quantity is not proportionate to the increase in price. At least two years are required for new trees to produce amounts of coffee sufficient to cover the costs of harvesting;[3] and several years must pass before newly planted trees reach full production. Present quantities are therefore a function of past prices. And because coffee trees produce for over a decade, farmers are reluctant to uproot them when coffee prices decline.

• The market is imperfectly competitive. A few large producers—Brazil, Colombia, and the Ivory Coast—account for over half the world's exports; and a few large roasting companies account for a large portion of the imports by nations consuming the commodity.[4]

And economists have documented how the characteristics of coffee consumption and production influence the formation of prices. The combination of highly inelastic demand and longer-run supply generates large swings in coffee prices. Rises in price are not compensated by immediate reductions in demand or increases in the stock of trees producing coffee. When prices rise, then, they stay at high levels for two years or more. In the longer run, however, increased prices lead to new plantings. And when the new trees enter production, prices fall. Demand being inelastic, consumers fail to respond by increasing their intake of coffee, however; and production being (in the intermediate run) inelastic, producers fail to reduce the stock of coffee-bearing trees. The result is a prolonged period of low prices.

Responses on both the consumer and producer side of the market therefore generate booms and busts in coffee prices, characteristics that the market for coffee shares with those for other primary commodities.

Studies of the economics of the coffee market fill important libraries in Rio de Janeiro, London, and Bogotá.[5] So distinguished are some that they have formed the basis for major careers in both academics and policy-making.[6] The quantity and quality of this economic research masks a deep irony, however. For it is precisely the surprising element of state-like, political controls exerted over the international coffee market that distinguishes trade in the product. And by comparison with the research into the international economics of coffee, relatively little research has been done into the international politics of coffee.[7] Fortunately, the few major studies that have been conducted have been of high quality,[8] and I will make ample use of them here. But they still leave important questions unanswered. In particular, they fail to explain the way in which the political institutions built around the coffee market influence the allocation of resources within it. Markets, as institutions, shape the way in which prices are formed and allocative decisions get made; but so, too, do the institutions of politics.

Notes

Preface

1. See, for example, Arjun Appadurai, *The Social Life of Things: Commodities in Cultural Perspective* (Cambridge: Cambridge University Press, 1986).

2. See the *Coffee Drinking Studies* commissioned by the International Coffee Organization and archived in the library of the ICO. See as well the data contained in Jorge Cárdenas Gutiérrez, "El Café en la Década de los Años 90," Bogotá: FNC, 6 de junio de 1991, mimeographed and the Economist Intelligence Unit, *Coffee to 1991*, Special Report No. 1086 (London: The Economist Publications Limited, 1987). Coffee habits in the United States have been studied in detail by the United States Coffee Council, an association of United States roasters. See the summary of their findings reported by H. L. Tower, President of Maxwell House, the coffee division of General Foods in *Revista do Comércio de Café*, maio 1976, pp. 42–44.

3. See Michael F. Jiménez, "From Plantation to Cup: The Beverage of North American Capitalism, 1830–1930," typescript, Princeton University.

4. Edmar Bacha, *Os Mitos de Uma Década* (Rio de Janeiro: Paz e Terra, 1978), pp. 161 ff.

5. C. F. Marshall, *The World Coffee Trade* (Cambridge: Woodhead-Faulkner, 1982), pp. 128–141.

6. See the charming discussions of manners in such books as Heinrich Eduard Jacob, *The Saga of Coffee: The Biography of an Economic Product*, trans. Eden and Cedar Paul (London: George Allen and Unwin, 1935); Andrés Uribe, *Brown Gold* (New York: Random House, 1954); and William H. Ukers, *The Romance of Coffee* (New York: The Tea and Coffee Trade Journal Company, 1948). The series of articles in *Atlantic Monthly* (May, June and July 1990) represents a welcome addition to this literature, as does the recent contribution by Ralph S. Hattox, *Coffee and Coffee Houses* (Seattle, Washington: University of Washington Press, 1991).

7. See the colorful accounts in Jacob, *The Saga*; Uribe, *Brown Gold*; and Ukers, *The Romance*. There exists a major primary literature on coffee in almost every territory in which coffee became a significant export crop. For a sample, consult C. F. Van Delden Laërne, *Brazil and Java: Report on Coffee-Culture to H. E. Minister of the Colonies* (The Hague: Martinus Nijhoff, 1885). See the extraordinary contribution: Jorge Dumont Villares, *O Café: Dos Partes* archived in the Centro do Comércio do Café. Villares's work possesses no place or date of publication, but appears to have been published in Rio de Janeiro in the 1920s.

Chapter 1

1. Peter Katzenstein, "International Relations and Domestic Political Structures: Foreign Economic Policies of Advanced Industrial States," *International Organization* 30 (Winter 1976): 1–45. See also Peter Katzenstein, ed., *Between Power and Plenty* (Madison: University of Wisconsin Press, 1978).

2. Stephan Haggard and Beth A. Simmons, "Theories of International Regimes," *International Organization* 41, 3 (September 1987): 513.

3. For contributions to this intellectual program, see Jeffry Frieden, *Debt, Development, and Democracy* (Princeton: Princeton University Press, 1991); Ronald Rogowski, *Commerce and Coalitions* (Princeton: Princeton University Press, 1989); Peter Gourevitch, *Politics in Hard Times* (Ithaca: Cornell University Press, 1986); Beth A. Simmons, *Who Adjusts? Domestic Sources of Foreign Economic Policy during the Interwar Years (Princeton: Princeton University Press, 1994);* and Daniel Verdier, *Democracy and International Trade* (Princeton: Princeton University Press, 1994). See also D. Michael Shafer, *Winners and Losers* (Ithaca: Cornell University Press, 1994). The contribution that has most influenced this book is Robert Putnam, "Diplomacy and Domestic Politics," *International Organization* 42, 3 (Summer 1988): 427–460.

4. International Coffee Organization, *Quarterly Statistical Bulletin on Coffee*, vol. 23 (July–September 1982), table VII–2, p. 136. Price data from F. O. Licht, *International Coffee Yearbook, 1993* (Ratzeburg, Germany: F. O. Licht, 1993), p. G.15. Throughout, I employ the standardized measure adopted by the International Coffee Organization, wherein one bag contains 60 kilograms of green coffee.

5. Based on an average price for robusta of $1.06 a pound. See the price data contained in Licht, *International Coffee Yearbook*, ibid.

6. Even assuming that over 80 percent of the border price was consumed by taxes, bribes, and transport costs. A bag of coffee weighs 60 kilograms, or 2.2 pounds. With a price at the border of $1 per pound, ten bags would be worth about $1320. The extent of government taxation is documented by Dudley Sears et al., *The Rehabilitation of the Economy of Uganda*, vol. 2 (London: Commonwealth Secretariat, 1979).

7. Oran R. Young, "International Regimes: Problems of Concept Formation," *World Politics* 32, 3 (April 1980): 331. The major contributions to the subfield of international political economy are collected in Helen Milner and Robert O. Keohane, eds., *The Library of International Political Economy*, 10 vols. (Aldershot, U.K.: Edward Elgar Publishing, 1993–95).

Many will note and most, I hope, will appreciate that I bypass the debates between realist and liberal theorists. I do so because the issues that are central to those debates are not central to this inquiry. For reviews, see Robert O. Keohane, ed., *Neorealism and Its Critics* (New York: Columbia University Press, 1986); David A. Baldwin, ed., *Neorealism and Neoliberalism* (New York: Columbia University Press, 1993); and Robert Powell, "The Neorealist and Neoliberal Debate," *International Organization* 48, 2 (Spring 1994): 313–44.

8. See Charles Kindleberger, *The World in Depression, 1929–1939* (Berkeley and Los Angeles: University of California Press, 1973), and Stephen D. Krasner, "State Power and the Structure of International Trade," *World Politics* 28, 3 (April 1976): 317–47. For reviews, see Robert Keohane, *After Hegemony* (Princeton: Princeton University Press, 1984), and Joanne Gowa, "An Epitaph for Hegemonic Stability Theory?" in *International Trade Policies*, ed. John S. Odell and Thomas D. Willett (Ann Arbor: University of Michigan Press, 1993).

9. Kindleberger, *The World*.

10. Mancur Olson, *The Logic of Collective Action* (Cambridge: Harvard University Press, 1965).

11. Kenneth N. Waltz, "Political Structures," in *Neorealism and Its Critics*, ed. Robert O. Keohane (New York: Columbia University Press, 1986), p. 88. The chapter is excerpted from Kenneth N. Waltz, *Theory in International Politics* (Reading, Mass.: Addison-Wesley, 1979).

12. See also the criticisms of Peter J. Katzenstein, "International Relations and Domestic Structures," *International Organization* 30, 1 (Winter 1976): 1–45; "Coping with Terrorism," in *Ideas and Foreign Policy*, ed. Judith Goldstein and Robert O. Keohane (Ithaca: Cornell University Press, 1993); and Robert Jervis, "Realism, Game Theory and Cooperation," *World Politics* 40, 3 (April 1988): 317–49. See also the clarifying comments of Robert Powell, "The Neorealist-Neoliberal Debate."

13. Kenneth N. Waltz, "Reductionism and Systematic Theories," in *Neorealism and Its Critics*, ed. Robert O. Keohane, p. 60.

14. See, for example, the collections of articles in Kenneth Oye, ed., *Cooperation under Anarchy* (Princeton: Princeton University Press, 1986).

15. See the discussion in chapter 4 of Eric Rasmussen, *Games and Information* (Oxford: Basil Blackwell, 1989).

16. As noted below, the principal one has to do with credibility and subgame perfection.

17. The same logic applies when the game terminates at randomly selected, and therefore uncertain, end points.

18. Drew Fudenberg and Eric Maskin, "The Folk Theorem in Repeated Games With Discounting or With Incomplete Information," *Econometrica* 54, 3 (May 1986): 533–54.

19. One of the clearest statements is contained in Goldstein and Keohane, eds., *Ideas and Foreign Policy*.

20. See Jervis, "Realism, Game Theory, and Cooperation." Perhaps the classic statement remains Putnam, "Diplomacy and Domestic Politics," 427–60.

21. For reviews of this vast and disparate body of writings, see Gabriel Palma, "Dependency: A Formal Theory of Underdevelopment or a Methodology for the Analysis of Concrete Situations of Underdevelopment," *World Development* 6 (1978): 886–924. Charles Wilbur has anthologized these writings in a series of editions of his reader: Charles Wilbur, ed., *The Political Economy of Development and Underdevelopment* (New York: Random House, 1973).

22. See, for example, Celso Furtado, *The Economic Growth of Brazil* (Berkeley and Los Angeles: University of California Press, 1963); Fernando Henrique Cardoso and Enzo Faletto, *Dependency and Development in Latin America*, trans. Marjory M. Urquidi (Berkeley and Los Angeles: University of California Press, 1979); and Peter Evans, *Dependent Development* (Princeton: Princeton University Press, 1979).

23. See the sources cited in the chapters that follow.

24. For a review, see R. E. Caves and R. W. Jones, *World Trade and Payments*, 3d ed. (Boston: Little, Brown, 1987).

25. Ronald Rogowski, *Commerce and Coalitions* (Princeton: Princeton University Press, 1989), and Jeffry Frieden, *Debt, Development and Democracy* (Princeton: Princeton University Press, 1991).

26. For a highly accessible review, see James E. Alt and Michael Gilligan, "The Political Economy of Trading States: Factor Specificity, Collective Action Problems, and Domestic Political Institutions," Typescript, 1993.

27. Stephen Maggee, in a study of the United States, finds support for the Ricardo-Viner version, employed by Frieden, as opposed to the Hechscher-Ohlin theorem, used by Rogowski. Stephen P. Maggee, "The Simple Tests of the Stolper-Samuelson Theorem," in Peter Oppenheimer, ed., *Issues in International Economics* (London: Oriel Press, 1980).

28. For key contributions to this literature, see Gene M. Grossman, ed., *Imperfect Competition and International Trade* (Cambridge: MIT Press, 1994), and Paul R. Krugman, *Rethinking International Trade*(Cambridge: MIT Press, 1994). For a highly accessible overview, see Paul R. Krugman and Maurice Obstfeld, *International Economics,* 2d ed. (New York: Harper Collins, 1994). Note that I am not assuming the existence of scale economies in coffee production, however.

29. I thus draw on the insights of Katzenstein, Cameron, and other students of the advanced industrial nations in viewing the role and structure of interest groups as endogenous. The structure of interest groups represents, in effect, the by-product of politicians' strategies, as they seek to stay in power while their political constituencies are shocked and buffeted by external economic forces. See David R. Cameron, "The Expansion of the Political Economy: A Comparative Analysis," *American Political Science Review* 72, 4 (December 1978): 1243–61; Peter J. Katzenstein, *Small States in World Markets* (Ithaca: Cornell University Press, 1985); and Geoffrey Garrett and Peter Lange, "The Politics of Growth," *Journal of Politics* 47 (1985): 792–827 and "Performance in a Hostile World," *World Politics* 38 (1986): 517–45.

See also Peter Gourevitch, "The Second Image Reversed: The International Sources of Domestic Politics," *International Organization* 32, 4 (Autumn 1978): 881–913; Alice Amsden, "Taiwan's Economic History: A Case of *Etatisme* and a Challenge to Dependency Theory," in *Toward a Political Economy of Development*, ed. Robert H. Bates (Berkeley and Los Angeles: University of California Press, 1988).

30. For further studies, see Tamassa Akiyama and Panayotis Varangis, "The Impact of the International Coffee Agreement's Export Quota System on the World Coffee Market" (Paper presented at the Twenty-fifth International Conference of the Applied Econometrics Association on International Commodity Market Modeling, World Bank, Washington D.C., 24–26 October 1988); C. L. Gilbert, "International Commodity Markets: Design and Performance," in *Primary Commodities in the World Economy: Problems and Policies*, Special Issue of *World Development* 15 (1987): 591–616; Roland Hermann, "Free Riders and Redistributive Effects of International Commodity Agreements: The Case of Coffee," *Journal of Policy Modeling* 8 (1986): 597–621; Roland Hermann, "The International Allocation of Trade-tied Aid: A Quantitative Analysis for the Export Quota Scheme in Coffee Scheme in Coffee," *Welwirtschaftliches Archiv* 124 (1988): 675–700; Roland Hermann, Kees Burger, and Hidde P. Smit, "Commodity Policy: Price Stabilization versus Financing," in *Primary Commodity Prices: Economic Models and Policy*, ed. L. Alan Winters and David Sapsford (Cambridge: Center for Policy Research, 1990); José Leibovich, "La Formación de Precio en el Mercado Mundial del Café," Fedesarrollo, typescript, April 1989; Franz C. Palm and Ben Vogelvang, "The Effectiveness of the World Coffee Agreement: A Simulation Study Using a Quarterly Model of the World Coffee Market," in *International Commodity Market Models* ed. Orhan Guvenen, Walter Labys, and Jean-Baptiste Lesouad (London: Chapman and Hall, 1991); J. K. Sengupta, "Asymmetry and Robustness in Stabilizing Policy for Imperfect Commodity Markets," *International Commodity Models and Policy Analysis,* ed. Orhan Guvenen (Dordrecht:

Kluwer Acdemic Publishers, 1988); J. K. Sengupta and R. E. Sfeir, "Control Theory Models in World Coffee: Some Empirical Tests," *International Journal of Systems Science* 14 (1983): 811–27; E. Volvang, *A Quarterly Econometric Model of the World Coffee Economy* (Amsterdam: Free University Press, 1988); J. Jesus Martinez Ruiz, "Los Convenios Internacionales Como Mechanismos Reguladores de los Mercados de Productos Basicos: El Caso de Café," Tesis Que Para Obtenir el Titulo de Liciendo en Economía, Universidad Nacional Autónoma de Mexico, 1982; Greta R. Boye, "The International Coffee Agreement: Past Accomplishments and Future Alternatives," in F. O. Licht, *International Coffee Yearbook, 1989* (Ratzburg, Germany: F. O. Licht, 1989); and Larry S. Karp and Jeffrey M. Perloff, "A Dynamic Model of Oligopoly in the Coffee Export Market," *American Journal of Agricultural Economics* 75 (May 1993): 448–457.

31. The measure of coffee "prices" is actually the unit value of exports, as recorded in International Coffee Organization, *W.P.—Agreement No. 1/88*, Rev. 2.

32. "I" actually refers to myself and Ms. (now Dr.) Dixie Reeves, my research assistant. For a development of the method followed, see Richard J. Larsen and Morris L. Marx, *Statistics* (Englewood Cliffs, N.J.: Prentice-Hall, 1990), pp. 486–87 and 496–97.

33. As seen in figure 1.2 and table 1.5, when quotas are not in place, prices in member markets fall below those in the markets of other countries. At such times, exporters seek hard-currency earnings by competing for sales in Europe and the United States.

The greater tendency for producers to sell low-quality coffees in the nonmember market constitutes a plausible alternative explanation of the price differentials. Research by economists at the Department of State concluded, however, that this behavior could not account for the magnitude of the differential (interview, U.S. Department of State, Washington D.C., June 1990). And a reanalysis of the data underlying table 1.5 suggests that the differential was as great for each quality of coffee; i.e., as great for robusta as for milds.

34. The coffees of Kenya and the Kilimanjaro region of Tanzania are also classified as Colombian coffees. Colombia produces a high-quality washed arabica. The category of coffees labeled "other milds" is also made up of washed arabicas, but of a slightly lower quality, on average, than the coffees of Colombia.

35. Also classified as "Brazilian" are the coffees of Peru, Bolivia, and Ethiopia. They share the characteristic of being arabicas that are not washed when being processed for export.

36. In fact, Andrew Mason of Stanford University and I. We wish to thank Jeffrey Williamson of the Food Research Institute, Stanford University, for his guidance in this portion of our work.

37. See the classic, Holbrook Working, "The Theory of Inverse Carrying Charge in Futures Markets," *Journal of Farm Economics* 30 (1948): 1–28, and "The Theory of the Price of Storage," *American Economic Review* 39, 6 (1949): 1254–62.

Chapter 2

1. Eduard Jacob, *The Saga of Coffee*, trans. Eden Paul and Cedar Paul (London: George Allen and Unwin, 1935), p. 314.

2. Ibid.

3. Antônio Delfim Netto, *O Problema do Café No Brasil* (São Paulo: University of São Paulo, 1959), p. 155.

4. As argued by Conybeare, Brazil could be expected to act not as a benevolent hegemon, maximizing the total value of production in the market, but rather as a self-interested price setter, maximizing its private earnings. See John Conybeare, "Public Goods, Prisoner's Dilemmas. and International Political Economy," *International Studies Quarterly* 28 (1984): 5–22.

5. The literature runs from Celso Furtado, *The Economic Growth of Brazil* (Berkeley and Los Angeles: University of California Press, 1965) to Peter Evans, *Dependent Development* (Princeton: Princeton University Press, 1979). For additional references, see below.

6. See Jeffry Frieden, *Debt, Development and Democracy* (Princeton: Princeton University Press, 1991); Deepak Lal and Sylvia Maxfield, "The Political Economy of Stabilization in Brazil," in *Political and Economic Interactions in Economic Policy Reform*, ed. Robert H. Bates and Anne O. Krueger (Oxford: Basil Blackwell, 1993). Barbara Geddes, *Politician's Dilemma* (Berkeley and Los Angeles: University of California Press, 1994), provides a politician-based exception to this genre. For a powerful and compelling analysis that mobilizes both neoclassical and Marxian categories, see Luiz Carlos Bresser Pereira, *O Colapso de uma Aliança de Classes* (São Paulo: Brasiliense, 1978).

7. The following section draws heavily from: Boris Fausto, "Brazil: The Social and Political Structure of the First Republic, 1889–1930," in *The Cambridge History of Latin America*, vol. 5, ed. Leslie Bethell (Cambridge: Cambridge University Press, 1986); Fernando Henrique Cardoso, "Dos Governos Militares a Prudente—Campos Salles," in *O Brasil Republicano: Estructura de Poder e Economia (1889–1930)*, ed. Boris Fausto (Rio de Janeiro: Editora Bertrand Brasil, 1989); Joseph Love, "Autonomia e Interdependência: São Paulo e a Federação Brasiliera, 1889–1937," in *O Brasil Republicano*, ed. Fausto, and *São Paulo in the Brazilian Federation*. Robert M. Levine, "Pernambuco e a Federação Brasiliera, 1889–1937," in *O Brasil Republicano*, ed. Fausto, and *Pernambuco in the Brazilian Federation, 1889–1937* (Stanford: Stanford University Press, 1978). I have found the most insightful treatments to be those of John Wirth: "Minas e a Nação: Um Estudo de Poder e Dependência Regional, 1889–1937," in *O Brasil Republicano*, ed. Fausto, and *Minas Gerais in the Brazilian Federation, 1889–1937* (Stanford: Stanford University Press, 1977). All acknowledge their debt to the foundational work of Victor Nunes Leal, *Coronelismo, Enxada e Voto*, 2d ed. (São Paulo: Editora Alfa-Omega, 1975).

8. Mauricio A. Font, *Coffee, Contention, and Change in the Making of Modern Brazil* (Oxford: Basil Blackwell, 1990), and Thomas H. Holloway, *Immigrants on the Land: Coffee and Society in São Paulo, 1886–1934* (Chapel Hill: University of North Carolina Press, 1980). See also the data reported in Love, *São Paulo*, p. 17.

9. Each state received 35 votes in the Senate.

10. Throughout this manuscript, I relate the power of groups to their capacity to be pivotal, which in turn is determined by the structure of the institutions in which the political game is played. This capacity has been given a measure by Lloyd Shapley and Martin Shubik, as well as by John Banzhaf; I employ the intuition underlying these measures. See the discussion in Steven J. Brams, *Game Theory and Politics* (New York: Free Press, 1975).

11. See Levine's account of the dramatic eclipse of Rosse e Silva and his political machine in Pernambuco: Levine, *Pernambuco*.

12. Love, *São Paulo*, p. 191.

13. Quoted in Elise Maria de Conceição Pereira Reis, "The Agrarian Roots of Authoritarian Modernization in Brazil, 1880–1930" (Ph.D. diss., Massachusetts Institute of Technology, 1979), p. 180.

14. Quoted in Stephen D. Krasner, "The Politics of Primary Commodities: A Study of Coffee, 1907–1970" (Ph.D. diss., Harvard University, 1971), p. 120.

15. Note how I have denominated the exchange rate as the number of mil-réis per unit of foreign currency. Conventions differ, with some authors allowing this convention and other employing the number of dollars or pence per mil-réis. This confusion permeates the broader trade literature, sometimes with serious consequences. See the discussion of exchange rates in Rudiger Dornbusch and F. Leslie C. H. Helms, eds., *The Open Economy* (New York: Oxford University Press, 1988).

The mil-réis remained the basic unit of Brazil's currency until 1942. Divided into one thousandths, it was replaced by the cruzeiro, which was divided into one-hundredths (the centavo). While the mil-réis provided a measure of prices, monetary and fiscal aggregates were generally measured in contos (de réis), which equaled 1,000 mil-réis. In 1967 Brazil introduced the cruzeiro novo, equal to 1,000 of the old cruzeiros.

Carlos Manuel Paláez provides one of the best discussions of the exchange rate controversy. See his "An Economic Analysis of the Brazilian Coffee Support Program: Theory, Policy and Measurement," in *Essays on Coffee and Economic Development*, ed. Carlos Manuel Paláez (Rio de Janeiro: Instituto Braileiro do Café, 1973). Delfim Netto, *O Problema,* provides another—indeed, the classic—discussion.

16. In his valuable work on the politics of this era, Steven Topik analyzes the politics of coffee policy separately from the politics of monetary policy and the exchange rate. My argument is that tactics deployed to influence the one often were in the service of attempts to alter the other, with the consequence that politics in the two domains must be analyzed simultaneously. See Topik, *The Political Economy.*

17. See the discussion in Wirth, *Minas Gerais,* pp. 45 and 221.

18. Wirth writes: after Minas Gerais's delegates in the legislature lowered freight rates, "Within two years, . . . beans, even rice from Minas, began to displace foreign imports in the Rio market. This was a brilliant use of the states' bargaining power." Wirth, *Minas Gerais,* p. 180.

19. Villela and Suzigan document the decline of food imports following the exchange rate manipulations of 1906. See Annibal V. Villela and Wilson Suzigan, *Government Policy and the Economic Growth of Brazil, 1889–1945* (Rio de Janeiro: IPEA/INPES, 1977), p. 80.

20. See Love, "O Rio Grande do Sul Como Fator de Instabilidade na Républica Velha," in *O Brasil Republicano,* vol. 1, ed. Boris Fausto.

21. Who had accumulated legislative power in part by accumulating satellite delegates through the judicious vetting of their candidates in the Credentials Committee. See Fausto, "O Expansão," pp. 217–18.

22. Wirth, *Minas Gerais,* p. 5.

23. Ibid., p. 30.

24. Ibid. See also Leal, *Coronelismo.*

25. Ibid., p. 177.

26. See W. M. Corden, *Trade Policy and Economic Welfare* (Oxford: Clarendon Press, 1974), and Paul M. Krugman and Maurice Obstfeld, *International Economics* (New York: Harper Collins, 1994).

27. I refer once again to Love, "O Rio Grande do Sul."

28. The valorization of 1906 has been the subject of several studies, most notably Thomas H. Holloway, *The Brazilian Coffee Valorization of 1906* (Madison: The State Historical Society of Wisconsin for the Department of History, University of Wisconsin, 1975). See also Delfim Netto, *O Problema do Café*.

29. Holloway, *The Brazilian Coffee Valorization*, p. 32.

30. The size of the harvest of 1907 remains a surprise, even taking into account the magnitude of the variables determining production behavior. A variety of factors appear to have been at play. As noted by Delfim Netto in chapter 1 of *O Problema do Café* and as amplified by Edmar Bacha and Robert Greenhill (*150 Years of Coffee* [Rio de Janeiro: Marcellino Martins & E. Johnston, 1992], pp. 36ff.), in the late nineteenth century, economic forces promoted an amplifying cycle of production—one that may have culminated in the 1907 harvest. The rapid inflation of the 1890s led to a depreciation of the currency even in a period of large inflows of foreign exchange resulting from large coffee harvests, resulting in positive incentives for further coffee planting.

31. Halloway, *The Brazilian Coffee Valorization*, p. 54.

32. Fausto, "Expansão," p. 217.

33. See Topik, *The Political Economy*, p. 40. It is notable that Campos was from São Paulo and Pena from Minas Gerais. The place of origin thus does not determine policy preferences, as interest-group explanations suggest; "coffee" often did better under non-Paulista presidents, who owed their political positions to the support they received on the margin from the coffee industry. It was "coffee's" ability to build coalitions and to offer pivotal support in maintaining presidents in power that counted.

34. Holloway, *The Brazilian Coffee Valorization*, Appendix, table 4. Brazil's exchange rate policy appears to represent an innovative adaptation to the norms of the gold standard. For a brilliant discussion, see Barry Eichengreen, *Golden Fetters* (New York: Oxford University Press, 1992); see also Giulio Gallarotti, *An Anatomy of an International Monetary Regime* (New York: Oxford University Press, 1995).

35. Delfim Netto, *O Problema do Café*, p. 69.

36. Delfim Netto, *O Problema*, p. 105. Nor was Pessoa from São Paulo; he was from Paraíba. He too illustrates that support at the margin, the ability to be pivotal, is what counted in the game of Brazilian politics. As stated by Topik (*The Political Economy*, p. 46): "Being from a poor, politically insignificant state, [Pessoa] depended on Paulista support to govern. Consequently, the bulk of his program was directed at the demands of the Center-South."

37. Calculated from Bacha and Greenhill, *150 Years*, Appendix, tables 1.1 and 1.2.

38. The average price of coffee imported in the United States' market fell from 19.50 cents per pound in 1920 to 10.7 cents per pound in 1921. Ibid., table 1.8.

39. Fritsch, *External Constraints*, p. 59.

40. Villela and Suzigan, *Government Policy*, p. 88.

41. Ibid., pp. 55 and 88.

42. Fishlow, Suzigan, and others document the expansion of industry and the increased pace of technical change at times in which the domestic currency is overvalued: Albert Fishlow, "Origins and Consequences of Import Substitution in Brazil," in *Industrial Economics and Development*, ed. Luis Eugenio di Marco (New York and

London: Academic Press, 1972); Wilson Suzigan, *Indústria Brasileira: Origen e Desenvolvimento* (São Paulo: Editora Brasilense, 1986). See especially Villela and Suzigan, *Government Policy*, p. 54.

This argument runs directly counter to that of Celso Furtado, *The Economic Growth of Brazil*. More about that below.

43. As is notorious, the most interesting and heated debate in Brazilian historiography turns on the relationship between industry and export agriculture. The discussion in the text barely skims the surface of this debate. In addition to sources noted above, and especially Celso Furtado, *The Economic* Growth, pp. 186 and 191, see Flávia Rabelo Versiani, *A Década de 20 na Industrialização Brasiliera* (Rio de Janeiro: IN-PEA/INPES, 1987). Recent work tends to argue that the rise of coffee promoted the rise of industry; that the agricultural and industrial bourgeoisie therefore possessed a commonality of interests; and that class conflict, rather than sectoral conflict, constitutes the fundamental contradiction of Brazilian politics. See, for example, Caio Prado Junior, *A Revolução Brasileira* (Rio de Janeiro: Editora Brasiliense, 1966). I am indebted to Luiz Carlos Bresser Pereira for his lucid discussion of these themes in conversations we held in June 1993.

44. Eduardo Kugelmas, "'Difícil Hegemonia': Um Estudo Sobre São Paulo Na Primera República" (Tese de Doctorado, Ciénca Política, Universidade de São Paulo, 1986), p. 91. For a useful general overview of the politics of this period, see Peter Flynn, *Brazil: A Political Analysis* (Boulder, Colo.: Westview Press, 1978).

45. Dean, *The Industrialization*, p. 137.

46. Fausto, "Brasil," in *The Cambridge History of Latin America*, vol. 5, p. 815.

47. In addition, the growing presidential aspirations of political leaders from Rio Grande do Sul rendered them increasingly unreliable supporters of the politicians from other states.

48. See the discussion in Dambaugh, "The Coffee Frontier"; Font, *Coffee, Contention, and Change*. See as well the classic: J.W.F. Rowe, *Studies in the Artificial Control of Raw Material Supplies No. 3: Brazilian Coffee* (London: His Majesty's Stationery Office, 1932).

49. See, for example, Maria Lígia Coelho Prado, *A Democracia Ilustrada: O Partido Democrático de São Paulo 1926–1934* (São Paulo: Editora Ática, 1986); Caio Prado Junior, *A Revolução*; Kugelmas, "'Difícil Hegemonia,'" pp. 215ff.

50. See this discussion in Font, *Coffee, Contention, and Change*.

51. Holloway, *Immigrants*, p. 128. As a series of scholars point out, the governing party also used its control over land rights to build a loyal constituency in the frontier regions. Love, *São Paulo*, p. 129; Font, *Coffee, Contention, and Change*, pp. 24ff.

52. Fritsch, *External Constraints*, p. 128; see also Topik, *The Political Economy*, pp. 80ff.

53. See the discussion in Ronato Augusto Frederico, "Brazil: Stabilization of the Exchange Rate and Coffee, 1927–1929" (M.Sc. thesis, Department of History, London School of Economics and Political Science, September 1985), p. 40.

54. The best discussion is contained in Frederico, "Brazil." See also Fritsch, *External Constraints,* and Villela and Suzigan, *Government Policy*.

55. This explanation represents my best effort at unscrambling the accounts presented in Rowe, *The Strategic*; Fritsch, *External Constraints*, pp. 145ff; Frederico, "Brazil"; Font, *Coffee, Contention, and Change*; Delfim Netto, *O Problema do Café*.

See also Mario Rolim Telles, *A Defeza do Café e a Crise Econômica de 1929* (São Paulo: n.p., 1931).

56. Frederico, "Brazil," p. 23.

57. Villela and Suzigan, *Government Policy*, p. 115.

58. Ibid., p. 116.

59. The phrase is that of Delfim Netto, *O Problema do Café*, p. 138.

60. Afonso de E. Taunay, *Historia do Café No Brasil*, vol. 15 (Rio de Janeiro: Departamento Nacional do Café, 1943), p. 60.

61. Delfim Netto, *O Problema do Café*, p. 164.

Chapter 3

1. Quoted in Krasner, "The Politics of Primary Commodities: A Study of Coffee, 1900–1970" (Ph.D. diss., Harvard University, 1971), p. 119.

2. Ibid.

3. Ibid., p. 120.

4. William Paul McGreevey, *An Economic History of Colombia, 1845–1930* (Cambridge: Cambridge University Press, 1971), p. 88.

5. For the foundations of this argument, see Mancur Olson, *The Logic of Collective Action* (Cambridge: Harvard University Press, 1965). See also Robert H. Bates, *Markets and States in Tropical Africa* (Berkeley and Los Angeles: University of California Press, 1981).

6. Robert Carlyle Beyer, "The Colombian Coffee Industry: Origins and Major Trends" (Ph.D. diss., University of Minnesota, 1974), p. 181. Also invaluable is Charles W. Bergquist, *Coffee and Conflict in Colombia, 1886–1910* (Durham: Duke University Press, 1978).

7. For the settlement of the west, see Jane J. Parsons, *Antioqueño Colonization in Western Colombia* (Berkeley and Los Angeles: University of California Press, 1949); Catherine Le Grand, *Frontier Expansion and Peasant Protest in Colombia, 1830–1936* (Albuquerque: University of New Mexico Press, 1986); Frank Safford, *The Ideal of the Practical* (Austin: University of Texas Press, 1976); and Marcos Palacios, *Coffee in Colombia, 1850–1970* (Cambridge: Cambridge University Press, 1960). See as well the contributions in Victor Alvarez, ed., *La Estructura Interna de la Colonizacíon Antioqueña* (Manizales: Biblioteca de Escritorios Caldenses, 1989); Carmenza Saldias, "La Contribucíon del Sector Cafetero al Desarollo Económico y Social de la Región Caldas," Manizales, 1992, typescript; Gonzales Paredes Hernadez y Herman Zambrano Ramirez, "El Café en la Colonización Antioqueño," Bogotá: FNC, 1992, typescript; Gonzales Paredes Hernandez and Hernan Zambrano Ramirez, "El Café en el Desarrollo de las Economías de Vertiente," Medellín: Universidad de Antioquia, 1987, typescript; Gonzalo Paredes Hernandez, "Regionalización de la Zona Cafetera Colombiana," Bogotá: FNC, 1992, typescript; and Jorge Orlando Melo, ed., *Historia de Antioquia* (Bogotá: Editorial Presencia Ltd., 1988).

8. In addition to the histories above, see Luis Ospina Vasquez, *Industria y Protección en Colombia, 1810–1930* (Medellín: FAES, 1987). Among the most illuminating and moving reminiscences are those of Mariano Ospina Pérez, contained in Acta No. 4 de la sesión del día 28 de abril de 1954, pp. 41ff., in XVIII Congreso de Cafeteros, *Actas, Acuerdos, Resoluciones*, Bogotá, 1954.

9. See the discussion in Beyer, "The Colombian Coffee Industry," pp. 97ff.

10. José Antonio Ocampo, "Los Orígenes de la Industria Cafetera, 1830–1929," en *Nueva Historia de Colombia*, vol. 5, ed. Alvaro Tirado Mejía (Bogotá: Planeta, 1969), p. 225.

11. For a fascinating discussion of the special characteristics of Caldas's economy—and therefore of its special political needs—see the comments of Caldas's representatives in Acta No. 2 del día 3 de junio de 1935, p. 2, in *Las Actas, Conferencia Cafetera, Junio de 1935*, archives of the Federación Nacional de Cafeteros. See as well Fernando Urrea, *Mercados de Trabajo y Migraciones en la Explotación Cafetera* (Bogotá: Ministerio de Trabajo y Seguidad Social, 1976).

12. Marco Palacios, *Coffee in Colombia*, pp. 207ff., and Vernon Lee Fluharty, *Dance of the Millions* (Pittsburgh: University of Pittsburgh Press, 1956).

13. Fluharty, *Dance of the Millions*, p. 32.

14. Jesús Antonio Bejarano Avila, "La Economía Colombiana entre 1926 y 1929," in *Nueva Historia de Colombia*, vol. 5, ed. Alvaro Tirado Mejía (Bogotá: Planeta, 1989), p. 55.

15. Miguel Angel Luzano, *Mariano Ospina Pérez* (Bogotá: Fundación Mariano Ospina Pérez, n.d.), p. 36. See also the discussion in Beyer, "The Colombian Coffee Industry," and McGreevey, *An Economic History*.

16. See the discussion in Michale F. Jiménez, "Traveling Far in Grandfather's Car: The Life Cycle of the Central Colombian Coffee Estates," *Hispanic American Historical Review* 69, 2 (1989): 185–219, and "At the Banquet of Civilization: Coffee Plantations and Policies in Early Twentieth Century Colombia," typescript, September 1988; Malcolm Deas, "A Colombian Coffee Estate: Santa Barbara, Cundinamarca, 1870–1912," in *Land and Labor in Latin America*, ed. K. Duncan and I. Rutledge (Cambridge: Cambridge University Press, 1977). See also J. Fred Rippy, "Dawn of the Railway Age in Colombia," *Hispanic American Historical Review* 33, 4 (November 1943): 650–63.

17. See the contributions to Alvaro Tirado Mejía, ed., *Nueva Historia de Colombia* (Bogotá: Planeta, 1989).

18. See the discussion in Jiménez, "Traveling Far," and "At the Banquet"; Deas, "A Colombian Coffee Estate."

19. In addition to the sources noted above, see the contributions of José Antonio Ocampo to *Nueva Historia de Colombia*, ed. Alvaro Tirado Mejía (Bogotá: Planeta, 1989). See as well Catherine Le Grand, "El Conflicto de las Bananeras," en *Nueva Historia de Colombia*, vol. 3, ed. Jorge Orlando Melo (Bogotá: Planeta, 1989). Another classic source is Roberto Junguito Bonnet, ed., "Federación para la Educación Superior y el Desarrollo," *Economía Cafetera Colombiana* (Bogotá: Fondo Cultural Cafetero, n.d.).

20. As written, the process of fragmentation may appear consensual and bloodless. It often was not. The references above review the violent struggle between tenants and landholders that took place in many portions of the central and eastern coffee zones.

21. This account draws heavily on Bennett Eugene Koffman, "The National Federación of Coffee Growers of Colombia" (Ph.D. diss., University of Virginia, 1969), and Junguito, ed., *Economía Cafetera Colombiana*.

22. Federación Nacional de Cafeteros, *Informe del Gerente de la Federación, 1930*, p. 17.

23. Ibid.

24. The levy was raised to 25 cents per bag in 1937. For a discussion of the origins of this institution, see Koffman, "The National Federation," and Ocampo, "Los Orígenes."

25. See the report of the New York representative of the FNC on his discussions with the Green Coffee Association of New York City, July 29, 1930, as excerpted in *Informe Rendido por el Gerente de la Federación, Dr. Mariano Ospina Pérez, Al Sexto Congreso Nacional de Cafeteros Reunido en la Ciudad de Pasto en Junio de 1934*, p. 18.

26. See the debates recorded in ibid.; Federación Nacional de Cafeteros de Colombia, *Actas del Comité Nacional de Cafeteros, 1932*; Conferencia de Delegados de los Comités Departamentales Reunida en Bogotá en el mes de febrero de 1932, *Actas, Acuerdos, Resoluciones*, 1932.

27. For a review of the literature, see Robert H. Bates, "Social Dilemmas and Rational Individuals: An Essay on the New Institutionalism," Working Paper IPR89, Institute for Policy Reform (April 1994). The most notable contribution to this line of argument remains Douglass North, *Institutions, Institutional Change, and Economic Performance* (Cambridge: Cambridge University Press, 1990).

28. For an informative discussion, see the contributions in Barry Eichengreen and Peter H. Lindert, eds., *The International Debt Crisis in Historical Perspective* (Cambridge: MIT Press, 1991). The best discussion is contained in José Antonio Ocampo and Santiago Montenegro, *Crisis Mundial, Protección y Industrialización* (Bogotá: CEREC, 1984).

29. Conferencia de Delegados de los Comités Departamentales Reunida en Bogotá en el Mes de Febrero de 1932, *Actas, Acuerdos y Resoluciones, 1932*, p. 2.

30. Ibid., p. 2. See also the debates in Federación Nacional de Cafeteros, *El Sexto Congreso Nacional de Cafeteros Reunido en la Ciudad de Pasto en Junio de 1934*, and Federación Nacional de Cafeteros, *Actas de Comité Nacional de Cafeteros, 1932*.

31. See the discussion in Jésus Antonio Bejarano Ávila, "La Economía Colombiana." See as well Federación Nacional de Cafeteros de Colombia, *Informe del Gerente de la Federación, 1930*, pp. 21ff.

32. See Germán Zea Hernández, "Proceso de las negociaciones de Colombia para la demarcación y señalamiento de sus fronteras terrestres," in *Nueva Historia Colombiana*, vol. 3, ed. Jorge Orlando Melo (Bogotá: Planeta, 1989).

33. For a description of this campaign, see Richard Stoller, "Alfonso López Pumarejo and Liberal Republicanism in 1930's Colombia" (Paper prepared for the International Congress of the Latin American Studies Association, Miami, Florida, 1989). See as well the speech by Ospina Pérez in Acta No. 6 del día 5 de mayo de 1935, p. 2, in Comité Nacional, *Actas, Acuerdos, Resoluciones 1935*; and Alvaro Tirado Mejía, *Aspectos Políticos del Primer Gobierno de Alfonso López Pumarejo, 1934–1938* (Bogotá: Instituto Colombiano de Cultura, 1981). See also discussions in Christopher Abel, *Política, Iglesia y Partidos en Colombia, 1886–1953* (Bogotá: Universidad Nacional de Colombia, 1987); and Eduardo Zuleta Angel, *El Presidente López Pumarejo* (Bogotá: Ediciones Gama, 1986).

34. As noted in the annual report of the Ministry of Finance:

An advantage of direct taxation is that its operation reminds the citizen that he is not an isolated entity but rather that he lives for and by means of the community and creates and strengthens in him . . . true patriotism. . . . It opens his eyes to a more elevated and noble conception of his own personality, forming in him a conception of his duties to the state. (Republic of Colombia, *Memoria de Hacienda 1935 y 1936*. Bogotá: Editorial Nueva, 1936, p. 33)

35. Alvaro Tirado Mejía, *Aspectos Políticos*, pp. 56–58.
36. Federación Nacional de Cafeteros de Colombia, *Informe de Gerente al Cinquo Congreso Nacional de Cafeteros* (Bogotá: Editorial Minerva, Junio de 1932), pp. 11ff.
37. "Manifiesto del Comité Nacional y la Gerencia de la Federación a los Cafeteros del País," en Federación Nacional de Cafeteros de Colombia, *Informe del Gerente de la Federación al VII Congreso Nacional de Cafeteros Reunido en Bogotá en Septiembre de 1935* (Bogotá: FNC, 1935). The account that follows is largely taken from this source.
38. Federación Nacional de Cafeteros, *Los Actas, Conferencia Cafetera*, Junio de 1935.
39. Some of its most prominent officers were themselves members of the legislature, most notably Mariano Ospina Pérez, who served in the Senate.
40. Federación Nacional de Cafeteros de Colombia, "Manifiesto de Comité Nacional."
41. This account of the battle between the FNC and the government is derived from the archival sources. See Federación Nacional de Cafeteros de Colombia, *VI Congreso Nacional de Cafeteros: Actas, Acuerdos y Resoluciones*, Junio 30 de 1934, and *VII Congreso Nacional de Cafeteros: Actas, Acuerdos, y Resoluciones*, Bogotá, 1935. The most lucid chronicle and analysis of the taxes levied on the coffee sector in this period is contained in José Antonio Ocampo, "La consoildación de la industria cafetera, 1930–1958," in *Nueva Historia de Colombia*, vol. 5, ed. Alvaro Tirado Mejía (Bogotá: Planeta, 1989), pp. 250–52.
42. See the comments of his Minister of Agriculture throughout the sessions of the 1935 Coffee Conference: Federación Nacional de Cafeteros de Colombia, *Los Actas: Conferencia Cafetera, Junio de 1935*.
43. See the analysis in Barry Eichengreen and Marc Uzan, "The 1933 World Economic Conference as an Instance of Failed International Cooperation," University of California, Berkeley, Department of Economics, Working Paper No. 90–149, October 1990. Interesting material is contained as well in Fiona Gordon-Ashworth, *International Commodity Control: A Contemporary History and Appraisal* (New York: St. Martin's Press, 1984).
44. See the discussion of this conference in Eichengreen and Uzan, "The 1933 World Economic Conference." See the discussion of López Pumarejo's views in Acta No. 11 de la sesión del día 2 de octubre de 1935, pp. 7ff., in Federación Nacional de Cafeteros de Colombia, *VII Congreso de Cafeteros: Actas, Acuerdos, y Resoluciones, 13 de Septiembre–10 de Octubre de 1935* (Bogotá: FNC, 1935) . See also his retrospective account of the development of his views in Acta 1 de la sesión del día 20 de junio de 1937, *VIII Congreso Nacional de Cafeteros: Actas, Tomo I, 1937*.
45. Acta No. 5 de la sesión del día 21 de junio de 1933, p. 3, in Federación Nacional de Cafeteros de Colombia, *Actas de las Sesiones de la Conferencia Cafetera Nacional Reunida en el mes de Junio de 1933*.

46. See the reports on Brazil's approach to Colombia in Washington, D.C., Acta No. 14, de la sesión del día 13 de mai de 1935, in Federación Nacional de Cafeteros de Colombia, *Comité Nacional: Actas, Acuerdos, y Resoluciones, 1935*.

47. Acta de la sesión del día 21 de junio de 1935, pp. 1–2, in Federación Nacional de Cafeteros de Colombia, *Los Actas: Conferencia Cafetera, Junio 1935*.

48. Acta No. 20 de la sesión del día 22 de junio de 1935, p. 4, in ibid.

49. Acta. No. 11 de la sesión del día 2 de Octubre de 1935, p. 8, in Federación Nacional de Cafeteros de Colombia, *VII Congreso Nacional de Cafeteros: Actas, Acuerdos, y Resoluciones*.

Alejandro López was a leading publicist of the Liberal movement in Colombia. A long-time resident of London, he had become deeply involved in debates about the Depression and wrote numerous works outlining the implications of these debates for Colombia. His numerous writings included *Problemas Colombianos* (Paris: Editorial Paris-Americana, 1927); *El Café: Desde el Cultivator al Consumidor* (London, 1929); and *El Desarme y La Usura* (London, 1933). See as well Alejandro López, *Obras Selectas* (Bogotá: Cámara de Representantes, 1983).

50. Acta No. 11 de la sesión del día 2 de octubre de 1935, pp. 7–8, en Federación Nacional de Cafeteros de Colombia, *VII Congreso Nacional de Cafeteros: Actas, Acuerdos, y Resoluciones*.

51. For details, see Bennett Eugene Koffman, "The National Federation of Coffee Growers of Colombia" (Ph.D. diss., University of Virginia, 1969).

52. Mariano Ospina Pérez, "Carta al Doctor Alfonso López," Noviembre 15 de 1933, p. 73, in Federación Nacional de Cafeteros, *Informe del Gerente al Sexto Congreso Nacional de Cafeteros, Junio 1934*.

53. Ibid., p. 53.

54. Roberto Londoño Covaleda, *Informe A La Federación Nacional de Cafeteros Sobre la Industria del Café en el Brasil* (São Paulo: n.p., 1933), p. 118

55. Ibid., p. 61.

56. The issue here, of course, is why there was no convergence in the beliefs of the two parties. The answer I offer would appear to be an example of what Fudenberg and Levine call "self-confirming equilibria." The behavior of the coffee producers' representatives on the Comité Nacional was consistent with the government's perceptions of their preferences, thus offering the government no incentive to revise its beliefs about the behavioral propensities of a third actor, Brazil. See Drew Fudenberg and David K. Levine, "Self-Confirming Equlibria," *Econmetrica* 61, 3 (May 1993): 523–47.

57. Federación Nacional de Cafeteros, *Conferencia Americana del Café* (Bogotá: FNC, 1936), typescript. See also Jorge Ramirez Ocampo y Silveria Perez Gomez, *83 Años de Política Cafetera Internacional y la Participación de Colombia en este Proceso* (Bogotá: Federación Nacional de Cafeteros, 1986).

58. Disagreements arose both within and between the Colombian and Brazilian delegations concerning the magnitude of the price band. The Brazilians wanted a margin of 2.5 cents; the Colombians, 1.5. Within Colombia's central committee, there were major differences as well. The representatives of the coffee producers lobbied for a price spread as small as 0.75 cents per pound; in this they were joined by the coffee Congress. The representatives of the government were willing to go as high as 1.5 cents—possibly 2—in order to provide for a "margin of error." Consult Acta No. 9 de la sesión del día 8 de octubre de 1936; Acta No. 20 de la sesión del día 14 de octubre

de 1937, in Federación Nacional de Cafeteros de Colombia, *Las Actas (sesiones secretas) Comité Nacional, 1936 y 1937.*

59. Acta No. 10 de la sesión del día 12 de noviembre 1936, p. 2, in Comité Nacional, Federación Nacional de Cafeteros, *Actas (sesiones secretas) 1936–1942.*

60. Ibid.

61. At 12 cents a pound, 300,000 bags would cost $4.75 million.

62. Acta No. 2 de la sesión del día 28 de enero de 1937, p. 2, in Comité Nacional, Federación Nacional de Cafeteros, *Actas (sesiones secretas) 1936–1942.* It is important to point out here that the loans from the Bank of the Republic were to be guaranteed by an increase in the export tax. A reason for the reluctance of the bank to cover the costs of the intervention was the government's failure to increase this tax. Scholars, such as Ocampo and Montenegro, tend to blame the bank for the collapse of the policy; but blame could just as well be put on the government that failed to provide the finances to back up its interventionist commitments. See José Antonio Ocampo and Santiago Montenegro, *Crisis Mundial, Protección e Industrialización* (Bogotá: CEREC, 1984), pp. 70–71.

63. Acta No. 2 de las sesión del día de 28 de enero de 1937, p. 1, in Comité Nacional, Federación Nacional de Cafeteros, *Actas (sesiones secretas) 1936–1942.*

64. Acta No. 17 de la sesión del día 7 de octubre de 1937, p. 5, in ibid.

65. Acta No. 2 de la sesión del día 28 de enero de 1937, in ibid.

66. Acta No. 4 de la sesión del día 29 de enero de 1937, p. 3, in ibid.

67. Acta No. 5 de la sesión del día 4 de febrero de 1937, p. 3, in ibid.

68. See the deliberations recorded in *Los Actas de la Junta Directiva del Banco de la Republica,* nos. 1037, 1038, 1041, 1056, and 1057, enero–mayo 1937. I am indebted to Fabio Sánchez for access to the transcripts of the meetings of the Junta.

69. Acta No. 1 de la sesión del día 14 de enero de 1937, p. 1, in Comité Nacional, Federación Nacional de Cafeteros, *Actas (sesiones secretas) 1936–1942.*

70. Acta No. 1 de la sesión del día 14 de enero de 1937 and Acta No. 4 de la sesión del día 29 de enero de 1937, in Comité Nacional, Federación Nacional de Cafeteros, *Actas (sesiones secretas) 1936–1942.*

71. Acta No. 9 de la sesión del día 8 de abril de 1937, p. 4, in ibid.

72. Acta No. 4 de la sesión del día 23 junio de 1937, *VIII Congreso Nacional de Cafeteros: Actas, Tomo I.*

73. "Instrucciones para los Delegados," Anexo Reservado, Acta No. 18 de la sesión del día 13 de julio de 1937, *VIII Congreso Nacional de Cafeteros: Actas, Tomo I.*

74. One of the best discussions of this series of incidents is contained in Carlos Lleras Restrepo, *Crónica de mi Propia Vida,* Tomo I (Bogotá: Stamato Editores, 1983), pp. 240–310.

75. Acta No. 19 de la sesión del día 13 de octubre de 1937, p. 1, in Comité Nacional, Federación Nacional de Cafeteros, *Actas (sesiones secretas) 1936–1941.*

76. Marco Palacios, *Coffee in Colombia, 1850–1970* (Cambridge: Cambridge University Press, 1980); Catherine Le Grand, *Frontier Expansion and Peasant Protest in Colombia, 1830–1936* (Albuquerque: University of New Mexico Press, 1986); Absalón Machado, *El Café: De la Aparcería al Capitalismo* (Bogotá: Tercer Mundo Editores, 1988); Mariano Arango, *Café e Industria, 1830–1930* (Bogotá: Carlos Valencia, 1977).

77. See also the evidence provided in José Antonio Ocampo, "La Consolidacción

de la Industria Cafetera, 1930–1958," in *Nueva Historia de Colombia*, vol. 5, ed. Alvaro Tirado Mejía (Bogotá: Planeta, 1989), pp. 236ff.

78. From its inception, the FNC chose as its Managing Director and chief executive someone from Antioquia or from Caldas.

79. The heads of the "state" governments in Colombia were appointed, not elected, as in Brazil. Nor could the departments, as these jurisdictions were known, recruit their own armed forces.

80. Acta 1, p. 6, Federación Nacional de Cafeteros de Colombia, *Informe del Gerente de la Federación* (Bogotá: FNC, Deciembre de 1930).

81. Acta 1, pp. 11–12, Federación Nacional de Cafeteros de Colombia, *Informe del Gerente al Cinco Congreso Nacional de Cafeteros* (Bogotá: FNC, Junio de 1932).

82. Marco Palacios, *Coffee in Colombia, 1850–1970* (Cambridge: Cambridge University Press, 1980), p. 138.

83. One of the best treatments of the electoral data from this period is contained in Patricia Pinzon de Lewin, *Pueblos, Regiones y Partidos: "La Regionalización Electoral"—Atlas Electoral Colombiano* (Bogotá: CEREC, 1989).

84. The best discussion is contained in Charles Bergquist, *Coffee and Conflict in Colombia* (Durham: Duke University Press, 1978).

85. The best analysis of the role of the church in political conflicts in twentieth-century Colombian politics is contained in Christopher Abel, *Política, Iglesia y Partidos en Colombia, 1886–1953* (Bogotá: Universidad Nacional de Colombia, 1987).

86. To posit a single-dimension issue space is to make a very strong assumption, one that determines the validity of much of the following argument. I have therefore taken special care to expose this portion of the argument to criticism by experts on this period in seminars in the United States and Colombia. The balance of the reactions supported the interpretation.

87. See the accounts in Jorge Orlando Melo, ed., *Historia de Antioquia* (Bogotá: Editorial Presence, 1988).

88. Abel, *Política, Iglesia, y Partidos*, p. 85.

89. Bergquist, *Coffee*.

90. See Thomas Tirado, *Alfonso López Pumarejo: El Conciliador* (Bogotá: Planeta, 1986), pp. 83ff.

91. Ibid., p. 84.

92. See, for example, Bates, *Markets and States*. The classic statement remains Karl Marx, *The 18th Brumaire of Luis Bonaparte* (New York: International Publishers, 1975), p. 123.

93. As a measure of the magnitude of the implied political threat, note the reaction of the Minister of Agriculture: "The government regards the Federación as a possible threat . . . it sees the Federación as possessing the power to overthrow it." Acta No. 11 de la sesión del día 2 de octubre de 1935, p. 7, in Federación Nacional de Cafeteros de Colombia, *VII Congreso Nacional de Cafeteros: Actas, Acuerdos, y Resoluciones*.

94. For an elaboration of this theme, see Ashutosh Varshney, *Democracy, Development, and the Countryside* (Cambridge: Cambridge University Press, 1995), and Ashutosh Varshney, ed., *Beyond Urban Bias* (London: Frank Cass, 1993).

95. Ibid.

96. Ministro de Hacienda, *Memoria de Hacienda 1940* (Brazil: Imprimador Nacional, 1940), p. 16.

NOTES TO CHAPTER 4

97. See, for example, Tercera Conferencia Panamericana del Café, *Cuadros Estadísticos Presentados por la Oficina Panamericana del Café* (Nueva York: Junio 1940), typescript from the files of the Federación Nacional de Cafeteros.

98. Jayme Fernandes Guedes, *Brazil Coffee in 1940* (Rio de Janeiro: Departamento Nacional do Café, 1941), pp. 25–26.

According to another source, Carlos Lleras Restrepo (the Minister of Finance), while punishment by Brazil may have been important, so too were the costs of waiting; their rapid growth drove the bargainers into an accord:

> Each country, naturally, hoped to secure the largest quota possible. But as this implied a decrease in the quota of other countries, it was not practicable to satisfy such aspirations. The struggle over quantities caused a considerable delay, a delay that impacted unsatisfactorily on prices. In the end, the necessity of a rapid settlement and the spirit of cooperation among the countries imposed themselves. (Ministro de Hacienda, *Memoria de Hacienda 1941*. Bogotá: Bogotá: Imprimador Nacional, 1941, p. 19)

99. See Acta No. 29 de la sesión del día 19 de Septiembre de 1940, in Federación Nacional de Cafeteros, Comité Nacional, Subcomité Ejecutiva, Gerencia, *Actas, Acuerdos, y Resoluciones*.

100. The best accounts are contained in Carlos Lleras Restrepo, *Política Cafetera, 1937/78* (Bogotá: Osprey Impresores, 1980), pp. 64ff. See also Part 10 of Roberto Junguito, ed., *Economía Cafetera Colombiana*, Bogotá: Fundo Cultural Cafetero. 1977).

Chapter 4

1. José Antonio Ocampo, "La Consolidación de la Industria Cafetera, 1930–1958," in Alvaro Tirado Mejía, ed., *Nueva Historia de Colombia* (Bogotá: Planeta, 1989), p. 236.

2. Ibid., p. 237.

3. One of the best studies of this program is contained in Wilson Ferreira, "Quando O Brasil Quiemo 80 Milhões de Sacas de Café," *Revista do Comércio de Café*, maio 1977, pp. 42–52.

4. See Diego Pizano-Salazar, "La Federación, el Fondo Nacional, y el Desarrollo de la Industria de Colombia," in Federación Nacional de Cafeteros, *II Seminario Sobre Economía Cafetera* (Manizales: Corporacion Autonema Universitaria de Manizales, 1980), p. 25.

5. Phillipe C. Schmitter, *Interest Conflict and Political Change in Brazil* (Stanford: Stanford University Press, 1971), p. 126. The quotation is from Oliveira Viana, *Problemas de Directo Syndical* (n.p., n.d.), n. 44, p. 64.

6. Michael Barzelay, *The Politicized Market Economy: Alcohol in Brazil's Energy Strategy* (Berkeley and Los Angeles: University of California Press, 1986). For a general discussion, see Ben Ross Schneider, "Politics Within the State: Elite Bureaucrats and Industrial Policy in Authoritarian Brazil" (Ph.D. Diss., University of California, Berkeley, 1987).

Similar agencies subsidized the costs and regulated the markets for other crops: wheat, rubber, cotton, and manioc, for example. See the discussion in Schmitter, *Interest Conflict*, p. 146.

To mediate relationships with industrialists in São Paulo, Vargas created the Confederation of Industries; its income came from a tax levied and administered by the government. Nathaniel H. Leff, *Economic Policy-Making and Development in Brazil, 1947–1965* (New York and London: John Wiley and Sons, 1968), p. 117.

7. Details of the crop plan were often published in the commercial press. See, for example, *Revista do Comércio de Café de Rio de Janeiro*, abril–maio 1951.

8. For background, consult the discussions of the monetary council in Thomas J. Trebat, *Brazil's State Owned Enterprises* (Cambridge: Cambridge University Press, 1983), pp. 120ff., and Werner Baer, *Industrialization and Economic Development in Brazil* (Homewood, Ill.: Richard D. Irwin, 1965), pp. 89ff.

9. See the discussion in Sergio Besserman Vanna, "Duas Tentativas de Estabilização: 1951–1954," in *A Orden do Progresso*, ed. Marcelo de Paiva Abreu (Rio de Janeiro: Editora Campus, 1990); Edmar Bacha, *Os Mitos de Uma Década* (Rio de Janeiro: Paz e Terra, 1988); and Fernando D. Homen de Melo and José Honório Accarini, *A Política Econômica e o Setor Agrícola no Brasil de Pós Guerra* (São Paulo: IPE/USP, 1979).

10. The best discussion of the coffee account is contained in Bacha, *Os Mitos*, pp. 140ff.

11. Consulate General, São Paulo to Department of State, Dispatch No. 192, March 8, 1954, file 832.2333/3–854, United States Archives.

12. For a complete list of the major frosts and droughts in Brazil's coffee regions and a rating of their severity, see C. F. Marshall, *The World Coffee Trade* (Cambridge: Woodhead and Faulkner, 1983), p. 42.

13. Following the breakup of the Inter-American Coffee Agreement, the government of Colombia renewed its agreement with the Federación Nacional de Cafeteros, conferring upon it the legal and financial power to regulate exports of coffee. The government of Brazil had not retained the DNC, citing the achievement of "statistical equilibrium" as reason to relax its regulation of coffee markets. In 1951, however, as prices rose, the government re-created the Instituto Brasileiro do Café (IBC) and endowed it with its former powers. The IBC offered a guaranteed minimum price: the higher that price, the greater the incentive for farmers to place their coffee in the stores of the Institute. It offered loans to farmers at terms that made it advantageous for them to store their coffee rather than sell it at prevailing market prices. And it regulated shipments to ports.

14. See the excellent history of policies in this period contained in *Revista do Comércio de Café de Rio de Janeiro*, abril 1955, pp. 8–10. See as well the accounts spread over ibid., abril–maio and junho–julho 1954. See also the analyses of these periods in Sérgio Besserman Vianna, "Duas Tentativas de Estabilização: 1951–1954," in *O Ordem do Progresso*; Edmar Bacha and Robert Greenhill, *150 Years of Coffee* (Rio de Janeiro: Marcellino Martins & R. Johnston, 1992), pp. 66–92; and Edmar Bacha, *Os Mitos de Uma Década*, pp. 161–62.

15. The standard treatments of this period remain Christopher Abel, *Política, Iglesia y Partidos en Colombia* (Bogotá: FAES—Universidad Nacional de Colombia, 1987); Robert H. Dix, *The Politics of Colombia* (New York: Praeger, 1987); and John D. Martz, *Colombia* (Chapel Hill: University of North Carolina Press, 1962).

16. *Semana*, octubre 28–noviembre 2, 1959, p. 12, quoted in Dix, *The Politics of Colombia*, p. 182.

17. Much of the most thoughtful work on the violence in this period is collected or reviewed in Charles Bergquist, Ricardo Peñorada, and Gonzalo Sánchez, *Violence in Colombia* (Wilmington, Del.: Scholarly Resources, 1992).

18. One of the best treatments of this period is contained in Silvia Galvis and Alberto Donadio, *El Jefe Supremo: Rojas Pinilla en la Violencia y el Poder* (Bogotá: Planeta, 1989).

19. *Revista do Comércio de Café de Rio de Janeiro*, maio 1945, pp. 7–9.

20. Ibid., abril 1944, p. 8.

21. The Inter-American Coffee Board, *Fourth Annual Report, 1944–1945* (Washington, D.C.: Inter-American Coffee Board, 1945), p. 65.

22. The Inter-American Coffee Board, *Fifth Annual Report, October 1, 1945, to September 30, 1946* (Washington, D.C.: Inter-American Coffee Board, 1946), pp. 10–14.

23. An example, albeit one taken from a later period, is provided in *Folha de Manha*, a newspaper published in São Paulo, October 22, 1952. The article provides data on the volume of exports by each firm in 1951 and 1952 and records their nationality. Indicative of the political significance of the price of coffee was that the article was deemed of sufficient importance that a summary was transmitted to the U.S. Department of State by the United States' consul in São Paulo. See Foreign Service Dispatch 140, AMCONSULATE GENERAL, São Paulo, to Department of State, in file 833.2333/8–2252,C5/A, United States' Archives.

24. *Who Was Who in America*, vol. 5 (Chicago: Marques's Who's Who, 1973), p. 220.

25. Acta No. 14 de la sesión del día 13 de abril de 1950, p. 2, in Comité Nacional, *Actas, Acuerdos, Resoluciones 1950*.

26. See the summary of the press coverage of Senator Gillette's subcommittee provided in Embassy Telegram No. 1173 to Department of State, December 14, 1949, in file 832.2333/1–2750, United States' Archives.

27. Ibid., p. 2.

28. Ibid., p. 4.

29. Ibid., p. 8.

30. Ibid. For comparison of reports on popular reactions in Colombia, see Department of State to Officer in Charge of American Mission, Bogotá, January 30, 1950, file 821.2333/1–3050, United States' Archives, and Bogotá to Department of State, January 13, 1950, "Reaction in Bogotá to Recommendations of Senator Gillette," June 20, 1950, file 82.2333/6–1350, United States' Archives.

Colombians expressed passions no less intense than those communicated by Brazilians. In discussions at the Department of State, the Colombian ambassador "said that he had been greatly alarmed by the report that legislation is pending in Congress to establish ceilings on coffee prices. He said that if true, this would be almost as disastrous news as a declaration of war." Department of State to Embassy, Bogotá, May 17, 1950, file 821.2333/5–1750, United States' Archives.

31. See the correspondence in file 832.233/4–154, United States' Archives.

32. See the correspondence in file 832.2333/2–1054, United States' Archives.

33. Memorandum, Mr. S. J. Cottrell to Msrs. Cabot, Atwood, and Cale, February 10, 1954, file 832.2333/2–1054, United States' Archives.

34. Memorandum, Mr. Sterling Cottrell to Msrs. Atwood and Bennett, February 4, 1954, file 832.233/2–454, United States' Archives.

35. A detailed account of this period is provided in Peter Flynn, *Brazil: A Political Analysis* (Boulder, Colo.: Westview Press, 1978). The classic treatment remains Thomas Skidmore, *Politics in Brazil, 1930–1964* (New York: Oxford University Press, 1967).

36. A transcript of the letter is contained in Dispatch No. 233, Acting Assistant Secretary to the Honorable Senator J. Glenn Beal, October 12, 1954, file 832.2333/10–1254, United States' Archives.

37. Ibid.

38. Dispatch No. 1118, Consulate General, Rio de Janeiro, to Department of State, January 30, 1951, p. 2, file 832.2333/1–3051, United States' Archives.

39. Dragoslav Avramovic, *El Problema del Café* (Washington, D.C.: Banco Internacional de Reconstrucción y Fomento, 1958), pp. 35–36.
In the seven years following the end of World War II, the number of trees bearing coffee in Paraná increased by 175 percent. Dispatch No. 1118, Consulate General, Rio de Janeiro, to Department of State, January 30, 1951, p. 3, file 832.2333/1–3051, United States' Archives. Surveying the coffee-producing municipalities of Paraná in 1953, one survey found them to be less than five years old. The state as a whole, it was calculated, could produce over 10 million bags of coffee per year, increasing Brazil's exportable production by over one-third! Rafael Parga Cortes, "La Situación Estadística del Café y el Cafetero Colombiano," in *Informe del Gerente de la Federación Nacional de Cafeteros de Colombia* (Bogotá: Federación Nacional de Cafeteros de Colombia, 1954), p. 94.

40. See Michael Sivetz, *Coffee: Origin and Use* (Corvallis, Oreg.: Corvallis Publications, 1977). See also Arthur Cordell, "The Brazilian Soluble Coffee Problem: A Review," *Quarterly Review of Economics and Business* 9, 1 (Spring 1969): 29–38, and the excellent analysis contained in *Revista do Comércio de Café de Rio de Janeiro*, julho 1957, pp. 7–10.

41. Acta No. 6 de la sesión del día 11 de febrero 1954, in Comité Nacional, *Actas, Acuerdos, Resoluciones 1954*. For Brazilian reports on this delegation, see *Revista do Comércio de Café de Rio de Janeiro*, março 1955, p. 8.

42. Insight into the negotiations is offered in Actas No. 37–40 dos meses septiembre hasta octubre 1954, in Comité Nacional, *Actas, Acuerdos, Resoluciones, 1954*.

43. Details of this important meeting are offered in Jerome Levinson and Juan de Onis, *The Alliance that Lost Its Way* (Chicago: Quadrangle Books, 1970), p. 46.

44. See the account in *Revista do Comércio de Café de Rio de Janeiro*, fevereiro 1954, pp. 13–14.

45. "In realty he will act there in the capacity of the representative of the coffee industry," as it was explained in the Comité Nacional. See Acta No. 9 de la sesión del día 13 de marzo de 1958, p. 3, in Comité Nacional, *Actas, Acuerdos, Resoluciones 1958*.

46. See, for example, *Revista do Comércio de Café de Rio de Janeiro*, augusto 1957, pp. 7–8.

47. AmEmbassy, Bogotá, to Department Of State, Dispatch 341, November 6 1958, file 821.2333/11–658, United States' Archives.

48. As stated by Fishlow, Kubitschek's "stabilization program failed in large part because of coffee policy. . . . The acquisition of coffee stocks in the second half of 1959 far in excess of the receipts of the coffee export tax led to greater monetary

expansion." Albert Fishlow, "Some Reflections on Post-1964 Brazilian Economic Policy," in *Authoritarian Brazil*, ed. Alfred Stepan (New Haven and London: Yale University Press, 1973), p. 75. As shown in the work of Díaz-Alejandro, the government of Colombia encountered similar difficulties. See Carlos F. Díaz-Alejandro, *Colombia* (New York and London: Colombia University Press, 1976), pp. 21ff.

49. Acta No. 20 de la sesión del día 25 de mayo de 1961, p. 5, in Comité Nacional, *Actas, Acuerdos, Resoluciones 1961, Vol. I.*

50. Ibid., p. 6.

51. See Robert Putnam, "Diplomacy and Domestic Politics," *International Organization* 42, 3 (Summer 1988): 427–60.

52. See Peter Gourevitch, "The Second Image Reversed: The International Sources of Domestic Relations," *International Organization* 32, 4 (August 1978): 881–911.

53. Kubitschek was president of Brazil 1956–1961.

54. Quotes in AMEMBASSY, Rio de Janeiro, Dispatch 596, to Department of State, November 4, 1955, p. 1, file 832.00/11–455, United States' Archives.

55. See the analyses in Luiz Ornstein and Antonio Claudio Sochaczewski, "Democracia Con Desenvolvimento: 1956–1962," in *A Ordem do Progresso*, ed. Marcelo de Paiva Abreu. See also Barbara Geddes, "Building 'State' Autonomy in Brazil, 1930–1964," in *Comparative Politics* 22 (1990): 217–35, and the discussions of BNDE contained in Schneider, "Politics Within the State," and Trebat, *Brazil's State Owned Enterprises.*

56. Skidmore, *Politics*, p. 170.

57. Schneider, "Politics Within the State," pp. 601–02.

58. From an account of the demonstration reported in AMCONGEN, São Paulo, to Department of State, Dispatch No. 225, November 12, 1958, file 832.2333/11–1253, United States' Archives. See also Telegram, Curtiba to Secretary of State, October 18, 1958, file 832.2333/10–1753, United States' Archives. As revealed in these accounts, the Minister of Defense characterized the march as subversive, dispatched troops, and suppressed it.

59. AMCONGEN, São Paulo, to Department of State, Dispatch No. 474, June 26, 1958, file 832.2233/6–2658, United States' Archives.

60. Albert Fishlow, "Origins and Consequences of Import Substitution in Brazil," in Luis Eugenio di Marco, *International Economics and Development* (New York and London: Academic Press, 1972), p. 345.

61. Excellent discussions of the structure and forms of protection are contained in Werner Baer, *Industrialization and Economic Development in Brazil* (Homewood, Ill.: Richard D. Irwin, 1965), and Nathaniel Leff, *Economic Policy Making and Development in Brazil, 1947–1964* (New York and London: John Wiley and Sons, 1968).

62. See Albert Berry, *Essays on Industrialization in Colombia* (Tempe: Arizona State University Press, 1983); Richard R. Nelson, T. Paul Schultz, and Robert L. Slighton, *Structural Change in a Developing Economy* (Princeton: Princeton University Press, 1971); Carlos F. Díaz-Alejandro, *Colombia* (New York and London: Columbia University Press, 1976); and José Antonio Ocampo, "Ciclo Cafetero y Comportamiento Macroeconómico en Colombia, 1940–1987," *Coyuntura Económica* 19 (3 octubre de 1989): 125–47, and 19, 4 (deciembre de 1989): 147–87.

63. John D. Martz, *Colombia: A Contemporary Political Survey* (Chapel Hill: University of North Carolina Press, 1962), pp. 224ff.

64. The best account remains Silvia Galvis and Alberto Donadio, *El Jefe Supremo* (Bogotá: Planeta, 1988). See also Tad Szulc, *The Twilight of the Tyrants* (New York: Henry Holt and Company, 1957); Martz, *Colombia*.

65. For details of these arrangements, see Jonathan Hartlyn, *The Politics of Coalition in Colombia* (Cambridge: Cambridge University Press, 1988); Jonathan Hartlyn, "Presidentialism and Colombian Politics," in *The Failure of Presidential Democracy: The Latin American Experience*, ed. Juan Linz and Arturo Valenzuela (Baltimore: Johns Hopkins University Press, 1994); and R. Albert Berry, Ronald G. Hellman, and Mauricio Salaúm, T*he Politics of Compromise: Coalition Government in Colombia* (New Brunswick, N. J.: Transaction Books, 1980).

66. See the history of taxes contained in Federación Nacional de Cafeteros, *Boletín de Información Estadística Sobre Café* (Bogotá: FNC, 1989), pp. 172–84; José Antonio Ocampo, "Ciclo Cafetero"; Federación Nacional de Cafeteros, "Contratos Existentes Entre la Federación Nacional de Cafeteros y El Gobierno Nacional," typescript, 28 de julio 1978, archives of the Departmental Committee of Caldas; Fernando Chavarro Miranda, *Política Monetaria, 1947–1958* (Bogotá: Siglo Ventiuno Editora, n.d.); and Robert M. Bird, "Coffee Tax Policy in Colombia," *Inter-American Economic Affairs*, 22 No. 1 (1968): 75–86.

67. U.S. Embassy, Bogotá to Department of State, Dispatch No. 953, June 4 1988, file 821.2333/6–458, United States' Archives.

68. U.S. Embassy, Bogotá, to Department of State, Dispatch No. 1006, June 4 1958, file 821.2333/6–458, United States' Archives.

69. Acta No. 11 de la sesión del día 20 de marzo de 1958, p. 3, in Comité Nacional, *Actas, Acuerdos, Resoluciones 1958*.

70. Ibid., p. 4.

71. Acta No. 9 de la sesión de clausura del día 20 de octubre de 1958, p. 2, in Federación Nacional de Cafeteros, XX Congreso Nacional de Cafeteros, 1958, *Actas, Acuerdos Resoluciones*.

72. Comité de Cafeteros de Caldas, Acta No. 38, septiembre 16 1958, p. 1.

73. Comité de Cafeteros de Caldas, Acta No. 8, 10 de mayo de 1958.

74. Ibid.

75. Comité de Cafeteros de Caldas, Acta No. 34, 22 agosto 1958, p. 1.

76. Acta 5a, sesión vespertina, octubre 5 de 1959, p. 14, in Federación Nacional de Cafeteros, XXI Congreso Nacional de Cafeteros, 1959, *Actas, Acuerdos, Resoluciones*.

77. Ibid.

78. Ibid., p. 20.

Chapter 5

1. Kenneth N. Waltz, "Political Structures," in *Neorealism and Its Critics*, ed. Robert O. Keohane (New York: Colombia University Press, 1986), p. 88. The chapter is excised from Kenneth N. Waltz, *Theory of International Politics* (Reading, Mass.: Addison-Wesley, 1979).

2. See Robert Axelrod and Robert O. Keohane, "Achieving Cooperation Under Anarchy: Strategies and Institutions," *World Politics* 38 (October 1985): 226–53.

3. With all due apologies to the coffee producers of Hawaii, who represent less than 1 percent of the world's total output of coffee.

4. For a superb recent treatment of these issues, see Jane Gowa, *Alliances, Adversaries, and International Trade* (Princeton: Princeton University Press, 1994).

5. As noted in the deliberations of the Comité Nacional of the Federación Nacional de Cafeteros de Colombia, "there could . . . be no interest nor any participation whatsoever of the leading consuming nations unless the problem were a grave political problem, not economic." Acta No. 1 de la sesión de instalación, octubre 23 de 1961, p. 6, in *XXII Congreso Nacional de Cafeteros, 1961*.

6. Ibid., p. 6.

7. See the account in Stephen J. Randall, *Colombia and the United States* (Athens and London: University of Georgia Press, 1992), p. 189.

8. See the untitled memorandum linking the Czech embassy in Cuba to the Bogatazo—the name given to the 1948 burning of Bogotá—in the possession of the Ospina family. See as well the review of the program of the Communist Party in Brazil in Telegram, Rio de Janeiro, to Secretary of State, January 4 1954, file 732.001/1–454, United States' Archives.

9. See the discussion in Cole Blasier, *The Hovering Giant* (Pittsburgh, Pa.: University of Pittsburgh Press, 1976).

10. See the discussion in Jerome Levinson and Juan de Onís, *The Alliance that Lost Its Way* (Chicago: Quadrangle Books, 1970), pp. 38–40.

11. A classic presentation of this argument is Graham T. Allison, *Essence of Decision* (Boston: Little, Brown, 1971). I offer here a reinterpretation, based upon the new institutionalism, as originally applied to the United States' Congress. I interpret the President as an agenda setter, with bureaucracies occupying the role of committees with monopoly jurisdictions and "outlier" preferences over particular policy dimensions. For a succinct and lucid presentation of this approach, see the contributions in Mathew D. McCubbins and Terry Sullivan, *Congress: Structure and Policy* (Cambridge: Cambridge University Press, 1987).

12. As described by Bruchey, drawing on his interviews with policymakers of that period: "In the early sixties, [Secretary of the Treasury George] Humphrey would be remembered as having abhorred commodity agreements so much that he would not allow that they be discussed in his presence." Stuart Bruchey, *American Business and Foreign Policy* (New York and London: Garland Publishing, 1987), p. 100. In a review of United States' policy in this period, the director of the Office of Inter-American and Regional Economic Affairs explained: "If the United States were to become associated . . . with men who . . . were operating a coffee cartel, it would be very difficult to persuade the American public that our membership was in the public interest." Director, Office of Inter-American Regional Economic Affairs to United States' Ambassador, La Paz, April 23, 1957, file 398.2331/8–255, United States' Archives.

13. It is notable that Nixon had come out in support of an international coffee agreement among producing nations as early as 1955. Acta No. 8 de la sesión del día de 24 de febrero de 1955, p. 2, in Comité Nacional, *Actas, Acuerdos, Resoluciones 1955*. See also interview with Thomas C. Mann by Marlyn P. Burg, Oral History, December 17, 1875, for the Dwight D. Eisenhower Library. The change was made easier, of course, by George Humphrey's departure from the Eisenhower Cabinet in 1957. See also R. Harrison Wagner, *United States Policy Toward Latin America* (Stanford: Stanford University Press, 1970).

As stressed by Skidmore, Vargas deeply feared being outcompeted from the Left, thus in part accounting for his "passionate crusade to ensure Brazil's 'emancipation' from the status of a 'colonial economy.'" Thomas E. Skidmore, *Politics in Brazil, 1930–1964* (New York: Oxford University Press, 1967), p. 97.

14. Two of the best discussions are contained in Alfred Stepan, *The Military in Politics: Changing Patterns in Brazil* (Princeton: Princeton University Press, 1971), and John W. F. Dulles, *Unrest in Brazil: Political-Military Crises, 1955–1964* (Austin and London: University of Texas Press, 1970). Both offer insights into the "official mind" of United States' policymakers.

15. Levinson and de Onís, *The Alliance*, p. 88. At the time, the United States' aid program in Brazil ranked as its fourth largest, lagging only behind its programs in Egypt, Pakistan, and Vietnam. Albert Fishlow, "Some Reflections on Post-1964 Brazilian Economic Policy," in Alfred Stepan, ed., *Authoritarian Brazil* (New Haven and London: Yale University Press, 1973), p. 83.

16. Peter Flynn, *Brazil* (Boulder, Colo.: Westview Press, 1978), p. 212.

17. See, in particular, Stephen D. Krasner, "The Politics of Primary Commodities: A Study of Coffee, 1900–1970" (Ph.D. diss., Harvard University, 1971), and "Business-Government Relations: The Case of the International Coffee Agreement," *International Organization* 27, 4 (Autumn 1973): 495–516. For his broader argument, see Stephen D. Krasner, *Defending the National Interest: Raw Materials Investments and U.S. Foreign Policy* (Princeton: Princeton University Press, 1978).

18. Levinson and de Onís, *The Alliance*, p. 63.

19. Quoted in Samuel E. Stavitsky, *Thirty-four Years of U.S. Coffee History* (Washington, D.C.: World Coffee Information Services, April 21, 1974), p. 20. Stavitsky and his "service" were the registered lobbyists for the coffee-producing nations. In this and other reports he documents the campaign mounted on behalf of the coffee agreement. See also the valuable documentation in World Coffee Information Center, *U.S. Support for Coffee Pact: The Development of Public Understanding for U.S. Senate Ratification of the International Coffee Agreement* (Washington, D.C.: World Coffee Information Center, 1963), and *Coffee: Economic Impact* (Washington, D.C.: World Coffee Information Center, 1970).

20. Acta No. 10 de la sesión del día 27 de fevereiro de 1964, pp. 1–2, in Comité Nacional, *Actas, Acuerdos, Resoluciones 1964*, vol. 1.

21. Lisa Martin also focuses on the role of Congress in foreign policy-making, although from a different perspective. See Lisa L. Martin, *Domestic Commitments: Legislatures and International Cooperation*, typescript, Harvard University, 1995.

22. Not yet in opposition to United States' intervention abroad.

23. U.S. Congress, Senate, Committee on Foreign Relations, *Brazil and United States Policies: Report of a Study Mission to Several of the American Republics*, 87th Congress, 2d Session, 1962.

24. Bruchey, *American Business*, p. 193.

25. Acta No. 22 de la sesión del día 12 de agosto, p. 4, in Comité Nacional, *Actas, Enero–Junio 1963*.

26. See the account in Acta No. 33 de la sesión del día 20 de agosto, in Comité Nacional, *Actas, Vol. II, Mayo–Septiembre 1964*.

27. With the exception of a very small crop in Hawaii, as noted above.

28. See Harvard Business School, *United States National Coffee Market* (Cambridge: Harvard University press, 1984), and International Coffee Organization, *Cof-*

fee Drinking Study, Winter 1987 (London: International Coffee Organization, 1987).

29. See the descriptions in Harvard Business School, *United States National Coffee Market*.

30. Ibid.

31. See John C. Hilke and Philip B. Nelson, "Strategic Behavior and Attempted Monopolization: The Coffee (General Foods) Case," in John E. Kwoka and Laurence J. White, *The Antitrust Revolution* (New York: Scott Foresman, 1989).

32. Frank M. Gallop and Mark J. Roberts, "Firm Interdependence in Oligopolistic Markets," *Journal of Econometrics* 10 (1979): 313–31.

33. Ibid., p. 326.

34. C. F. Marshall offers insight into the complex and fascinating commercial practices that prevail in the world of coffee. See C. F. Marshall, *The World Coffee Trade* (Cambridge: Woodhead and Faulkner, 1983). Stephen D. Krasner, "The Politics of Primary Commodities," and "Business-Government Relations," remain the standard treatments of the political role of the roasting companies. See also Bruchey, *American Business*.

35. See, for example, the correspondence between Mr. Edward Aborn, president of the National Coffee Association, and the Secretary of State, contained in file 821.2333/1–1653, United States' Archives.

36. See the discussion in Bruchey, *American Business*, pp. 103ff. Important insights into the politics of this period are also contained in Bart Fisher, *The International Coffee Agreement: A Study in Coffee Diplomacy* (New York: Praeger, 1972).

37. The National Coffee Association holds an annual conference in Boca Raton, Florida, to which it invites government officials from the United States and abroad.

38. The organization of the coffee study group is contained in file 398.2333/2–1955, United States' Archives.

39. Bruchey, *American Business*, pp. 163–64.

40. For example: United States Congress, Senate, Committee on Foreign Relations, 88th Congress, 1st Sess., *On Executive H*, 87th Congress, 2d Sess., International Coffee Agreement, 1962, 1963. United States Congress, Committee on Foreign Relations, 90th Congress, 2d Sess., *International Coffee Agreement: Hearings before the Committee on Foreign Relations, 90th Cong., 2d Sess., On Executive D, 90th Cong., 2d Sess.*, 1968. U.S. Congress, Senate Committee on Finance, 88th Cong., 2d Session, Coffee— *Hearings on H.R.8864*, February 25–27, 1964, and Report No. 941, *Report on the International Coffee Agreement Act of 1963*, 1963. See also United States Congress, Congressional Record, vol. 110, p. 17572, "Impact of Consumer Price Increase." United States Congress, Senate, Committee on Finance, 89th Congress, 1st Sess., *Coffee Agreement, Hearings on S701*, January 27, 1965. United States Congress, House of Representatives, 90th Cong., 2d Sess., *Report No. 1704, International Coffee Agreement Act of July 1968*, July 1968. See as well the discussion in Fisher, *The International*; Krasner, *The Politics*. The most lucid critic of United States' entry into the International Coffee Agreement was, of course, Senator Paul Douglas.

The line of argument advanced here represents, of course, an amendment to the arguments advanced in Theodore Lowi, *The End of Liberalism* (New York: W. W. Norton, 1979), and Grant O'Connell, *Private Power and American Democracy* (New York: Knopf, 1960).

41. Under the agreement, Brazil limited its exports of green coffee, thereby raising its price in international markets. The government then sold the coffee it withheld from export to domestic manufacturers of soluble coffee, who then exported that processed coffee to the United States at the low prices resulting from the abundance of coffee in Brazil's domestic market. United States' producers of solubles bought their coffee at the higher international price, and Brazil's exports were therefore able to undercut them in the United States' market. General Foods got the House Ways and Means Committee to suspend the agreement until Brazil changed its export policies. See Arthur Cordell, "The Brazilian Soluble Coffee Problem: A Review," *Quarterly Review of Economics and Business* 9, 1 (Spring 1969): 29–38.

42. Bruchey, *American Business*, p. 202.

43. The modern version of this literature is contained in R. Douglas Arnold, *Congress and the Bureaucracy* (New Haven and London: Yale University Press, 1979); Morris P. Fiorina, *Congress: Keystone of the Washington Establishment* (New Haven: Yale University Press, 1989); and John A. Ferejohn, *Pork Barrel Politics* (Stanford: Stanford University Press, 1974).

Clearly, however, I am using an informational, rather than a distributive politics, approach to the study of Congress. See Keith Krebhiel, *Information and Legislative Organization* (Ann Arbor: University of Michigan Press, 1991); D. Roderick Kiewiet and Mathew McCubbins, *The Logic of Delegation* (Chicago: University of Chicago Press, 1991). See also Thomas Gilligan and Keith Krebhiel, "Asymmetric Information and Legislative Rules with Heterogeneous Committees," *American Journal of Political Science* 33(1989): 459–90, and Helen Milner and B. Peter Rosendorf, "Divided Government and International Cooperation: A Signaling Model" (Paper presented for the American Political Science Association, Annual Meetings, Washington, D.C., September 2–5, 1993).

Chapter 6

1. The classic remains Stephen D. Krasner, ed., *International Regimes* (Ithaca: Cornell University Press, 1983).

2. Indeed, the recognition of the significance of nonstate actors antedated, and helped to spark interest in, the study of regimes. See Robert O. Keohane and Joseph Nye, *Power and Interdependence* (Boston: Little, Brown, 1977).

3. For the entire definition of a regime, see Stephen D. Krasner, "Structural Causes and Regime Consequences: Regimes as Intervening Variables," in *International Regimes*, ed. Krasner, p. 2.

4. The best overview remains Stephen Haggard and Beth A. Simmons, "Theories of International Regimes," *International Organization* 41, 3 (Summer 1987): 491–517.

5. Robert O. Keohane, *After Hegemony* (Princeton: Princeton University Press, 1984).

6. The best statement is Stephen D. Krasner, "Global Communications and National Power: Life on the Pareto Frontier," *World Politics* 43, 3 (April 1991): 336–66.

7. This is the core of the logic behind the hypothesis of hegemonic behavior. See David A. Baldwin, ed., *Key Concepts in International Political Economy*, vol. 1 (Aldershot, U.K.: Edward Elgar Publishing Co., 1993). For a game theoretic formulation,

see Mancur Olson, *The Logic of Collective Action* (Cambridge: Harvard University Press, 1965).

8. Drew Fudenberg and Eric Maskin, "The Folk Theorem in Repeated Games with Discounting or with Incomplete Information," *Econometrica* 54, 3 (May 1986): 533–54.

9. See Eric Van Damme, *Stability and Perfection of Nash Equlibria* (New York: Springer-Verlag, 1987).

10. See the important contribution of Beth V. Yarbrough and Robert M. Yarbrough, *Cooperation and Governance in International Trade* (Princeton: Princeton University Press, 1992).

11. For an analogous set of studies, see the recent literature on the European community. Examples would include Robert O. Keohane and Stanley Hoffman, eds., *The New European Community* (Boulder, Colo.: Westview, 1991), and especially the chapter by Andrew Moravcsik entitled "Negotiating the Single European Act." See also the debates in *International Organization* between Geoffrey Garrett and Anne-Marie Slaughter and Walter Mattli: Geoffrey Garrett, "International Cooperation and International Choice," *International Organization* 46 (Spring 1992): 533–56 and "The Politics of Legal Integration in the European Union," *International Organization* 49 (Winter 1995): 171–81; Anne-Marie Burley and Walter Mattli, "Europe Before the Court," *International Organization* 47 (Winter 1993): 41–76 and Walter Mattli and Anne-Marie Slaughter, "Law and Politics in Europe," *International Organization* 49 (Winter 1995): 183–90.

See also Wayne Sandholtz and John Zysman, "1992: Recasting the European Bargain," *World Politics* 42 (October 1989): 95–128, and Wayne Sandholtz, "Monetary Politics and Mastricht," *International Organization* 8 (Winter 1992): 1–40. Lastly, consult the special issue of *Economics and Politics* 5 (July 1993).

12. See James M. Buchanan and Gorden Tullock, *The Calculus of Consent* (Ann Arbor: University of Michigan Press, 1962).

13. More accurately, proportionately to their quota, which was itself based on historical market shares (see below).

14. The best analysis of the voting rules is contained in a memorandum forwarded to headquarters by Colombia's permanent representative to the International Coffee Agreement. See Delegación Permanente, Memo No. 005, febrero 14 1975, in Convenio International del Café, *Copiador Memorandos, 1975*. See also Bart S. Fisher, *The International Coffee Agreement* (New York: Praeger, 1975), p. 66.

15. Delegación Permanente ante la Organización International del Café Para Gerencia General, Federación Nacional de Cafeteros, enero 19 de 1976, Annexo 1: Votos, p. 3. See as well Delegación Permanente, Memo No. 005, febrero 14, 1975, in Convenio International del Café, *Copiador Memorandas, 1975*; Bart S. Fisher, *The International Coffee Agreement* (New York: Praeger, 1975), p. 66.

16. Acta No. 21 de la sesión del día 24 de marzo de 1962, p. 5, in Comité Nacional, *Actas, Acuerdos, Resoluciones 1962*.

17. Ibid.

18. See discussions in Memorandum, octubre 9 de 1963, and marzo 9 de 1964, Comisión International del Café, *Copiador Memorandos, 1963–1964*.

19. Memorandum No. 12, p. 3, in Convenio International del Café, *Copiador Memorandos, 1970–71*.

20. ICO, "Rules for the Application of Certificates of Origin When Quotas Are in Effect," EB-1628/78 Rev. 2, January 1987.

21. Memorandum No. 013, abril 26 de 1972, in Convenio International del Café, *Copiador Memorandos, 1972–73.*

22. Memorandum No. 039, deciembre 20 de 1974, p. 6, in Convenio International del Café, *Copiador Memorandos, 1974.* See also International Coffee Organization, "Rules: Composite Indicator Price, 1979," EB-1956/81 (E) Rev. 1, 20 July 1982.

23. See, for example, Memorandum 008, 29 noviembre de 1966, p. 3, in Convenio International del Café, *Copiador Memorandos, 1964–1966.*

24. Whom, through the Executive Board, they hired, fired, and superintended.

25. Through our study of monitoring, we thus gain further insight into the relationship between the notions of domination and "rational legality" in the literature on bureaucratic organization. See, for example, H. H. Gerth and C. Wright Mills, *From Max Weber: Essays in Sociology* (New York: Oxford University Press, 1958).

26. It can be seen that the United States was in fact entitled to 529 votes: (5 + (905 × .5793) = 529). Other countries were not willing to take part in an agreement in which a single member held such a preponderance of votes. The rule was therefore adopted that no country could control an excess of 400 votes. Given that this number of votes still conferred veto powers, the United States was willing to abide by this modification of the rules.

27. See, for example, the discussion in Memorandum, noviembre 16 de 1965, pp. 6–7, in Convenio International del Café, *Copiador Memorandos, 1964–1966.* For additional examples of effective enforcement, see *Wall Street Journal,* 14 November and 5 December 1983.

28. Acta No. 15 de la sesión del día 28 de abril, p. 11, in Comité Nacional, *Actas, Acuerdos, Resoluciones,* vol. 1, enero–abril 1966.

29. Details are contained in Memorandum, noviembre 16 de 1965, Convenio International del Café, *Copiador Memorandos, 1964–1966.* This ruse was used to ship robusta coffees to the United States' market as well.

30. See, for example, Antônio Delfim Netto and Carlos Alberto de Andrade Pinto, *O Café Do Brasil,* Estudos ANPES No. 3 (São Paulo: ANPES, 1967).

31. Which runs October 1 to September 30.

32. Memorandum No. 007, abril 14 de 1970, p. 3, in Convenio International del Café, *Copiador Memorandos, 1970–71.*

33. Memorandum, abril 2 de 1965, pp. 6–7, Convenio International del Café, *Copiador Memorandos, 1964–1966.*

34. Memorandum, abril 6 de 1966, Convenio International del Café, *Copiador Memorandos, 1964–1966.*

35. Expenditures from the fund were to be repaid from export taxes, thereby protecting the aid agencies against charges that taxpayer dollars were being spent to assist producers in their efforts to raise the price of coffee to United States' consumers. Acta No. 1 de la sesión del día 4 de enero de 1961, in Comité Nacional, *Actas, Acuerdos, Resoluciones,* 1962.

36. Acta No. 5 de la sesión del día 7 de febrero de 1963, p. 3, in Comité Nacional, *Actas, Acuerdos, Resoluciones,* vol. I, enero–junio 1963.

37. One of the clearest expressions of this fear is to be found in Acta No. 4a, sesión

secreta del día 26 de octubre de 1961, pp. 8ff., in Comité Nacional, XXII Congresso Nacional de Cafeteros, *Los Actas*, 1961.

38. Edmar Bacha and Robert Greenhill, *150 Years of Coffee* (Rio de Janeiro: Marcellino Martins and E. Johnston, 1993), Appendix, table 1.2.

39. The classic model of the noncooperative sources of collusive behavior is Edward Green and Robert Porter, "Non-cooperative Collusion Under Imperfect Price Information," *Econometrica* 52 (1984):87–100. For an application to the coffee market, see Amy Farmer Curry, "Essays in Applied Micoeconomic Theory: Cartel Stability, Followers' Gains from Leadership Strategies, and Voting Over Independent Attributes" (Ph.D. diss., Duke University, 1991).

40. Acta No. 18 de la sesión del día 12 de mayo de 1960, p. 4, in Comité Nacional, *Actas, Acuerdos, Resoluciones 1960*.

41. Acta No. 8 de la sesión del 25 día de febrero de 1960, p. 7, in Comité Nacional, *Actas, Acuerdos, Resoluciones, 1960*.

42. Citations to specific threats would include Acta No. 10 de la sesión del día 10 de marzo de 1960, p. 4; Acta No. 14 de la sesión del día 7 de abril de 1960, p. 6, in Comité Nacional, *Actas, Acuerdos, Resoluciones 1960*. Acta No. 15 de la sesión del día 18 de abril de 1961, p. 2, in Comité Nacional, *Actas, Acuerdos, Resoluciones*, vol. 1, 1961. Acta No. 13 de la sesión del día 14 de abril de 1966, in Comité Nacional, *Actas, Acuerdos, Resoluciones*, Vol. I, enero–abril 1966; Memorandum, septiembre 1 de 1971, pp. 9ff., in Convenio International del Café, *Copiador Memorandos, 1970–71*; and Memorandum, 8 septiembre de 1966, p. 10, in Convenio International del Café, *Copiador Memorandos, 1964–1966*.

I cite the following instance:

A Brazilian source indicated that Brazil would be liable to launch a price war if her program for stabilizing the world market was not approved. This information produced an enormous impact, in spite of it being illogical to announce in advance one's determination to undertake such an action, as it would probably cause a paralysis in sales until it was acted upon. (Acta No. 10 de la sesión del día 4 de marzo de 1965, p. 2, in Comité Nacional, *Actas, Acuerdos, Resoluciones*, vol. 1, enero–abril 1965)

43. This and the following discussion are based on a series of memoranda written by the Colombian representative to the ICO, Hernán Jaramillo Ocampo, the most probing of which is Memorandum, noviembre 26 de 1965, Convenio International del Café, *Copiador Memorandos, 1964–66*.

44. Ethiopia's coffees are classified along with Brazil's as unwashed arabicas. And coffee from Kenya and the Kilimanjaro region of Tanzania were classified as Colombian milds. But the dominant producers accounted for more than 85 percent of the exports in each instance.

45. So constant was the presence of Robbins that I failed to record each notice of his arrival. For a Brazilian example, see the coverage given his 1948 visit in *Revista do Comércio de Café de Rio de Janeiro*, fevereiro e março 1948. For examples from Colombia, see Actas No. 38, 42, 43. 44, 30 de octubre–18 de deciembre de 1952, in Comité Nacional, *Actas, Acuerdos, Resoluciones 1952*. See as well records of the visit of his successor, Paul Keating, to Manizales, in Federación Nacional de Cafeteros, *II*

Seminario Sobre Economía Cafetera (Manizales: Corporación Autonema Universiatria de Manizales, 1980).

46. This account is drawn from Federación Nacional de Cafeteros, Comité Nacional, *Actas II, Julio–Deciembre 1963*.

47. See the transcripts of the meetings in ibid.

48. Acta No. 4 de la sesión del día 28 de enero de 1960 and Acta No. 18 de la sesión del día 12 de mayo de 1965, in Comité Nacional, *Actas, Acuerdos, Resoluciones 1960 and 1965*.

49. See John Sutton, *Sunk Costs and Market Structure: Price Competition, Advertising, and the Evolution of Competition* (Cambridge: MIT Press, 1991), and John C. Hilke and Philip B. Nelson, "Strategic Behavior and Attempted Monopolization: The Coffee (General Foods) Case," in John C. Kwoka and Laurence J. White, eds., *The Antitrust Revolution* (New York: Scott Foresman, 1989).

50. The situation most clearly resembles the Penington case. See Oliver E. Williamson, "Wage Rates as Barriers to Entry: The Penington Case in Perspective," *Quarterly Journal of Economics* 83, 1 (February 1968): 85–116. The impact of the industry-wide shift in the costs of production upon competitors in the industry is magnified in this instance by the rebates. See as well Steven C. Salop and David T. Scheffman, "Raising Rivals' Costs," *American Economic Review* 72, 2 (May 1983): 267–71.

51. Acta No. 16 de la sesión del día 11 de mayo de 1967, p. 6, in Comité Nacional, *Actas, Acuerdos, Resoluciones*, vol. 2, mayo–agosto 1967.

52. October 27, 1982.

53. Antonio Delfim Netto y Carlos Alberto de Andrade Pinto, "O Café do Brasil," *Estudos ANPES No. 3* (São Paulo: ANPES, 1967); Antonio Delfim Netto y Carlos Alberto de Andrade Pinto, "Brazilian Coffee: Twenty Years of Set Backs in Competition on the World Market, 1945/65," in *Essays on Coffee and Economic Development*, ed. Carlos Manuel Peláez (Rio de Janeiro: Instituto Brasileiro do Café, 1973); Antonio Delfim Netto, "Consideraçoes Sobre A Elasticidade de Demanda dos Cafés Brasileiros," in *Ensaios Econômicos* (Rio de Janeiro: APEC Editôra, 1972).

54. This section draws heavily upon Robert H. Bates and Da-Hsiang Donald Lien, "On the Operation of the International Coffee Agreement," *International Organization* 39 (1985): 553–59, and Da-Hsiang Donald Lien and Robert H. Bates, "Political Behavior in the Coffee Agreement," *Economic Development and Cultural Change* 35, 3 (1987): 629–36. The articles contain the data underlying this analysis.

For treatments of closely related issues, see Geoff Fielding and Hans Liebeck, "Voting Structure and the Square Root Law," *British Journal of Political Science* 5 (1975): 249–63, and Madeline O. Hosli, "Admission of European Free Trade States to the European Community: Effects of Voting Power on the European Community Council of Ministers," *International Organization* 47, 4 (1993): 629–43.

55. The producer nations could choose either period. Brazil, for example, chose the first and Colombia the second, as the former lost market share following the frost of 1975 while the latter gained.

56. For a discussion, see R. Duncan Luce and Howard Raiffa, *Games and Decisions* (New York: John Wiley and Sons, 1957), chapter 11. For illuminating critiques and discussions, see Alvin E. Roth, *The Shapley Value: Essays in Honor of Lloyd S. Shapley* (Cambridge: Cambridge University Press, 1988).

57. We: Da-Hsiang Donald Lien and I.

58. Memorandum No. 001, enero 22 de 1982, pp. 1–2, Convenio Internacional de Café, *Copiador Memorandos*, 1982.

Chapter 7

1. Ronald Rogowski, *Commerce and Coalitions* (Princeton: Princeton University Press, 1989), and Jeffry Frieden, *Debt, Development and Democracy* (Princeton: Princeton University Press, 1991).

2. See Philippe C. Schmitter, *Interest Conflict and Political Change in Brazil* (Stanford: Stanford University Press, 1971). See the classic: Anne O. Krueger, "The Political Economy of the Rent-Seeking Society," *American Economic Review* 64 (1974): 291–303.

3. I therefore join Geoffrey Garrett and Peter Lange in their criticisms of Frieden and Rogowski. See Geoffrey Garrett and Peter Lange, "Internationalization, Institutions, and Political Change," *International Organization* 49 (Autumn 1995): 625–55. See also Jeffry Frieden and Ronald Rogowski, "The Impact of International Economy on National Politics: An Overview," in Robert O. Keohane and Helen V. Milner, eds., *International and Domestic Politics* (Cambridge: Cambridge University Press, forthcoming).

The Colombian case provides a closer approximation of the Frieden model. Land in Caldas, the core of the coffee sector, possessed very little value in its next best use, a fact well known to producers and government alike. As Frieden's model would suggest, Caldas indeed became the militant center of coffee politics. Nonetheless, the producers of Caldas were not always successful spokesmen for the industry. The government sometimes adopted policies favorable to their interests; at other times, it did not. As will be argued below, it too therefore illustrates the need for political analysis.

4. Gene M. Grossman, ed., *Imperfect Competition and International Trade* (Cambridge: MIT Press, 1994); Paul R. Krugman, *Rethinking International Trade* (Cambridge: MIT Press, 1994); Paul R. Krugman and Maurice Obstfeld, *International Economics*, 2d ed. (New York: Harper Collins, 1994).

5. Douglas Nelson, "Endogenous Tariff Theory: A Critical Survey," *American Journal of Political Science* 32, 3 (August 1988): 796–837.

6. Peter Gourevitch, *Politics in Hard Times* (Ithaca: Cornell University Press, 1986).

7. Peter J. Katzenstein, *Small States in World Markets* (Ithaca: Cornell University Press, 1985); David Cameron, "The Expansion of the Public Economy: A Comparative Analysis," *American Political Science Review* 72, 4 (1978): 1243–61; Geoffrey Garrett and Peter Lange, "Performance in a Hostile World: Economic Growth in Capitalist Democracies, 1974–1982," *World Politics* 38, 4 (1989): 676–98.

8. Early assertions of the significance of institutions were made by Peter J. Katzenstein, ed., *Between Power and Plenty* (Madison: University of Wisconsin Press, 1977); they were renewed by such "statists" as Stephen D. Krasner, *Defending the National Interest* (Princeton: Princeton University Press, 1978). See Judith Goodstein, "The Political Economy of the Tariff," *American Political Science Review* 80 (1986): 161–84; Wendy Hansen, "The International Trade Commission and the Politics of Protectionism," *American Political Science Review* 84, 1 (March 1990): 21–46; and John Mark Hansen, "Taxation and the Political Economy of the Tariff," *International Orga-*

nization 44, 4 (Autumn 1990): 527–51; Ronald Rogowski, "Trade and the Variety of Domestic Institutions," *International Organization* 41, 2 (Spring 1987): 203–23; and Beth A. Simmons, *Who Adjusts?* (Princeton: Princeton University Press, 1994). See also Daniel Verdier, *Democracy and International Trade* (Princeton: Princeton University Press, 1994).

9. We are thus placing institutional structure to game theoretic conceptions of domestic politics. In this sense, we are placing flesh on the skeleton outlined in Robert Putnam, "Diplomacy and Domestic Politics," *International Organization* 42, 3 (Summer 1988): 427–60.

10. Gary King, Robert O. Keohane, and Sydney Verba, *Designing Social Inquiry* (Princeton: Princeton University Press, 1994).

11. For a variety of contributions to theory-driven studies of narratives, see Peter Abell, *The Syntax of Social Life* (Oxford: Clarendon, 1987); Andrew Abbott, "Notes on Narrative Positivism," *Sociological Methods and Research* 20, 4 (May 1992): 428–55; Margaret R. Somers, "Norms, Narrative Identities, and Social Action," *Social Science History* 16, 4 (Winter 1992): 591–630.

12. Adam Przeworski and Henry Teune, *The Logic of Comparative Social Inquiry* (Malabar, Fla.: Krieger Publishing Company, 1982); Harry Eckstein, "Case Study and Theory in Political Science," in *Handbook of Political Science*, vol. 1, ed. Fred I. Greenstein and Nelson W. Polsby (Reading, Mass.: Addison-Wesley, 1975).

13. Uganda Government, *Report of the Committee of Inquiry into the Coffee Industry, 1967* (Entebbe: Entebbe Government Printer, 1967).

14. R. M. Van Zwanenberg and Anne King, *An Economic History of Kenya and Uganda, 1800–1970* (London: Macmillan, 1975), p. 222.

15. Ibid., p. 223.

16. See the analysis of the 1968 Produce Marketing Act in Stephen Bunker, *Peasants Against the State* (Urbana: University of Illinois Press, 1987), pp. 198ff., and of the 1969 Coffee Marketing Act in Titterud, "Prices, Policies, and Products," pp. 19ff. See as well H. J. van Hilten, "The Coffee Sub-Sector—Marketing and Related Recommendations, Uganda Rehabilitation Credit," Consultancy Report, June 1982; and Robert H. Bates, Robert W. Hahn, and John G. Kreag, "The Reorganization of the Marketing and Processing of Crops in Uganda," Consultancy Report, November 1981.

17. Interview, Minister of Cooperatives, Kampala, November 1982. See also, Uganda Government, *Report of the Commission of Inquiry into the Coffee Industry*, pp. 54ff.

18. See the estimates in Bates, Hahn, and Kreag, "The Reorganization," table 5.

19. This approach is fulsomely and lucidly exposited by King, Keohane, and Verba, *Designing Social Inquiry*.

20. Consult Leonard Lardaro, *Applied Econometrics* (New York: HarperCollins, 1993).

21. I say compelled because the transformation of the data into first differences results in a loss of information: reductions in variation and, of far less significance in this instance, a loss of observations as well.

22. PRTCOMP assigns a 0 to all years beginning with the presidency of Laureano Gómez and ending in 1972, two years before the restoration of partisan presidential elections (the elections of 1974), when the parties began to select rival presidential candidates. We experienced a variety of other cutting points, and the results were somewhat sensitive to the choices. Thus our subsequent use of another measure (see below).

23. The best detailed coverage of this period is contained in Roberto Junguito and Diego Pizano, coordinadores, *El Comercio Exterior y la Política Internacional del Café* (Bogotá: Fondo Cultural Cafetero y Fedesarrollo, 1994).

24. Nestlé purchased Hills Brothers.

25. "Report of the Foreign Affairs Committee, Board of Directors, National Coffee Association," February 1988, p. 4.

26. Interviews, former Under Secretary for Economic Affairs Allen Wallis, 12 June 1990, and Dr. Martin Bailey, 6 June 1990. There is a methodological and theoretical core to this argument: that the bureaucratic politics model of policy-making can be formalized in the same manner as the literature on the impact of structures upon legislative decisions. See the discussion in Graham Allison, *Essence of Decision* (Boston: Little, Brown, 1971), and the work on structure-induced equilibria in Kenneth A. Shepsle and Barry R, Weingast, "Positive Theories of Congressional Institutions," in *Positive Theories of Congressional Institutions,* ed. Kenneth A. Shepsle and Barry R. Weingast (Ann Arbor: University of Michigan Press, 1995).

27. Interview, Washington, 12 June 1990.

28. Interviews, London, 8–10 March 1990.

29. Memorandum de Delegación Permanente ante la O.I.C., 20 junio de 1989, p. 22.

30. Ibid., p. 28.

Appendix

1. Leading studies of the economics of the coffee market would include T. Akiyama and R. C. Duncan, *Analysis of the World Coffee Market* (World Bank Staff Commodity Working Paper No. 7, Washington, D.C.: 1982); Edmar Bacha, "An Econometric Model for the World Coffee Market" (Ph.D. diss., Yale University, 1968); Derek James Ford, "Coffee Supply, Trade, and Demand: An Economic Analysis of the World Market, 1930–1969" (Ph.D. diss., University of Pennsylvania, 1977); A. H. Gelb, "A Spectral Analysis of Coffee Market Oscillations," *International Economic Review* 20 (1979): 495–514; Montague J. Lord, *Market Price Models for Latin America's Major Commodity Exports* (Washington, D.C.: Inter-American Development Bank, 1986); A Parikh, "A Model of the World Coffee Economy: 1950–1968," *Applied Economics* 6 (1974): 23–43; M. Th. A. Pieterse and H. J. Silvia, *The World Coffee Market and The International Coffee Agreement* (Wageningen, Belgium: Agricultural University, 1988); Mark A. Renné, "An Econometric Model of the World Coffee Economy" (Ph.D. diss., State University of New York at Buffalo, 1987); Blair Eugene Rourke, "Causes and Predictability of Annual Changes in Supplies and Prices of Coffee" (Ph.D. diss., Stanford University, 1969); M. R. Wickens and J. N. Greenfield, "The Econometrics of Agricultural Supply: An Application to the World Coffee Market," *Review of Economics and Statistics* 55, 1 (1973): 433–40.

Essential overviews are contained in: F. G. Adams and J. R. Behrman, *Econometric Models of World Agricultural Commodity Markets* (Cambridge, Mass.: Ballinger Publishing Company, 1976); Economic Research Unit, Center for Analysis of Developing Countries, University of Pennsylvania, *Econometric Models of the World Commodity Market, ELSA Technical Report 1* (Philadelphia, Pa.: Institute of Developing Economies, University of Pennsylvania, 1984); Robert L. Thompson, *A Survey of Recent*

Developments in International Agricultural Trade Models (Washington, D.C.: U.S. Department of Agriculture, Economic Research Service, 1981); and L. Alan Winters and David Sapsford, *Primary Commodity Prices: Economic Models and Policy* (Cambridge: Cambridge University Press, 1990).

Additional studies by Latin American scholars would include those published in the following: Instituto Brasileiro do Café, *Essays on Coffee and Economic Development* (Rio de Janeiro: Instituto Brasileiro do Café, 1973); Fundación Para La Educación Superior y el Dessarrollo, *Economía Cafetera Colombiana* (Bogotá: Fondo Cultural Cafetero, 1978); and Roberto Junguito y Diego Pizano Salazar, *Producción de Café en Colombia* (Bogotá: Fondo Cultural Cafetero, 1991).

An excellent review of the leading models is contained in Diego Pizano-Salazar, "Economic Policy in Coffee Producing Countries: Aspects of the Experience of Colombia and Brazil," in *Terms of Trade and the Optimum Tariff in Latin America*, ed. Interamerican Development Bank (Washington, D.C.: Interamerican Development Bank, 1982).

2. Perhaps the most notable contribution is Felipe Jaramillo, "Supply Response and Optimal Pricing for a Perennial Crop: The Case of Colombian Coffee" (Ph.D. diss., Stanford University, 1989).

3. Before the early 1970s, longer periods were required. Technical innovations by plant breeders and geneticists have reduced the maturation period. Recent investigations suggest that fixed costs represent over two-thirds of the total costs of production. See Landell-Mills Commodity Studies, *A World Survey of Coffee Production Costs* (Oxford: Landell-Mills, 1990).

4. See the data in C. F. Marshall, *The World Coffee Trade* (Cambridge: Woodhead-Faulkner, 1983).

5. I refer to the library of the Instituto do Café, now held by the Ministry of Finance in Rio de Janeiro; the library of the International Coffee Organization on Berners Street in London; and that of the Federación Nacional de Cafeteros in Bogotá.

6. Edmar Bacha, Roberto Junguito, Felipe Jaramillo, and José Antonio Ocampo, to name but a few, have all entered the highest reaches of policy-making. Each began his career researching the economics of coffee. Works by Bacha and Jaramillo are cited above; later chapters extensively cite those of Ocampo. Antônio Delfim Netto is perhaps the most notable graduate from the ranks of coffee researchers. The policies he adopted as Minister of Finance are widely credited with producing Brazil's economic miracle. Delfim's dissertation, published as *O Problema do Café no Brasil* (São Paulo: Faculdade de Ciências Econômicas e Administrativas da Universidade de São Paulo, 1959), remains a classic.

7. Several important works emphasize the less than perfectly competitive structure of the world coffee market. They fail, however, to analyze the ICO as a political entity. See Thomas Geer, *An Oligopoly: The World Coffee Economy and Stabilization Schemes* (New York: Dunnellen, 1971); Roland Hermann, *Internationale Agarmarktabkommen: Analyse ihrer Wirkungen auf deb Märkten für Kaffee und Kakao* (Tübingen: J.C.B. Mohr, 1988); and the excellent series of papers by Mary Bohman and Lovell Jarvis, which are referenced in the central contribution to this project: Mary Elizabeth Bohman, "The Impact of the International Coffee Agreement on Policy in Exporting Countries" (Ph.D. diss., University of California, Davis, 1991).

8. See, for example, Stephen D. Krasner, "The Politics of Primary Commodities:

A Study of Coffee 1900–1970" (Ph.D. diss., Harvard University, 1971); Stephen D. Krasner, "Manipulating International Commodity Markets: Brazilian Coffee Policy 1906 to 1962," *Public Policy* 21, 4 (Fall 1973): 493–523; Stephen D. Krasner, "Business Government Relations: The Case of the International Coffee Agreement," *International Organization* 27, 4 (Autumn 1973): 495–516; and Bart S. Fisher, *The International Coffee Agreement: A Study in Diplomacy* (New York: Praeger Publishers, 1972).

Index

About the Author

ROBERT H. BATES is Eaton Professor of the Science of Government in the Department of Government and a Faculty Fellow in the Institute of International Development at Harvard University. His most recent books include *Beyond the Miracle of the Market* and a volume he coauthored and coedited with Anne O. Krueger, *Political and Economic Interactions in Economic Policy Reform.*